Asian Immigration to the United States

For W. Z. Y.

Asian Immigration to the United States

Philip Q. Yang

polity

First published in 2011 by Polity Press

Polity Press
65 Bridge Street
Cambridge CB2 1UR, UK

Polity Press
350 Main Street
Malden, MA 02148, USA

ISBN-13: 978-0-7456-4502-5
ISBN-13: 978-0-7456-4503-2 (pb)

A catalogue record for this book is available from the British Library.

Typeset in 11 on 13 pt Sabon
by Servis Filmsetting Ltd, Stockport, Cheshire
Printed and bound in Great Britain by MPG Books Group Limited, Bodmin, Cornwall

The publisher has used its best endeavours to ensure that the URLs for external websites referred to in this book are correct and active at the time of going to press. However, the publisher has no responsibility for the websites and can make no guarantee that a site will remain live or that the content is or will remain appropriate.

Every effort has been made to trace all copyright holders, but if any have been inadvertently overlooked the publisher will be pleased to include any necessary credits in any subsequent reprint or edition.

For further information on Polity, visit our website: www.politybooks.com

Contents

List of Figures

List of Figures

List of Tables

List of Tables

Preface

No one can deny that Asian Americans are a permanent and growing part of multiracial and multiethnic America. Today, the majority of Asian Americans are foreign born. As documented in this book, more than 1 million Asians had moved to the United States before the 1965 immigration reform. Since 1965, roughly 9.6 million Asians have immigrated to this land of opportunity.[1] Asia has become one of the two main sources of immigration since 1965.[2] One in three immigrants in America now is of Asian descent.

Although the past four decades have produced a prodigious amount of information on Asian immigration and immigrants, systematic social science research on post-1965 Asian immigration remains meager. While a wealth of information on pre-1965 Asian immigration exists, book-length studies covering the post-1965 period are countable. Among the few existing volumes, quite a few pursue the subject from a legal perspective (Hing 1993; Park and Park 2005), a social work perspective (Segal 2002), or a public policy perspective (Hing and Lee 1996). Ong, Bonacich, and Cheng's book (1994) does take a social science approach, but its scope is confined largely to Los Angeles. Min's edited volumes (1995, 2006a) also take a social science approach and include a significant amount of information on Asian immigration, but the focus of his books is Asian Americans. In the pre-1965 period, the terms Asian immigrants and Asian Americans may be used interchangeably to a great extent without much impact on research findings. However, in the post-1965 period these are not synonyms because a significant proportion of Asian Americans are not immigrants and, in particular, the majority of Japanese Americans are US born. Moreover, Min's books do not aim at developing a theory of Asian immigration and do not address its impacts since 1965. Overall, there is a lack of a comprehensive theoretical framework that can explain Asian immigration to the United States, and research on the demographic, economic, political, and social impacts on American society after 1965 is very thin. Despite a plethora of research on the adaptation of post-1965 Asian immigrants and their children, rarely has any single study examined simultaneously all the important dimensions – cultural, structural, socioeconomic, marital, identificational, and political – for all major groups using data from representative samples at the national level. This social science book represents an attempt to fill these gaps in the literature.

The book addresses three central questions: What causes Asian immigration to the United States? How do post-1965 Asian immigrants impact American society? How do new Asian immigrants and their children adapt to American life? Instead of targeting solely academics and specialists, it aims to reach a broader audience who can grasp the fundamental issues of Asian immigration to America without any special training. I have sifted out material from the broad literature to offer a synthesis of major aspects of Asian immigration. I have also pulled together data from various nationally representative samples to supply the latest empirical evidence whenever possible. Notwithstanding an emphasis on the years after 1965, I have sought to shed light on current realities with a historical perspective and in the contexts of competing theories.

A book on Asian immigration to the United States has been in my mind since my years as a graduate student at the University of California at Los Angeles (UCLA). While working on my dissertation on post-1965 immigration, I contemplated the directions of my next major research project. Post-1965 Asian immigration and post-1965 Chinese immigration were both in my mind. However, over the years, as other projects such as *Post-1965 Immigration* to the United States: *Structural Determinants* (Yang 1995) and *Ethnic Studies: Issues and Approaches* (Yang 2000a) took precedence, the Asian immigration project was placed on the back burner, albeit never forgotten.

It was a meeting with Dr Emma Longstaff, senior commissioning editor at Polity Press, at the annual meeting of the American Sociological Association in New York in August 2007 that prompted me to rethink about the subject more deeply and so rekindled my passion and commitment to this topic. I believed that this was a book that was badly needed in the fields of both Asian American studies and international migration studies and that it was more important than anything else I had been working on. So I decided to put aside other books to concentrate on this project, and the external proposal reviews by three anonymous reviewers reinforced my conviction about its necessity and importance. I am immensely indebted to Emma and the editorial board at Polity, who placed full confidence in me by giving me the contract and increasing the potential length of the book. I would also like to express my sincere gratitude to the reviewers for their enthusiasm for, and appreciation of, this project and highly constructive comments and suggestions.

Jonathan Skerrett, commissioning editor at Polity, has provided me with detailed guidance and vital support throughout the whole process of writing during Emma's maternity leave. I very much appreciate his dedication, patience, and professionalism. I would especially like to thank the three anonymous manuscript reviewers who carefully read the manuscript and offered positive feedback and highly constructive critiques and suggestions, many of which have been incorporated into the final draft. Special thanks are also due to production editor Clare Ansell, and editorial assistant Lauren Mulholland. Huping Ling read the entire manuscript and offered her endorsement and helpful suggestions, for which I am grateful.

At Texas Woman's University, a faculty development leave award in the spring semester of 2009 gave me much needed time to complete the bulk of the manuscript.

An earlier version of chapter 2 appeared in the *Journal of Asian*

American Studies (Volume 13, Issue 1, February 2010, pages 1–34. Copyright © 2010, The Johns Hopkins University Press).

Last but certainly not least, the support of my family has been indispensable throughout the span of this project. My late mother, Ma Xuan, was a staunch supporter of my pursuits from my childhood until her last breath. She learned of this project in fall 2007, but could not wait to see its fruition. I know she would be in seventh heaven if she could see this book. My wife, Jianling Li, read the draft of the manuscript and gave me her candid reactions. She also provided technical support for formatting the tables and graphs. My daughter Ming Yang consistently showed interest in the progress of this project while a very busy student in medical school. My son William Zeus Yang joined the family as a godsend in 2003. He gives me joy and energy and makes my day every day. He has been a perfect nudger with the question: "Daddy, are you done with your book yet?" This book is dedicated to him.

1

Introduction

Some mini-stories

This book is mainly about post-1965 Asian immigration to the United States. Let us begin with some mini-stories in order to get some tangible feelings about the experiences of these new immigrants. Stories abound, but because of a limit on space, only a handful have been selected from personal interviews or some other specified sources.[1] Names are pseudonymous unless indicated otherwise.

Who they are and why they come

Min Zhou[2] is professor of sociology and Asian American studies at UCLA. After receiving her bachelor's degree in English in 1982 from Sun Yat-sen University (named after the founder of the Republic of China and also known as Zhongshan University, the no. 1 university in Southern China), she was assigned a faculty position as a *zhujiao* (literally, "teaching assistant," but equivalent to assistant professor in America) in the newly established sociology department at her alma mater. In 1984, she left her infant child in the care of her family in China and came to the United States to study for her PhD in sociology at the State University of New York at Albany. She had every intention of returning to China afterwards to be reunited with her family (her toddler son) and resume her teaching position at Sun Yat-sen University. Indeed, she shipped her belongings back to China and left the United States two days after her graduation ceremony in late May 1989, but made a detour to Europe for a short vacation. The Tiananmen Square incident that June destroyed her plan. Like many Chinese students studying in the United States at the time, she decided not to return home in such an uncertain situation. After being stranded in Switzerland for a year, in 1990 she accepted an assistant professorship from Louisiana State University (LSU) at Baton Rouge, which allowed her to obtain an H-1B temporary work visa and eventually permanent resident status.[3]

Meili Zhang, 28 years old and pretty, came illegally from a village in Fujian. Her husband arrived in the United States more than ten years ago and has been running a Chinese restaurant. In her hometown, almost every family has at least one member abroad, and *toudu* (illegal migration) is a way of life. America is perceived as a paradise, and even jail in the USA is considered better than life in China. Led by the snakeheads, and in a group of more than ten others all with genuine passports, Meili flew from Beijing to Cuba, to a few other small countries, and finally to Mexico. They then dropped all their luggage, ran through a forest for about five hours, and crossed the border to the United States. There they were caught and put into jail. Meili spent $100,000 on this journey.[4]

Yoshi Yamaguchi is a Japanese immigrant living in Los Angeles. His Japanese father married a Taiwanese woman while doing business in Taiwan before World War II. Yoshi was born in Taiwan and grew up there until he was eight years old. After his parents' divorce, he moved with his father to Japan, where he finished university education and went on to obtain an advanced degree in culinary arts, and worked as a chef. However, because he was concerned that the smoky and oily environment could affect his health he decided to take up acupuncture, and received a master's degree. In 1989, Yoshi immigrated to the United States and settled in Los Angeles, hoping for a better life.

Kazuko Miller is a "war bride" from Japan. She was born in 1942 and grew up in difficult circumstances after the death of her father in World War II. She worked at a navy commissary store and met a US serviceman at the navy base. Despite the objection of her family, Kazuko married the soldier in 1974 without a ceremony because "he was really nice" and they got along well. In 1975, she followed her husband to America upon his completion of service in Japan. She really likes the abundant open space in America compared to Japan.[5]

Ashok Shah was a graduate of the chemical engineering program at the Indian Institute of Technology (IIT Madras) – an elite engineering school in India. He came to the United States in 1975 to pursue a PhD degree in chemical engineering at a large Midwestern university and also received an MBA degree. The United States was a popular destination for most students at the IIT at that time. Ashok landed a job at a computer company, which enabled him to get a green card, and worked his way up to become vice-president of the global marketing division. At the time of the interview he had been in America for 26 years. He never thought of returning to India because half of the faculty at the IIT were American and all the professors who taught him there taught him again in the United States. Being immersed in the American education system in India, he felt almost "like a second-generation Indian, being in America." His individual qualities, his world-class undergraduate education in science and technology, his American consciousness, and his networks with the American professors ensured his passage to the USA first for study and later for settlement.[6]

Born into a family of teachers in Manila, Diwata Lopez worked in a private nursery before coming to America, having obtained her nursing degree from the University of the Philippines in 1963. The education system in the Philippines was modeled on America's, most professors had a master's degree from the United States, and textbooks were all American. Upon graduation, Diwata was curious to go to another country, and she got a visa to the United States under the Visitor's Exchange Program for nurses in 1964. She chose to work as a nurse at Cook County Hospital in Chicago because that was where many graduates from the University of the Philippines worked. Her initial purpose was to get a master's degree in nursing, but she had to abandon her plan because the schools available were all too far away, so she simply stayed in Cook County Hospital. Diwata finally adjusted her immigration status to permanent resident (green card holder) in 1971.[7]

Dug Nguyen was a farmer in a Catholic family in South Vietnam. After the United States became involved in the Vietnam War, he found a job as a security guard at the US consulate in a city in the northern part of South Vietnam. When the US troops withdrew from South Vietnam in 1975, he and his family qualified for evacuation. In fear of persecution on account of his religion, he decided to move the whole family to the United States, and they left Saigon on April 28, 1975, in a US military cargo plane. They stayed in the Philippines for a few days and then flew to Guam. Shortly afterwards they moved to Camp Pendleton. After a month, the family found a sponsor in a Catholic parish in Oregon and settled in the town of Woodburn. In 1978, they relocated to Oceanside, California, where Dug Nguyen's sister's family lived.[8]

Len Kath was a Cambodian refugee who settled in Chicago in 1980. Since he had worked as a clerk for a shipping company, he fell foul of Pol Pot's government; both his brother and his uncle were arrested. Len was viewed as a member of the urban elite and not part of the peasant revolution. By 1979 he had no job and no money, and because of the famine his family had little food. So he had no choice but to escape. His family – his wife and two young children – took weeks to reach Thailand. But at the Phnom Chat camp there they were bombed by the Vietnamese and almost died. They were fortunate to come to America.[9]

Takae Jeong worked in real estate in Korea before moving to the USA. He had a bachelor's degree in law from Korea University and was married with three children. The family lived a comfortable life in their own home before emigration. His three brothers already lived in the United States: two as doctors and one as a pharmacist. The constant contact with his brothers helped him come to the conclusion that America was a better place to live, with more economic opportunities, a higher quality of life, and a better education for his children. With the sponsorship of one of his brothers, his entire family immigrated in 1976 and settled in

Flushing, New York, in an apartment in the same building as his brother's family.[10]

Josh Jung Hyung Shave was born in Seoul, South Korea, in 1973, and as an infant was abandoned in a box on the doorstep of an orphanage. In 1979, he was adopted by a white American couple living in Massachusetts with three children. His adoptive father was an engineer and his adoptive mother was a schoolteacher.

How they have impacted America

Paul Hsu[11] is nicknamed "the king of American ginseng." He emigrated from Taiwan in 1969 to pursue a master's degree in social work at the University of Denver and discovered a golden business opportunity while a social worker in Wisconsin (Hsu 2005). In 1974, he started Hsu's Ginseng Enterprises (HGE), Inc., in Wausau and became the first Chinese ginseng grower in America, selling small quantities of dried roots to expatriate Chinese. After 36 years of hard work, HGE is now the largest ginseng company in the United States, supplying more than 400,000 pounds a year and accounting for more than 20 percent of the ginseng produced in the country. Hsu's products are sold worldwide, especially in the United States, Canada, China, and Hong Kong. HGE's annual sales revenues totaled more than $40 million in 2009. Because of his tremendous success, Hsu has received many awards and honors, including the Wisconsin Governor's Award for Export Excellence in 1986, the US Small Business Administration's National Small Business Exporter of the Year in 1992, the Award for Distinguished Achievement as an Asian Farmer from the US Department of Agriculture in1995, and a visit by President George W. Bush in 2002.[12]

Steve Cheung and his wife immigrated to the United States from Hong Kong in the early 1970s and decided to make their home in San Luis Obispo, central California, where they started the first Chinese restaurant in the city, the Imperial China Restaurant. Their delicious Cantonese cuisine, unique dim sum, spacious and neat environment, outstanding service, and reasonable prices have kept both Chinese and non-Chinese customers coming back again and again. The restaurant is also a pleasant venue for wedding banquets and birthday parties. Despite competition from other Chinese restaurants, the Imperial has remained one of the best Chinese restaurants in San Luis Obispo.

Le Van Truong was among the Vietnamese refugees who arrived in America in 1985. Having lived in Minnesota for five years, he moved to San Francisco to join his brothers and worked as a mechanic in an auto repair shop. But he wanted to have a better life. In 1997 he decided to move to Arlington, Texas, and opened an auto shop. Because of his reliability and lower charges, he has regular clients. He is making a much better living than in San Francisco.

Dr Azar Kamran received an MD degree from Allama Iqbal Medical College at the University of Punjab in Pakistan in 1986 and came to the United States to pursue the American dream shortly afterwards. After four years of residency at Temple University Hospital, the UAB Montgomery Health Center, St Johns Episcopal Hospital-South Shore, and Muhlenberg Regional Medical Center, he started to practice gastroenterology and internal medicine in Georgia. He moved to North Texas in 2005. Dr Kamran has two offices in two North Texas cities, serving a large number of patients and providing language support in Punjabi, Urdu, and Vietnamese. He has won the praises of many patients.

"Jenny" Lang Ping[13] was a celebrity icon nicknamed "Iron Hammer" in China in the 1980s because she was one of the key players who helped the Chinese Women's National Volleyball Team capture four successive women's volleyball world championships. She came to America for graduate study in sports administration at the University of New Mexico in 1987 while working as an assistant coach for the school's volleyball team (1987–9 and 1992–3). She got married, had a daughter, and owns a home in Tustin, California. She lives in two worlds. As head coach, she led the Chinese women's national volleyball team to the bronze medal in the 1995 World Cup, the silver medal at the 1996 Atlanta Olympic Games, and the silver medal in the 1998 World Championship. Jenny accepted the job of head coach of the

US women's volleyball team in 2005 and led the team to the silver medal in the 2008 Olympic Games.[14]

How they adapt to American life

For Min Zhou, the first year at LSU was especially challenging. She had little teaching experience, had to care for her six-year-old son while her husband worked in Switzerland, had to teach four extra courses on Saturdays, between semesters and in summer session to support her family financially, and had to learn to adapt to a culturally different environment. On top of all this, she had to publish (or perish). Under such pressure, she reserved the hours of 3 to 6 every morning to work on her first book, *Chinatown*, and completed the manuscript in six months. She joined the faculty of sociology and Asian American studies at UCLA in 1994. To date, Zhou has published seven books and more than 100 articles in peer-reviewed journals and edited volumes. Over the years she has received many academic awards and honors, including the 2007 Chiyoko Doris '34 and Toshio Hoshide Distinguished Teaching Prize in Asian American Studies at UCLA, a fellowship at the Russell Sage Foundation, and a fellowship at the Center for the Advanced Study of Behavioral Sciences at Stanford University. In 2009, she was appointed the first Walter and Shirley Wang Endowed Chair of US–China Relations and Communications at UCLA and a Chang Jiang Scholar Lecture Professor by the Chang Jiang Scholars Program funded by the Ministry of Education of the People's Republic of China and the Hong Kong Li Ka-Shing Foundation.[15]

After arriving in Los Angles in 1989, Yoshi Yamaguchi opened his own acupuncture clinic. But he soon found that, after all his costs were taken into account, he could only just break even, and so he became a driver for a well-known tourist company. Despite this downward occupational mobility, he felt satisfaction. His income is significantly higher than previously, and he can enjoy the tours himself. He is more relaxed. He married a Chinese woman and had two children.

Diwata Lopez met her husband, also a Filipino immigrant,

through his niece. They had children and purchased a house. They ate Filipino food almost every day. She spoke Tagalog to her husband at home, though they did not speak Tagalog to their children because they believed it would be better for them to speak English without an accent. However, they did raise their children in Filipino ways, with more parental guidance. They still went to Catholic Church. Diwata was satisfied with her nursing job, which paid well and offered good benefits. She had good relationships with her colleagues, but most of her friends remained Filipinos. In 1976 she became a US citizen. She was interested in American politics and registered as a Democrat. She planned to retire in the Philippines because it is cheaper and safer there.[16]

During his first two years in New York City, Takae Jeong tried several jobs, including taxi driver and warehouseman, while his wife worked as a seamstress in a garment factory. Two years later, hoping for better economic opportunities, he moved the family to Alameda, California, where he had been invited by a friend to manage a liquor store. However, after seven years the family returned to Flushing because the liquor store went out of business and Takae could not find another job. Even during times of financial hardship, Takae always found money for his children's activities and managed to send them to the best schools possible. His son obtained a law degree from George Washington University Law School and became an assistant district attorney in the Kings County District Attorney's Office in Brooklyn. His children learned to retain some Korean largely because they had to communicate with their mother, whose English was very poor. Takae and his wife moved to Texas in the 1990s. Even though he did not have great personal success, he was proud of the achievements of his children.[17]

Ajoy Hussain immigrated from Bangladesh with his family. After the attacks of September 11, the United States set up the Special Registration Program, which required certain male non-citizens aged 16 or older from 25 countries to register with the immigration authorities. Ajoy was summoned and deported because of some irregularity with his visa. He called his wife from Bangladesh: "I am here; they put me on a plane." He was not allowed to return, and his family in America did not know whether they should leave or stay.[18]

Jeong Dae moved with his parents from South Korea at a very young age and settled in Tarrant County, Texas. During his time at school he had found that teachers and classmates alike seemed to have trouble pronouncing his name correctly and that classmates often distanced themselves from him. That had bothered him a lot. At the age of 18, he decided to change his name formally, to "John Doe," hoping to solve the problem and gain acceptance among his peers as well as to make it easier to find a job. While the social difficulties have all but disappeared, Jeong has discovered that, much to his surprise, every time he boards an airplane he is called in by the authorities for thorough questioning. He encounters the same trouble every time he has to go through a security checkup. He finally realized that it is his new name that is causing the problem.[19]

The above stories are "ordinary," but they mirror the normal life of new Asian immigrants. They are by no means representative of post-1965 Asian immigrants, but they provide a glimpse of the causes and effects of Asian immigration and the adaptation of Asian immigrants to American life. They will also help the reader to understand the statistical data presented later in this book.

Aim of the book

This book seeks to offer a comprehensive examination of Asian immigration to the United States with an emphasis on the post-1965 period. To the lay mind, Asian immigration naturally means immigration of people from the continent of Asia. In the context of racial/ethnic politics, however, the US government does not define "Asians" or "Asian Americans" as people who originated from the continent of Asia. Currently, the US Office of Management and Budget (OMB), the federal agency in charge of racial and ethnic categorization, defines Asian Americans as those who can trace their origins to the Far East (i.e., East Asia), Southeast Asia, and the Indian subcontinent (i.e., South Asia) (OMB 1997a).

Thus, those who originate from Southwest Asia (sometimes also called West Asia – namely, west of Pakistan) – including Israelis, Afghans, Iranians, Iraqis, Kuwaitis, Bahrainis, Qataris, Syrians, Lebanese, Jordanians, Saudi Arabians, Emiratis, Omanis, Yemenis, Turks, and Cypriots – are not considered Asian Americans. Nor are those originally from the Asian part of Russia and some of the former Soviet republics (i.e., Kazakhstan, Uzbekistan, Kyrgyzstan, Tajikistan, Turkmenistan, Georgia, Armenia, and Azerbaijan). Racially, such people are normally categorized in the United States as white. Historically, the term "Asian American" did not appear until the 1960s. At that time, Asians meant East Asians and perhaps Southeast Asians, but not South Asians or others. Asian Indians were not recognized as Asian Americans until the late 1970s, following the reclassification movement.[20] Pacific Islanders in the 1980 and 1990 US censuses were tallied together with Asian Americans. The racialized term "Asian and Pacific Islander" was therefore used during that period, sometimes shortened to "Asian American" or "Asian Pacific American." The lumping of Asians and Pacific Islanders together was challenged after the 1990 census, and the splitting of the two groups was proposed. The argument was that Pacific Islanders and Asians differed largely in terms of culture and socioeconomic status and that the relatively disadvantageous position of Pacific Islanders has been concealed in the combined category (OMB 1997b). Another proposal was to separate Native Hawaiians from the "Pacific Islander" category and to include them in the "American Indian or Alaskan Native" category because they shared more in common with Native Americans in terms of their non-immigrant status and experiences of colonization (Skerry 2000). This proposal was rejected by the OMB partly for technical reasons,[21] but it also met with objections from Indian tribal organizations, who argued that lumping Native Hawaiians with Native Americans would artificially raise their socioeconomic status and undermine the unique claims and status of Indians in America. As a result of negotiations and reconstruction, the OMB decided to single out "Native Hawaiian and other Pacific Islander" as a separate racial category, starting in the 2000 US census.

This book uses the OMB's definition of "Asian" or "Asian American," since this is the official definition commonly used in American society. Hence, "Asian" refers to East Asians, Southeast Asians, and South Asians, but not people who originated from other parts of Asia. Accordingly, "Asian immigration" refers to the immigration of people from East Asia, Southeast Asia, and South Asia only.

Thus, I will not cover immigration to the United States from Southwest Asia and Northwest Asia (or the Asian part of the former Soviet Union). Some of the peoples from Southwest Asia are from the Arab world, as defined by the membership in the League of Arab States – Iraq, Kuwait, Bahrain, Qatar, Syria, Lebanon, Jordan, Saudi Arabia, the United Arab Emirates, Oman, Yemen, Djibouti, Comoros, Palestine, Egypt, Libya, Tunisia, Algeria, Morocco, Mauritania, Sudan, and Somalia. The people from these countries are called "Arab Americans," and they overlap with but are not identical to "Middle Easterners" – Israelis, Iranians, Iraqis, Kuwaitis, Bahrainis, Qataris, Syrians, Lebanese, Jordanians, Saudi Arabians, Emiratis, Omanis, Yemenis, Egyptians, and sometimes Libyans, Tunisians, Algerians, Moroccans, Turks, and Cypriots. Arab Americans also overlap with but are not the same as Muslim Americans, who are defined in terms of their religion (the believers of Islam). "Many Arab Americans are not Muslims, and most Muslim Americans are not Arabs" (Schaefer 2008: 301). Hence, this book will not discuss immigration of Arabs, Middle Easterners, or Muslims either.

I will not address the immigration of Pacific Islanders for several reasons. First, since 2000 Native Hawaiians and other Pacific Islanders have been categorized by the US government as a separate racial group. Second, Native Hawaiians and other Pacific Islanders are very different from Asians in their experience of immigration. Many Asian groups of the post-1965 period comprise largely immigrants, but Native Hawaiians are an indigenous group and the immigration of other Pacific Islanders is very small. Third, Pacific Islanders are concerned more about issues related to American colonialism, island sovereignty, and the rights of indigenous peoples (e.g., Kauanui 2008; Rogers 1996; Silva 2004), but

Asian Americans are interested more in issues pertaining to immigration, civil rights, and political representation. Finally, and more importantly, because of the different experiences, Pacific Islanders deserve a systematic treatment in a separate volume.

It should be noted that analytical distinction is different from racial or ethnic community building. Separating Asians and Pacific Islanders helps sharpen the focus of analysis and serves the purpose of this book well. Nevertheless, distinguishing Asians from Pacific Islanders in a scholarly book by no means suggests that the Asian community and the Pacific Islander community have no common interest and need not engage in building alliances. In fact, there have been genuine and consorted efforts over the last three decades to construct the Asian and Pacific Islander community, both scholarly and politically.[22]

Asian immigration to the United States attempts to answer three central research questions: (1) What causes Asian immigration to the United States? (2) How does Asian immigration impact American society in the post-1965 period? (3) How do post-1965 Asian immigrants and their children adapt to American life?

A central argument is that Asian immigration can best be understood as the outcome of an interactive and cumulative process of inequality between Asian countries and the United States in economic, political, social, and environmental conditions; multilevel connections between the United States and Asian countries and between prospective Asian immigrants and their social networks across the nations of origin and destination; and migration policies in both the home and host countries. Pre-1965 Asian immigration can be explained by this macro–micro interactive and cumulative causation framework and should be viewed as interrelated movements of Asian groups rather than as separate and isolated migration flows. This macro–micro interactive and cumulative causation theory can also account very well for post-1965 Asian immigration to the United States. Another important argument is that post-1965 immigration has profound demographic, economic, sociocultural, and political impacts on American society that should be researched and fully understood. The final principal argument is that the classic assimilation paradigm cannot adequately capture the adaptation experiences of post-1965 Asian immigrants and their children, and alternative theories, including cultural pluralism theory, segmented assimilation theory, and revisionist assimilation theory, can do this better.

A *few words about data*

This book draws on a variety of existing data from various sources. Statistical data, mainly from the US Citizenship and Immigration Service (CIS) and its predecessor the US Immigration and Naturalization Service (INS), are the best available source of information for the purpose of analyzing the trends, levels, settlement patterns, and types of Asian immigration in both the pre-1965 and post-1965 periods. The latest or longitudinal data from the US centennial population censuses, the American Community Surveys (ACS), and the Current Population Surveys (CPS) collected by the US Bureau of the Census are used to address the demographic, racial/ethnic, and economic impact of post-1965 Asian immigration, as well as the cultural, structural, socioeconomic, marital, identificational, and political adaptation of such immigrants and their children. The US census data used here are based on the long form collected from 5 percent of the population. The ACS data are available starting in 2000 and replaced the long form in the US census beginning in 2010. The data from the latest (2006–8) ACS are used whenever possible to provide the most up-to-date information. The CPS is conducted every month, and the data from the March and November surveys are used in this project. The General Social Surveys (GSS), the American National Election Study (ANES), and the Pilot National Asian American Political Survey (PNAAPS) provide additional supplemental data to examine the cultural and political adaptation of post-1965 Asian immigrants and their children, as well as the political impact of post-1965 immigration. The GSS, conducted since 1972, is a representative sample of the US adult population and contains a wealth of information. The ANES (since 1948) is also a nationally representative sample and includes some useful information related to political partisanship and orientation. The PNAAPS, conducted by Pei-te Lien in 2000–1, is a semi-random sample survey of Chinese, Filipino, Japanese, Korean, South Asian, and Vietnamese households in the five major metropolitan areas of the United States, where about 40 percent of the nation's Asian-American population resided in 2000, and it provides useful information on the voter registration, voting turn-out, political orientation, and political party affiliation of major Asian American groups. In general, these data sets are of good to excellent quality. Whenever possible, I provide the most up-to-date data. Other sources, such as historical data and the Survey of Business Owners (SBO), are also utilized when appropriate. The existing literature is used to analyze topics not covered in the foregoing data sets.

Organization of the book

Chapter 2 seeks to develop a comprehensive theoretical framework for explaining Asian immigration to the United States. It begins with a critical review of competing theoretical perspectives on international migration, with an emphasis on their relevancy, usefulness, and limitations in explaining Asian immigration. It then reviews existing explanations of Asian immigration and discusses the need for a comprehensive theory. The balance of this chapter proposes my own theoretical framework, which integrates some contesting theories. This theoretical framework is intended to guide a major part of the analyses in the next two chapters.

Chapter 3 examines the period before 1965, when Asians were excluded or restricted from immigration to the United States. It follows a chronological order of entry by various Asian groups into America, starting with Chinese immigration, in particular the Exclusion and post-Exclusion eras. This is followed by Japanese immigration and the Gentlemen's Agreement – the exclusion of Japanese laborers. Since Korea was colonized by Japan between 1910 and 1945, and historically Korean immigration was confounded with Japanese immigration, the examination goes next to Korean immigration and disguised exclusion. The chapter then analyzes the immigration of a relatively small number of Asian Indians and their exclusion. The final section delves into Filipino immigration and the Tydings–McDuffie Act, which virtually excluded Filipinos from immigration. One important point to be demonstrated is that the successive Asian immigration flows and the dreadful experiences of the immigrants were interrelated and had common sources.

Chapter 4 opens with a brief description of the immigration reform since 1965, which has contributed to the phenomenal growth in Asian immigration. It then documents the trends in post-1965 Asian immigration in comparison with total immigration, European immigration, and Latin American immigration and among major Asian sending countries. This is followed by an analysis of the settlement patterns of post-1965 Asian immigrants. The types of post-1965 Asian immigrants are also analyzed in terms of sponsorship, occupational preference, refugee adjustment, and diversity immigrants, as well as new arrivals versus adjustments of status, the brain flow, and adoptees. The focus then shifts to the causes of post-1965 Asian immigration, guided by the macro–micro interactive and cumulative causation theory developed in chapter 2. This chapter also briefly discusses Asian immigrant transnationalism – a growing phenomenon of people who live their lives in two or more countries – among post-1965 Asian immigrants. The final section addresses the scope, trends, and causes of undocumented Asian immigration. Although this chapter is organized thematically, information on major Asian immigrant groups is presented whenever possible.

Chapter 5 has its own conceptual considerations and examines the various impacts of post-1965 Asian immigration on US society. It first analyzes the demographic impact of Asian immigration on the growth of the total Asian population and of each major Asian American group, as well as on the US population. It also examines the impact of Asian immigration and population growth on US racial/ethnic relations. As part of this discussion, the issue of whether Asians are becoming white is considered. The chapter then looks into the economic influence of Asian immigration, including its impact on the quality of the US labor force and labor market and financial effects. It discusses the sociocultural impact of Asian immigration, such as the effects on the American diet, American health practices, science and technology, and US competitiveness in sports events. The final section addresses the impact of post-1965 Asian immigration on political partisanship and political orientation in America.

Chapter 6 addresses how post-1965 Asian immigrants and their children adapt to American life – a different question from those posed in chapters 2 and 5. The first section briefly reviews some important theories of adaptation to provide theoretical guidance for later discussion. The next section considers to what extent Asian immigrants and their children become assimilated to American culture and retain their ethnic cultures, using such indicators as English competence, native language abilities, and religious affiliation. The following section assesses the socioeconomic adaptation of immigrants and their children in terms of education, occupational status, income, entrepreneurship, and poverty. Structural adaptation based on available data such as residential integration or segregation is examined. The literature on intermarriages between Asian immigrants and non-Asians and among Asian groups is surveyed, and identity formation and change are discussed. The chapter examines the political incorporation and participation of Asian immigrants and their children by analyzing their acquisition of citizenship, voter's registration, and voting rate. Whenever possible, the analyses are broken down by ethnicity, generation, and gender. The final section assesses which theories of adaptation can best capture the experience of post-1965 Asian immigrants and their children.

The final chapter revisits the three important themes of this book and looks into the future. The first theme is explanations of Asian immigration. The emphasis here is on the utility of the macro–micro interactive and cumulative causation theory in explaining Asian immigration and perhaps other immigration flows. The second theme is the impacts of post-1965 Asian immigration on US society, including the demographic, economic, sociocultural, and political dimensions. The third theme is the adaptation of

Asian immigrants, which assesses the extent to which theories of adaptation are useful for understanding real experiences. In the end, the book discusses several possible future trends in Asian immigration to the United States and points to the need for future research.

2

A Theory of Asian Immigration

Asians have been an integral part of immigration to the United States since the mid-nineteenth century and one of the two dominant groups of post-1965 immigration. Since the majority of Asian Americans are foreign born,[1] immigration is a very important part of their experience. However, the theoretical base for understanding Asian immigration remains weak. As reviewed below, currently there exist mostly underdeveloped propositions, assumptions, assertions, or explanations concerning why Asians immigrate to America, often bounded by a specific level of analysis, a specific part of the migration process, a specific discipline, and/or a specific time period. There is no single, coherent, well-developed theory of Asian immigration to the United States that takes into account multilevel processes, multiple causes, initiating and sustaining forces, and historical and contemporary flows. A full understanding of Asian immigration calls for a synthetic theory that incorporates all important determinants at different levels for both historical and contemporary periods. The lack of a single comprehensive theory incorporating multilevel processes, multiple causes, initiating and sustaining forces, and historical and contemporary flows is not just a prime weakness of the literature on Asian immigration to the United States, but remains a major limitation in the literature on international migration in general as well, despite some progress as reviewed below. Hence, the significance of developing a synthetic theory may very well go beyond the field of Asian immigration to the general field of international migration – of course with some apposite modifications.

The goal of this chapter is to develop such a comprehensive theoretical framework. Toward this end, it critically reviews contesting theories of international migration to lay out the broader backdrop relevant to later discussions, examines existing explanations of Asian immigration to the United States, analyzes the needs for a comprehensive theory, and formulates a synthetic theory to explain Asian immigration.

Theories of international migration

For a better understanding of the causes of Asian immigration to the United States, it is necessary to gain a general understanding of why international migration takes place. Many theories have been proposed to answer this question, and these may be pigeonholed into four categories: classical push–pull theory, economic models, sociological models, and integrated theories.

Classic push–pull theory

The earliest, classical approach to the explanation of migration is push–pull theory. This can be traced back to the pioneering work of Ernest Ravenstein (1889), who analyzed internal migration in England from 1871 to 1881, and the refinement of the American demographer Everett Lee (1966), who formulated it as a general theory for both internal and international migration. The basic idea is that migration takes place because push factors (e.g., natural disasters, population pressures, economic hardship, political turmoil or disturbances, environmental disadvantages) in places of origin cause people to leave and pull factors (e.g., economic opportunities, political preferences, environmental advantages) in places of destination attract people to those locations. For Ravenstein, pull factors play a more important role in causing migration than push factors. It is true that the most important factor motivating people to migrate is a desire to improve their lives rather than to escape from unpleasant conditions. However, push and pull factors are relative and may be considered as two sides of the same coin, since often a pull from the receiving country is also a push from the sending country along the same dimension (e.g., a higher wage in the receiving country versus a lower wage in the sending country). Lee also considered intervening obstacles, such as the distance between places of origin and destination, other physical barriers, immigration laws, and so on.[2]

Push–pull theory seemingly offers a commonsense, timeless, and ubiquitous list of conditions that influence migration. Empirically, it is not difficult to pick up some push or pull factors that can contribute to a specific migration flow or an individual's decision to migrate. However, its straightforward, eternal, and universal nature has also met with criticism. Some argue against the simplicity of this theory, since it simply lists push and pull factors. Others criticize its ahistorical and omnipresent nature, charging that it does not take into account the role of specific historical development in particular countries contributing to international migration, and so cannot explain why, with similar push or pull conditions, some countries have large immigration flows while others do not (Portes and Bach 1985). Furthermore, its ability to predict migration is seriously questioned. For example, according to this theory, the poorest countries should have the highest level of emigration because push factors are the strongest there. Nonetheless, many African countries – the poorest in the world – have very low levels of immigration to the United States. Large sending countries, such as Mexico, the Philippines, China, India, Korea, and so on, are not very poor at all. At the individual level, people of lower socioeconomic status are supposedly pushed and pulled more to other places, but in reality they are less likely to migrate. Migrants are not the poorest people from the poorest places. Other conditions beyond push–pull factors, such as cross-national connections, migrants' social networks, ability to migrate, and migration policy, must be taken into account in order to predict international migration.

Economic models

Since international migration is to a great extent economically based, economists have proposed a number of theories to explain it. Among the most influential are equilibrium theory, human capital theory, the new home economics of migration, and dual labor market theory.

Equilibrium theory

Equilibrium theory can trace its origin to economic models developed to explain internal labor migration in the process of economic development (Lewis 1954; Todaro 1969). It attributes rural–urban migration within a country to the disequilibrium (or imbalance) between rural areas and urban areas in labor supply and demand as well as in wages. When applied to international migration, the key argument of this theory is that international migration is caused by the imbalance between the sending country and the receiving country in the supply of and demand for labor and the resulting wage differences; international migration will restore equilibrium (or balance) to labor supply and demand as well as to wages. Specifically, in the receiving country there is a shortage of labor, leading to higher wages, while in the sending country there is a surplus or oversupply of labor, causing wages to be lower. As a result, workers in the country with a labor surplus and lower wages will move to the country with a labor scarcity and higher wages. Migration is thus a process of labor and wage adjustment from disequilibrium to equilibrium.

This theory makes perfect sense from an economic standpoint, especially for internal migration. However, when extended to international migration, it is handicapped by three major limitations. First, it does not consider immigration and emigration policies, which are crucial in international migration (Zolberg 1989). Regardless of imbalance in labor supply and demand as well as in wages, if a receiving country does not allow workers to enter, they cannot come; if the home country does not allow workers to leave, they cannot leave, unless illegally. Second, economic disparities in wages and employment are only a necessary condition, not a sufficient one. For example, this theory cannot explain why, with large employment and wage differences between the United States and many countries, quite a few African countries send few immigrants to the United States and why a particular migration flow (e.g. from Korea and the Philippines) started at a particular point but not earlier or later. Conditions other than employment and wage differences must be at play. Migrants do not always move to places with the highest wages. Third, contrary to this theory's predictions, migrants can sometimes move from a place of origin with a higher wage to a place of destination with a lower one – a telling example being the migration of large numbers of Taiwanese and South Koreans to mainland China.[3] In addition, this is a macrotheory that explains international migration mainly at the national level, not at the individual level, although one can infer that workers migrate in order to maximize their wages.

Human capital theory

Larry Sjaastad (1962) was the first to suggest a human capital theory of migration. His is a neoclassic economic theory, a microtheory of migration, and "a resource allocation framework." It views "migration as an investment increasing the productivity of human resources, an investment which has costs and which also renders returns" (Sjaastad 1962: 83). Both costs and returns can be monetary or non-monetary (e.g., opportunity and psychic costs and improved amenities). Returns can be positive or negative. The theory suggests that people migrate from one place to another because they expect a positive net return in the future. In other words, expected future returns or better opportunities (e.g., better jobs, higher wages, and a more satisfying lifestyle) motivate people to move to places where those expected future returns are the greatest. Framing it as a cost–benefit model, DaVanzo (1981) later elaborated on this theory and expanded its applications to different types of migration.

Human capital theory was proposed to explain human migration in general, both internal and international. This approach captures the essence of migration: people move because they want to be better off. Human capital theory recognizes that the costs and benefits of migration are not just economic, and it emphasizes expected future returns, not actual current income – a major difference between it and other neoclassic economic theories. Nevertheless, while it can explain why people want to move, it does not explain why they can move across national boundaries. Like equilibrium theory, it does not consider the role of migration policy.

The new home economics of migration
Migration is often analyzed at the individual level. Challenging this traditional strategy, economists Oded Stark and David Bloom (1985) shifted the focus of analysis from the individual to the household and proposed a new approach called the new home economics of migration. The key idea is that migration decisions are not made by isolated individuals, but often by larger units of related people, typically families or households but sometimes communities, in order to maximize expected income and minimize risks. Hence, migration can best be viewed as a calculated strategy to increase household income and to overcome constraints on household production or consumption caused by failures in insurance, capital, or consumption credit markets (Massey et al. 1998). This theory can be applied to both internal and international migration. Similar to human capital theory, it also talks about the maximization of expected future income and the minimization of risks associated with migration. However, it differs in that it uses the household rather than the individual as the unit of analysis. Thus, costs and returns are shared. Migrants depend upon "network and kinship capital."

The new home economics of migration recognizes the important role of the family or household in migration decisions. Moreover, it stresses that international migration seeks to improve not only absolute income but income relative to other households (Stark and Taylor 1989, 1991). However, it also shares many of the limitations of neoclassic economic theories. It does not emphasize the role of government migration policy; it is a micro-level theory; and it does not consider other, non-economic determinants of migration.

Dual labor market theory

Dual labor market theory was proposed by the economist Michael Piore (1979).[4] This theory argues that, because of the unlimited supply of labor from developing countries, international migration is caused not by push factors in sending countries (e.g., low wages and unemployment) but by an inherent demand for immigrant labor in developed countries (pull factors). However, the demand is not from the entire labor market or just from the lowest positions. Piore divides the labor market into two sectors – primary and secondary. He contends that the demand for immigrant labor comes mainly from the secondary labor market, where jobs tend to be unskilled and carry generally lower wages, fewer benefits, worse working conditions, considerable insecurity, low social status, and little opportunity for promotion. Since it is harder to attract workers into this market, immigrants are needed to fill the vacancies. Piore also contends that international migration is usually initiated through recruitment of laborers by employers (or their agents) in developed countries or by governments acting on their behalf. Employers, rather than workers, are critical. Such recruitment activities explain both the timing of particular migration movements and the particular areas to which migrants move.

Dual labor market theory recognizes the important role of demand for cheap labor in developing countries in explaining immigration to developed countries and highlights the role of employers' deliberate recruitment in the initiation of international migration flows. Nevertheless, the limitations of this theory should be noted. First, albeit important, the demand for cheap labor is not the only factor; cross-country connections, government policy, and people's motivations to improve their lives are important as well. Second, at least in the United States, the demand for cheap labor is not limited to the secondary labor market. Some immigrants are in the primary labor market, although often in its lower ranks (Portes and Rumbaut 1996); some are in ethnic enclaves (Portes and Bach 1985; Zhou 1992); and some are in the international labor market (Yang 2006a). Third, labor recruitment is not omnipresent in all migration movements. Finally, the role of migration policy is

24

treated as limited to the regulation of the receiving country's labor recruitment programs.

Sociological models

While economists seek to understand international migration using economic factors such as supply and demand, cost and benefit, and price and utility, sociologists tend to emphasize the importance of social factors in the initiation and continuation of migration. The most influential sociological theories of migration are world system theory and migrant social network theory.

World system theory

A number of important works have contributed to the formulation and development of world system theory for international migration. Elizabeth Petras (1981), one of the earliest world system theorists, treated international migration as a component of labor, commodity, and capital exchanges between core countries and peripheral/semiperipheral countries and an outcome of the development of the world capitalist system. Portes and Walton (1981) also viewed international migration as a part of the internal dynamics of the world capitalist system. In the same vein but in a more lucid and cogent fashion, Cheng and Bonacich (1984) argued that world capitalist development inevitably leads to imperialism, which generates both the demand for immigrant labor in the core countries and the supply of migrant labor in the peripheral countries; the very same forces of demand and supply therefore engender international migration from the peripheral countries to the advanced core countries. While earlier world system theorists explained international labor migration solely in terms of economic exchanges between peripheral and core countries, Sassen (1988) expanded the analysis to include military, political, and ideological linkages. She also considered foreign direct investment to be "a migration push factor." All different versions of world system theory view international migration as an integral part and a consequence of the development of the modern world economic system, within which exists a complex network of cross-national movements of capital, commodities, and labor. Labor moves from peripheral/semiperipheral countries to core countries, while capital moves in the opposite direction.

World system theory as a general theoretical framework makes several unique contributions to the understanding of international migration. First, it sees the linkages among the mobility of capital, technology, commodities, and labor. Second, it views international migration as a historical process. Third, it takes into account the demand for cheap labor, the supply of labor, income differential, employer recruitment, and government migration policy. Finally, perhaps its greatest contribution lies in its emphasis on intercountry connections as the most important factor in shaping international migration. Hence, one can predict that, all else being equal, the closer the relationship between a sending country and a receiving country, the higher the level of migration between them. Nonetheless, most theorists tend to reduce international migration to uneven economic exchanges between countries but pay less attention to other factors. The greatest limitation is that this is only a macro-theory that gives little consideration to the micro-processes of migration.

Social network theory
Another influential sociological theory of international migration is social network theory. The important role of social networks in international migration was recognized by early sociologists (Thomas and Znaniecki 1918–20; Tilly and Brown 1967). The seminal work of MacDonald and MacDonald (1974) concerning the chain migration from southern Italy to the northern cities of the United States at the turn of the twentieth century explicitly labeled these types of ties "social networks." The contribution by Massey et al. (1987) on the social organization of Mexican migration to the United States is also significant.

Migrants' social networks are their interpersonal relationships in places of origin and of destination through the connections of their relatives, friends, and ethnic communities and institutions. They are critical in explaining why people in one country can migrate to another country and why migration flows continue even after the initial driving forces stop. Migration is a process of network building, which depends on and, in return, reinforces social relationships across spaces (Portes and Bach 1985). Migration takes on a life of its own and becomes a self-sustaining process. Once started, it may have very little to do with the supply of, and demand for, labor. In the context of the United States, migrants' social networks are a crucial determinant of immigration, because under US laws the major modes of entry through family reunification or occupational preferences rely on the sponsorship of prospective migrants' relatives, friends, or employers in the United States. Without these connections, legal immigration is impossible. Furthermore, for survival and success after immigration, new immigrants depend on their networks for travel arrangements, room and board, job searching, language assistance, and other information. Social networks increase the likelihood of migration because they lower the costs and risks of movement and increase the expected returns (Massey et al. 1993). Massey et al. (1987: 170) were the first to treat migrant networks as a form of social capital, which can be converted into financial capital through foreign employment, higher wages, and remittances.

Social network theory is a unique contribution of sociology to international migration. It underscores that migration is not only an economic and political product, but, more importantly, a social product, as it relies on the existence of personal networks (Boyd 1989). It also recognizes the importance of social resources in the migration process. That is, migration depends not just on motivation, but also on resources, particularly social resources.

One of the limitations of social network theory is that it is more powerful in explaining the continuation of migration than its initiation. Another inadequacy lies in its inability to address the motivation for migration, as it stresses the social resources. Finally, social networks are only one type of migration resource, but others, such as migrants' financial capital and human capital (e.g., higher education, greater occupational skills, and more labor market experience), also play certain roles. It should also be noted that migrant social network theory is a micro-theory that aims to explain migration at the individual or household level.

Integrated theories

In the last two decades there have been attempts to integrate existing micro- and macro-theories of migration and to link how structural factors affect individual motivations and behaviors and therefore lead to migration. Two of these theories are structural determination theory and cumulative causation theory.

Structural determination theory
Portes and Rumbaut (1996) sketched a framework of undocumented international migration, which, in my opinion, is largely applicable to legal immigration as well. To explain migration, this framework considers the "promigration cycle" of structural societal changes, deliberate labor recruitment, changes in individual lifestyles, and relative deprivation.

According to Portes and Rumbaut (1996), structural changes caused by external intervention and/or internal restructuring will disrupt the economy of the sending country and link it to the core receiving country, causing changes in consumption patterns. Structural changes are followed by labor recruitment from the receiving country. At the individual level, macro-structural forces cause the disruption of traditional lifestyles and a growing gap between new consumption aspirations and the means to fulfill them. People who want better lives and opportunities look for alternatives – one of which is international migration. The first group of migrants moves, and others follow. Over time social networks develop, linking origin with destination. Networks sustain migration, and migration becomes cumulative.

This theory considers macro- and micro-level determinants and connections in causing migration. A major problem is that Portes and Rumbaut limit its applicability to undocumented migration. Partly because of this consideration of undocumented immigration, the role of intercountry disparities and migration policies is deemphasized, although the authors properly recognize the role of structural changes. In addition, they provide only an outline, without much elaboration.

Cumulative causation theory

Another theory along the same lines is cumulative causation theory. The concept of "the cumulative causation of migration" was first suggested by Myrdal (1957) and Massey (1990) and is systematically articulated by Massey et al. (1993, 1994). This theory argues that migration is a process that sustains itself in a cumulative fashion through the expansion of networks, the distribution of income, the distribution of land, the organization of agriculture, the culture of migration, the regional distribution of human capital, the social meaning of work, and the structure of production. Causation is cumulative because each act of migration changes the subsequent context within which migration decisions are made. Migration causes motivational, structural, and cultural changes that lead to more migration. It becomes self-perpetuating and increasingly independent of the initial causes.

This theory represents an integration of international migration theories, especially those dealing with the continuation of migration. It incorporates different strands of theories such as social network theory, neoclassic economic theories, and structural theories. It describes the whole process of international migration from initiation to ending. It specifies the mechanisms of migration. It considers both micro- or individual-level factors and macro- or community- and societal-level factors in sustaining migration. However, cumulative causation theory basically does not deal with the initiation of migration. Moreover, it does not directly address the role of migration policies.

The theories reviewed above pertain to international migration in general. To what extent have they been used to explain Asian immigration to the United States, and what are the gaps in the existing explanations of Asian immigration? These are the questions to which we now turn.

The need for a comprehensive theory of Asian immigration

Asian immigration to the United States has been distinguished by such unique characteristics as "the bachelor's society," "paper sons" or "paper families," "picture brides," "war brides," "mail-order brides," "extended family," and, most importantly, exclusion and restriction. Nonetheless, like other international migration flows, it has been driven by similar economic, political, military, social, and policy forces at both macro- and micro-levels.

Explanations of Asian immigration to the United States

Although volumes have been written on the subject, there have been only meager efforts towards developing a theory of Asian immigration to the United States. Currently, there are mostly sketchy explanations of why Asians come to this country, either historically or contemporarily, applying some theories of international migration reviewed in the preceding section. Earlier works drew mostly on a push–pull framework. For example, Coolidge ([1909] 1969), who was among the first to write systematically about Chinese immigration to the United States, depicted pre-Exclusion Chinese immigration as a result of the pushes of the Taiping Rebellion, famine, and poverty and the pulls of the Gold Rush in the Sacramento Valley and high wages in America. Lasker (1969: 325–6) also attributed the emigration of early Filipinos to the pushes of "social restrictions" and the pulls of "larger earnings and a higher standard of living" and attractions of "a more developed form of civilization." Tsai (1986) attributed early Chinese immigration to heavy taxation, corruption, oppression, population pressure, bureaucratic incompetence, natural disasters, social unrest, and rebellion.

The push–pull framework is still used by some researchers today because of its convenience. Takaki (1989) described the reasons for earlier Chinese, Japanese, Korean, Filipino, and Indian immigration largely in terms of push and pull factors, but he adeptly placed these in historical context. In his analysis of early

Chinese and Japanese immigration, Daniels (1988) used a similar approach with skills of historical analysis. Even as late as the early twenty-first century, Segal (2002) still employed this framework to account for Asian immigration to the United States. Her list of push factors includes lack of opportunity, war, political-legal-religious persecution, natural disasters, personal dissatisfaction, sparse individual resources, and personal constraints; her list of pull factors encompasses increased opportunity, freedom/safety, family reunification, and adventure. With almost no reference to previous works, she further applied this framework to explaining each of the migration flows from China, Japan, India, the Philippines, and Korea in the pre-1965 period. While some push–pull factors no doubt influence Asian immigration, this explanation remains simplistic, without considering the historical and structural processes. It does not take into account the new developments in the field of international migration.

Cheng and Bonacich (1984) developed a general world system theory of migration with the intention of accounting for Asian immigration to the United States before World War II. Although they did not directly explain Asian immigration, the other articles in their edited volume all employed their world system framework in their analyses. Cheng and Bonacich did not treat pre-World War II immigration simply as a result of discrete pushes and pulls in the Asian homelands and the receiving country. Rather, they viewed it as an outcome of US imperialism in Asia, which simultaneously created potential emigrants by displacing peasants from the traditional economies and a demand for a cheap labor force in the United States, especially on the West Coast, that could be filled by these emigrants. This theory provides an elegant historical-structural explanation of pre-World War II Asian immigration, but it is limited to historical immigration and does not address micro-level determinants.

Continuing the world system approach in Cheng and Bonacich's (1984) volume, but recognizing changes in new Asian immigration, Ong, Bonacich, and Cheng (1994) developed a restructuring approach to explain post-World War II Asian immigration. They maintained that this new immigration, particularly since 1965, is a product of the restructuring in the global capitalist system and in the United States. The restructuring has impacts on two major strands of immigration. Immigration from Latin America is used to accomplish the cheap labor strategy, and Asian immigration is used to achieve both "investment-in-innovation" and cheap labor strategies. The authors also contended that Asian immigration is a force that contributes to the restructuring. This restructuring perspective takes into account new developments in the world capitalist economy in shaping new Asian immigration, but its explanation remains at the macro- and structural level. It does not go beyond economic variables. Chan's (1991) analysis of historical and contemporary Asian immigration also reflects a similar approach, which goes beyond a simple list of push–pull factors and takes into account the involvements of foreign imperial powers, although it does not develop a theoretical framework.

While focusing on the impact of immigration laws and policies on Asian American communities rather than explaining immigration, Hing (1993) demonstrated that US immigration laws and policies have shaped Asian immigration. Before 1965, US laws allowed the admission of Asians only for specific purposes, excluded them altogether if necessary, and always kept them in control. However, since 1965 the United States has established a uniform egalitarian framework for the admission of all people without considering race or ethnicity, thereby opening the door to Asians. Nonetheless, Erika Lee (2004) suggested that, even after 1965, race or ethnicity remains an implicit consideration in admission, although class and immigrant status have been given more weight in determining immigration opportunities and treatment. Park and Park's (2005) recent book also showed the effect of immigration laws on Asian immigration. Works along these lines demonstrate that immigration laws and policies have great impact and should be taken into account for any explanation (albeit not the only determinant) of Asian immigration.

In an attempt to integrate the literature, Min (2006a: 7–9) sketched an analytical framework of Asian immigration by including four factors: (1) push factors (e.g., economic difficulties caused by famine or change in industrial structure, a change in government, or war), and pull factors (e.g., better economic and career opportunities, better opportunities for children's education, or political freedom); (2) US immigration policy and the emigration policies of Asian countries; (3) the military, political, and economic linkages between the United States and Asian countries; and (4) the globalization of the economic system, education, travel, and the media and the ease of population movement. This framework provides an expanded list of the factors that influence Asian immigration. Nevertheless, the interaction of these factors ought to be taken into account, as, for instance, US involvement may initiate or exacerbate pushes or generate pulls, and globalization may lead to changes in migration policies. Globalization and the US–Asian country linkages are intertwined and hard to separate as different processes. Moreover, this is still only a macro-approach, and factors at the community and individual levels should be taken into consideration. Overall, more theorization and integration are needed in order to create a seamless comprehensive theory of Asian immigration.

Limitations of the existing explanations

The foregoing review of the existing explanations of Asian immigration reveals several major limitations. First and foremost, all of them address the initiation of Asian immigration but not its continuation. In particular, social network theory has not been incorporated into the theoretical formulations and has seldom been reflected in empirical analysis. Second, associated with the first limitation, these explanations rarely consider both the macro- and the micro-processes together. Third, they are not comprehensive because they do not take into account all, or at least important, determinants of Asian immigration. Fourth, except for the works of Cheng and Bonacich (1984) and Ong, Bonacich, and Cheng (1994), explanations are normally sketchy and underdeveloped, often only in a few paragraphs or less. Finally, push–pull theories excepted, these theories ordinarily explain either historical (pre-World War II or pre-1965) or new (post-World War II or post-1965) Asian immigration, but not both.

Thus, in order to gain a better understanding of Asian immigration to the United States, developing a comprehensive theory is a desideratum. The new theory must consider the following elements:

1 the integration of theories concerning the initiation and theories concerning the continuity of Asian immigration;
2 the integration of macro- and micro-theories of migration (we need a dynamic model that includes both societal-level and individual-level factors and allows interactions between macro-processes and micro-level decisions);
3 a comprehensive coverage of important conditions that influence Asian immigration;
4 a fully developed theory with not only skeleton but also meat;
5 a theory that considers both historical and contemporary Asian immigration in a single model.

Indubitably, a synthetic theory is more powerful than the coexistence of different theories that can explain only certain aspects, levels, or periods of Asian immigration. It is also possible and feasible to develop such a synthetic theory by integrating the useful elements of existing theories.

A synthetic theory of Asian immigration

Based on the considerations in the preceding section, this section proposes a comprehensive theory of Asian immigration to the United States labeled "macro–micro interactive and cumulative causation theory."[5] The basic idea of this theory is that Asian immigration to the United States can best be seen as the result of an interactive and cumulative process of disparities between Asian countries and the United States; multilevel connections between the United States and Asian countries and between potential immigrants and their families and communities at the origin and their social networks at the destination; and migration policies in both the sending and receiving countries. Analytically, this theory highlights three clusters of determinants: intercountry disparities, multilevel connections, and migration policies. But, in reality, these factors operate at several levels in a cumulative and interactive fashion. The balance of this section elaborates these clusters and then outlines the cumulative and interactive process involving them.

Intercountry disparities

A fundamental premise of this theory is that people do not normally engage in international migration if conditions or life opportunities in their home country are the same as or similar to those in another country. People migrate across national borders because of differences in economic, political, social, and environmental conditions or in life chances; they move to improve their lives. This is true universally across space and time.

Significant or substantial differences exist, historically and contemporarily, between Asian sending countries and the United States in economic, political, social, and environmental conditions. Economic disparities in employment, income, and quality of life are usually the most important factors that motivate migration. This basic idea is underlined by push–pull theory (Lee 1966) and neoclassic economic models (Lewis 1954; Sjaastad 1962; Todaro 1969) and recognized by world system theory (e.g., Petras 1981), cumulative causation theory (Massey et al. 1993, 1994), and some other theories. Asian immigration has been motivated by fewer employment opportunities, lower income, and a lower quality of life in the sending countries, on the one hand, and more job opportunities, higher wages, and a higher quality of life in the United States, on the other (see, for example, Chan 1991; Melendy 1977; Min 1995, 2006a; Takaki 1989). It is important to understand that relative deprivation plays a more important role in migration decisions than absolute poverty, since many Asian immigrants in the post-1965 period are neither the poorest nor the unemployed but educated middle-class people. It is income relative to that of fellow citizens and of people (especially relatives and friends) in the country of destination that is crucial. The gap between life aspirations and the means to fulfill them must be a very important determinant in the decision of any international migration.

Political conditions are pertinent to international migration because personal safety, freedom, and democracy are some of the basic human needs. International disparities in political conditions are also important stimuli for Asian emigration. Historically, political uprisings (e.g., the Taiping Rebellion (1851–64) in China; the Sepoy Mutiny of 1857, also known as India's First War of Independence) and ethnic warfare (e.g., from 1855 to 1868 between the Hakka (guest people) and the Punti (local people) in China) directly or indirectly provoked the exodus of Asians from their homelands (see, for example, Chan 1991; Chen 1980; Ingram and Girod 2004; Melendy 1977; Takaki 1989). More recently, the civil war (1945–9) in China, the Korean War (1950–3), and the Vietnam War (1965–75), as well as a lack of personal freedom, personal security, political stability, and democracy in many sending countries, pushed Asians to leave (see, for example, Min 1995, 2006a; Zhou 1992). Peace, democracy, political stability, the rule of law, and individual freedom in the United States have attracted Asians here.

Inequalities in social conditions also spur immigration. In particular, in the post-1965 period many Asians migrated to the United States because of a lack of college education opportunities for their children in their homelands and much greater opportunities in the United States (Min 2006a). At least until the 1990s, in almost all Asian countries only a small proportion of high-school graduates were able to enroll in college following intense competition through standardized college entrance examinations, but in the United States a college education is essentially open to any student. Although in recent years a significantly higher percentage of high-school graduates in South Korea, Taiwan, Hong Kong, and China can obtain higher education, the gap between these countries and the United States remains large.

Differences in environmental hazards can also encourage immigration. Natural or man-made disasters (e.g., flooding, drought, epidemic, pollution) can exacerbate living conditions and drive people away. The effects of disasters on historical Asian immigration have been cited in the literature (see, for example, Chan 1991; Melendy 1977; Takaki 1989), although the impact of disasters and other environmental hazards on new immigration has rarely been documented. While natural or man-made disasters also occur from time to time in the United States, their impact is less severe because of disaster management and prevention. Because of stricter environmental controls, the United States is a better place to live than most Asian countries in terms of pollution and physical environment.

Demographic disparities are sometimes mentioned as determinants of international migration. Nonetheless, in my view demographic *disparities* are not pertinent at all. As Massey et al. (1998: 11) pointed out, "people do not migrate because they perceive demographic differences." Most immigrants do not come from countries with the highest fertility rates, the fastest population growth rates, or the highest population density. High fertility and high mortality rates, coupled with high population growth in sending countries, however, may indirectly influence migration through their effect on employment, housing, schooling, infrastructure, national resources, and life satisfaction.[6]

Economic, political, social, and environmental disparities can be considered push and pull factors along the same dimensions. Worse conditions in the home country (e.g., a higher unemployment rate, lower wages, a higher poverty rate, lack of democracy, lack of personal freedom, lack of college education opportunities) are push factors, while better conditions in the receiving country (e.g., a lower unemployment rate, higher wages, a lower poverty rate, democracy, personal freedom, college education opportunities) are pull factors. In other words, disparities reflect both push and pull factors. They are both sides of the same coin.

These disparities at the macro-level translate into individual and family migration decisions at the micro-level. Disparities mean different life chances for individuals and families. Disparities explain individual and family motivations for migration. Disparities push people to leave worse economic, political, social, and environmental conditions for better living conditions. Humans always want to have a better life. It is this longing for a better life that underlies the migration decisions of individuals and families from one country to another.

Multilevel connections

However, mere cross-country disparities will not automatically cause migration, and they serve only as potential motivators for migration. There must be forces that initiate migration and forces that sustain it. These initiating and perpetuating forces entail connections at both macro- and micro-levels. At the macro-level, there must be international connections between sending and receiving countries. In fact, intercountry connections can be conceptualized as a network of countries linked by interactions (Kritz and Zlotnik 1992). US involvement in Asian sending countries acts to establish US–Asian ties and creates a conducive social environment that renders immigration possible or more likely to occur. It helps activate the effect of disparities between the Asian countries and the United States, and it causes the formation of a pool of potential migrants and the emergence of emigration as an actual option. The higher the level of US involvement in Asian countries, the higher the level of immigration to the United States, *ceteris paribus*. This is the essence of world system theory (Sassen 1988; Light and Bonacich 1988). Intercountry connections can be economic, military, political, or cultural. Each dimension of these connections or involvements affects immigration through specific mechanisms.

The most common form of US–Asian connections is economic involvement, including US trade, US direct investment, the establishment of US-owned factories in Asia, the operation of US transnational corporations in Asia, the training of Asian management and technical personnel, and so forth. This involvement displaces people from traditional economies and creates an emigrant pool; it heightens potential migrants' awareness of the disparities between the United States and their own country; and it consolidates the objective and ideological linkages with the receiving country (Yang 1995). It therefore becomes a factor pushing Asians to leave their homelands and pulling them to the United

States. Such effects before World War II were well documented in Cheng and Bonacich's (1984) volume. The Western powers, including the United States, imposed unequal treaties concerning trade, tariffs, and labor flow on all the Asian countries; shook slack Asians from their traditional economic base, rendering them available for labor recruitment; and actively recruited Asians as cheap labor to meet the demand on the US Pacific Coast and Hawaii. The impact of US economic involvement on new Asian immigration after World War II was analyzed by Ong, Bonacich, and Cheng in 1994 and needs more documentation. But one basic fact is that major Asian sending countries in the post-1965 period all have close economic ties with the United States.

Another important dimension is US military involvement in Asian countries, encompassing military bases overseas, military intervention in other countries, and temporary occupation of foreign countries. The most important impact of US military bases is the generation of a large number of "international marriages" between US servicemen and local residents (Yang 1995). US military bases also hire many supporting personnel from the local civilian population, who may one day become immigrants via their personal relationships with US service personnel. Additionally, a US military presence helps disseminate American culture through movies, television programs, and popular culture and strengthens potential migrants' material and ideological linkages with the United States, thereby motivating migration. The evidence on the large effect of US military occupation and bases on the immigration of Asian women as war brides is well documented (Glenn 1986; Kim 1977; Min 2006b; Williams 1991; Yuh 2002). Examples include a significant number of Japanese war brides after the brief US occupation of Japan and the establishment of military bases there after World War II (Glenn 1986; Williams 1991), a large number of Filipino war brides from the end of the war until the abandonment of military bases in the Philippines in the early 1990s, Chinese war brides from Taiwan after China's civil war and the founding of US military bases there, and Korean war brides after the Korean War (Kim 1977; Kim 1987; Yuh 2002). The adoption of Korean orphans after the Korean War is a telling example of the result of US military intervention. The Vietnam War also created a large number of refugees from Indochina. Indeed, the numbers of Vietnamese, Cambodian, and Laotian immigrants did not really become significant until US involvement in Vietnam, and especially after its withdrawal in 1975.

Political connections represent another dimension of inter-country links. These may include the establishment of diplomatic relations and US influence in the formation of political systems. The establishment of formal diplomatic relations greatly facilitates immigration. The normalization of Sino-US diplomatic relations in 1979 is a case in point. This normalization immediately jump-started significant immigration from mainland China to the United States and has facilitated major immigration since then. The restoration of diplomatic relations between Vietnam and the United States in 1995 also significantly increased Vietnamese immigration. The US government has played a significant role in the formation of political systems in a number of Asian countries, such as the Philippines, Japan, and South Korea, and the establishment of a democratic system may impact immigration by strengthening the ideological linkages between people in these countries and the United States.

The final dimension of intercountry connections is US cultural involvement in Asian countries. This may comprise sending students to study abroad, the exchange of scholars and students, the availability of movies and television programs across countries, and cross-country cultural performance activities. It affects immigration to the United States mainly via the diffusion of American norms, values, lifestyles, and ideologies (Yang 1995). Such cultural dissemination strengthens the ideological linkages of potential migrants with American society, reduces social distance between prospective migrants and Americans, and therefore encourages migration. Although all forms of US cultural involvement have some impact on Asian immigration, Asian students studying in American colleges and universities probably have the greatest effect for a couple of reasons. First, returnees are usually in an important position to influence their homeland's population, culture, and behavior, and their behavior often consciously or unconsciously reflects American culture. Second, many Asian students become immigrants after completing their education by adjusting their status to that of permanent resident. This is especially true at earlier stages of development in their home countries after World War II, although an increasing number of them have returned to their homelands in recent years. Taiwan, South Korea, and, most recently, China are cases in point.

To be sure, the ties between the United States and Asian sending countries are not isolated. They are part of the globalization process in the world capitalist system and reflect the relationships between core and periphery and semiperiphery. Especially as a superpower in the post-World War II era and the sole superpower in the post-Soviet era, the United States has been involved economically, politically, militarily, and culturally around the world, and its involvement in Asia is only part of this. Major immigration comes from wherever the United States is heavily involved (Yang 1995).

At the micro-level, there must also be interpersonal connections/relationships or social networks linking prospective migrants in the country of origin with their relatives, friends, and/or ethnic communities and institutions in the country of destination. There are three types of social networks that influence migration. The most basic type is a kinship-based network consisting of family members and relatives, and the second type is a friendship-based network. Often neglected and inadequately researched in the international migration literature, the third type is a network based on ethnic communities and institutions (e.g., churches, alumni associations, townspeople's associations). In the literature, social networks are treated only, or largely, as a force sustaining migration but not as an initiating force (see, for example, Massey et al. 1993, 1994, 1998). However, it is my contention that social networks have both a migration-generating and a migration-sustaining function. Social networks generate migration through two mechanisms. First, they provide information on economic, political, social, and environmental conditions in the country of destination. Oftentimes, selective, positive, successive, migration-inducing images from family members, friends, and employers are transmitted to prospective migrants, while negative, migration-dampening images are omitted or downplayed. Second, the networks provide an indispensable pass for admission to the United States through sponsorship. Since 1965, potential migrants must be sponsored either by their relatives for family reunification or by employers for occupational preferences. Without these sponsorships, Asian immigration is almost impossible. Not only do social networks help generate migration, but more often they help sustain it, even in the fading or absence of the initiating forces that motivated individuals to move. Social networks sustain migration by helping immigrants maximize their returns and minimize their losses through the conduits of information and social and financial assistance for their survival and upward mobility. Migration often starts with one or a few members of a family and then expands to other members of the family, to the extended family, and even to an entire community. This is the process of "chain migration," which took place historically and most importantly in the post-1965 period in many Asian families. Among the three types of social network, the kinship-based network generally plays the most important role in spawning and sustaining migration through information, assistance, and family-based sponsorship. While friendship-based networks and community/institution-based networks do not directly sponsor immigrants, they can indirectly induce migration and sustain it through information, assistance, and employment-based sponsorship. Albeit not consciously conceptualized, there is some evidence from the literature that, historically, Asian immigration was influenced by social networks based on kinship, friendship, and ethnic community/institutions (see, for example, Chan 1991: ch. 4). Also note that migration is not only a network-dependent process but also a network-generating and network-expanding process, which can lead to more migration.

A social network is not static but can expand, and individuals with a higher level of human capital and other personal resources can build up their networks faster than those with a lower level of such capital and resources. People who have more human capital and other resources are more capable of moving than those with less human capital and fewer resources. Since 1965, the relatively high levels of education, occupational skills, and physical capital of many Asians help them reconnect with their kinship-based networks or build anew their friendship-based and institution/ community-based social networks in the destination, and therefore facilitate their immigration.

The notion of connections or linkages is crucial in any explanation of international migration. Since international migration transfers people from one place to another, there must be forces that tie the two places together – connections. Linkages at both macro- and micro-levels are necessary for migration to occur. Intercountry connections engender pushes and pulls and help set migration in motion, while connections at the micro-level involving individuals, families, and perhaps communities can provide an impetus and especially keep migration going on. International migration is caused and sustained by a network of countries linked by interactions and by migrant social networks. Multilevel connections embody the essence of transnationalism because the classic transnationalism approach emphasizes the maintenance of ties linking countries of origin and destination (Basch, Glick Schiller, and Szanton Blanc 1994), although it does not extend to cross-national connections.

Migration policies

International inequalities, intercountry connections, cross-border social networks, and individual motivations and abilities are not sufficient to generate international migration because, unlike internal migration, international migration is governed by rules of entry and exit in both home and host countries. Hence, migration policies of sending and receiving countries must be an integral part of the explanation for any international migration.[7]

The immigration policy of the receiving country is perhaps most crucial. One policy option is exclusion or restriction. If the receiving country shuts its doors, no one can enter, except illegally, or, if it imposes restrictions, immigration will decrease. This is evident throughout the history of Asian immigration to the United States. US open-door immigration policy before 1882 enabled tens of thousands of Chinese to come, but the Chinese

Exclusion Act of 1882 and a series of acts that extended it effectively reduced Chinese immigration to a trickle until 1943, when all the Exclusion laws were repealed. The Gentlemen's Agreement of 1907–8 banned the entry of Japanese laborers but allowed those already in the United States to bring in their spouses, children, and parents. The Immigration Act of 1917 established the "Asiatic barred zone" and prevented the immigration of all Asian laborers except for Filipinos, who were US nationals at the time, and Japanese laborers, whose entry was governed by the Gentlemen's Agreement. The Emergency Quota Act of 1921 and its permanent replacement, the National Origins Act of 1924, set an annual quota of 100 for each of the Asian countries and so severely restricted their immigration. A second policy option is passive acceptance – namely, the granting of access without facilitation or hindrance (Portes and Rumbaut 2006). One example is the Immigration and Nationality Act of 1965, which, without the intent of encouraging Asian immigration, lifted the restrictions, offered Asians equal opportunity, and has led to a tremendous increase in immigration. The third policy alternative is active encouragement (ibid.). Examples include deliberate government involvement in recruiting Japanese, Korean, and Filipino laborers to Hawaii in the late nineteenth and early twentieth centuries.

The emigration policies of some Asian countries also play certain roles in immigration, albeit relatively minor in comparison to the role of US immigration policy. For example, the Qing Dynasty in China punished emigration with decapitation. This law actively deterred the emigration of many Chinese until 1860 and was finally repealed in 1894 (Chen 1980: 7). Japan forbade emigration before 1885. The Korean kingdom also had an anti-emigration policy before 1903, but relaxed it between 1903 and 1905, making Korean emigration possible during that period (Min 2006b). The People's Republic of China (PRC) imposed many restrictions on leaving the country until 1979, so that it was very difficult for a Chinese to obtain a passport (Zhou 1992). However, the PRC has since gradually relaxed its restrictions on emigration and foreign travel. The Republic of Korea (South Korea) enacted an Overseas Emigration Law in 1962 to encourage emigration in order to alleviate unemployment, control the population, earn foreign exchange, and acquire knowledge of advanced technology (Light and Bonacich 1988). The following year it started the export of Korean contract laborers to earn foreign currency and obtain new technology. These actions certainly stimulated Korean emigration. Nevertheless, South Korea restricted the emigration of draft resisters, convicts, diseased persons, political dissidents, persons who might damage the country's reputation, and the elite (e.g., former National Assembly members, military officials holding rank above colonel, government officials above the rank of bureau director, and people with property values over $100,000) (ibid.). Most of these restrictions have been rescinded. Such laws and policies no doubt had some impact on emigration from these countries. However, since many Asian countries currently impose no restrictions on exit, the effect of emigration policy is generally small.

Migration policies reflect intercountry relationships and/or intracountry developments. For example, US open-door immigration policy in the pre-Exclusion era mirrored the country's needs for economic development and cheap labor. The exclusion and restriction policies reflected racial/ethnic tensions and class struggles and differential relations between the United States and different Asian countries. The repeal of the Exclusion laws and restrictive immigration policies was the outcome of changes in US relations with its allied countries and other nations. The enactment of the Immigration and Nationality Act of 1965 was a result of the ineffective national origins quota system, the increasingly tolerant attitudes of Americans toward ethnic minorities, Americans' growing rejection of discrimination against their fellow citizens and immigrants not from northwestern Europe after the passage of the Civil Rights Act of 1964, and the fading opposition to immigration as a result of continuing postwar prosperity (Yang 1995).

The cumulative and interactive process

The three clusters of conditions presented above represent the important determinants of Asian immigration to the United States.

As mentioned earlier, dissected for analytical purpose notwith-standing, these factors operate at different levels in a cumulative manner to shape Asian immigration. This section outlines how these factors bring about and sustain Asian immigration cumulatively and interactively.

The process began with economic, political, social, and environmental disparities between Asian countries and the United States, which has a much shorter history than most Asian countries. These disparities existed because of historical, spatial, and/ or structural reasons. However, the emergence of the United States as a world imperial power in the capitalist system in the second half of the nineteenth century (Barraclough 1978) gave rise to US advantages over Asian nations. In the nineteenth and early twentieth centuries, the American quest for expanded territories, cheap raw materials, and cheap labor in the less developed world led to its penetration into some Asian countries. This economic penetration resulted in the displacement of agricultural workers, making them potential emigrants. Natural or human-made disasters, political turmoil, economic hardship, and social inequity further exacerbated the displacement of peasants. Economic development in the United States, particularly in the West and Hawaii, also produced a high demand for cheap labor. US companies or their agents actively recruited Asian workers from China, Japan, Korea, and the Philippines to fill their labor needs, often with the lure of higher wages, large houses, and opportunities to get rich. These pushes and pulls generated by US–Asian disparities and the economic penetration of the United States into the Asian sending countries were felt by prospective Asian migrants and families as well as their communities. Seeking opportunities to improve their lives, the earliest groups of Asians, normally men, decided to migrate to the United States. They often originated from a few communities where US involvement was the deepest and were directed to the regions of America where labor needs were the greatest, such as the West Coast and Hawaii. The US open-door immigration policy in the early period imposed no barriers. These early immigrants gradually built their communities and social networks in the areas of settlement. They visited their home villages once in a while and later sent for their fathers, brothers, and uncles, then their grown-up sons, and eventually their wives and daughters. Their social networks expanded and continued, and immigration was reproduced again and again. Their home communities became emigrant communities. But the economic competition of Asian immigrants with white workers, racism, and international relations resulted in a series of laws or policies that excluded or restricted the immigration of Asian labor groups one after another, reducing Asian immigration to a very low level.

US participation in World War II changed the dynamics of Asian immigration. America's alliance with China and the Philippines in the war, the repeal of the Chinese exclusion laws in 1943, and the granting of US citizenship rights to Filipinos and Indians in 1946 improved the status of these groups. But the attack on Pearl Harbor and the US declaration of war against Japan, together with racism, devastated the Japanese community and sent most of the Japanese to concentration camps. A number of special laws or policies, such as the War Brides Act of 1945, the Alien Fiancées and Fiancés Act of 1946, the Chinese Alien Wives of American Citizens Act of 1946, the Displaced Persons Act of 1948, the Refugee Relief Act of 1953, the Refugee-Escapee Act of 1957, and the Executive Order of May 1962, brought more than 33,000 Chinese, especially women, to the United States (see chapter 3 for details). US military bases in Japan and the Philippines after the war resulted in large numbers of Japanese and Filipino war brides. US educational and cultural involvements in the Philippines also led to the immigration of many Filipino nurses. The Korean War, with its US military bases, set in motion the immigration of many Korean war brides and orphans. The international contexts, US involvements, US–Asian disparities, Asian migrants' social networks, and laws or policies pertaining to migration all interacted to result in the movement of these immigrants in the postwar period. The influx of many women also transformed the Asian communities in America.

The Immigration and Nationality Act of 1965 marked a fundamental change in US immigration policy, which eliminated almost all historical restrictions on Asian immigration. Similarly, most Asian countries have removed obstacles to emigration or loosened exit policies. Large economic, political, social, and environmental differences between the Asian sending countries and the United States have continued to motivate many Asians to leave their homelands. Some significant political events in Asian countries (e.g., the Chinese Cultural Revolution of 1966–76; the Tiananmen Square incident on June 4, 1989) also deepened crises in those countries and precipitated emigration. US economic, military, political, and cultural involvements in Asia have resulted in a large number of people who are ready to emigrate to America. Specifically, the ongoing presence of US military bases in South Korea, the Philippines (until 1992), and Japan has continued to generate significant numbers of "war brides." America's involvement in the Vietnam War and its withdrawal in 1975 produced a huge number of Indochinese refugees, who later adjusted their status to that of permanent resident. The normalization of Sino-US relations in 1979 and Vietnamese–US relations in 1995 has since facilitated Chinese and Vietnamese immigration. Ongoing or growing economic ties between the United States and Japan, South Korea, the Philippines, China, India, Vietnam, and so forth have also engendered pushes and pulls, as have continuous US cultural influences in Asian countries. In particular, the vast number of Asian students studying in American colleges and universities has become a major source of Asian brain flow, since many of them have later found jobs and become permanent residents. Earlier Asian immigrants (social networks) have sponsored their relatives and friends through family renunciation and occupational preferences. US immigration policy advocating family reunification and occupational preferences has increased the role of social networks in producing Asian immigration and has shaped the strategies of Asians and their families to improve their life chances. Previously established Asian communities have provided a variety of assistance for new immigrants and helped sustain continuous immigration. New Asian immigrants further sponsor their relatives and friends, leading to chain migration.

Summary

Many theories have been proposed to explain why international migration occurs. Among the most influential are push–pull theory, equilibrium theory, human capital theory, the new home economics of migration, dual labor market theory, world system theory, social network theory, structural determination theory, and cumulative causation theory. Each of these theories has merits and limitations, as discussed earlier.

Applying some of these theories, researchers have attempted to explain Asian immigration to the United States by the push–pull framework, world system theory, the restructuring perspective, and a hybrid approach. With a couple of exceptions, these explanations are normally sketchy and underdeveloped. They are inadequate, focusing on only the initiating forces, the macro-process, and either historical or contemporary migration. A comprehensive theory of Asian immigration must incorporate both the initiating and sustaining forces, both the macro- and micro-processes, and both historical and contemporary Asian immigration.

The new theory of Asian immigration, which may be labeled "macro–micro interactive and cumulative causation theory," proposed in this chapter argues that, in order for Asian immigration to occur, there must be three clusters of factors: economic, political, social, and/or environmental disparities between Asian sending countries and the United States;[8] economic, political, military, and/or cultural linkages between the sending and receiving countries, and social networks of potential migrants and their families and communities in the places of origin and destination;[9] and the immigration and emigration policies of the USA and Asian countries respectively. Moreover, these factors affect Asian immigration cumulatively and interactively at different levels.

This theory integrates the useful ideas of world system theory, migrant social network theory, the migration policy perspective, push–pull theory, neoclassic economic theories, structural determination theory, and cumulative causation theory into one body by highlighting international inequalities, multilevel connections, and immigration and emigration policies as the fundamental forces leading to Asian immigration to the United States and by considering the cumulative and interactive effects of these forces. It treats intercountry disparities and intercountry connections as push and pull factors. It considers connections between historical and contemporary processes in the world capitalist system, both macro- and micro-factors, both structural and policy factors, and both migrants' motivations and abilities to immigrate. It is believed that this theory provides a general framework that can better explain Asian immigration to the United States. The validity of this theory is subject to empirical verification when pre-1965 and post-1965 Asian immigration is examined in the next two chapters.

3

Pre-1965 Asian Immigration

Before 1965, Asian immigration to the present-day United States was largely restricted, and several groups of laborers experienced exclusion. Many Asians still managed to come to America. Asian groups that saw significant immigration during this period were Chinese, Japanese, Koreans, Filipinos, and Asian Indians. A total of more than 1 million Asians arrived in the United States and Hawaii between 1820 and 1965 (table 3.1), including the foregoing major groups and a small number of other Asian groups (not shown in the table). Since collapsing years will conceal some important historical patterns, I deliberately leave the annual data intact, although this makes the table longer. Basically following the chronological order of arrivals by group, this chapter examines who arrived, where they hailed from, where they settled, why they came, and what they experienced in the pre-1965 period.

Chinese immigration and exclusion

The pioneers

This chapter begins with the Chinese because they were the first Asian group that immigrated to the United States in large numbers. Oftentimes, many books treat the Chinese arrivals during the Gold Rush in the mid-nineteenth century as the beginning of Chinese America. While it is correct that this was the first

Table 3.1 Number of immigrants to the United States and Hawaii from major Asian sending countries, 1820–1965

Year	China[d]			Japan		Philippines		Korea		India
	US	SF	Hawaii	US	Hawaii	US	Hawaii	US	Hawaii	
1820–9	3									9
1830–9	8									38
1840	0									1
1841	2									—
1842	4									2
1843[a]	3									2
1844	3									—
1845	6									0
1846	7									4
1847	4									8
1848	0	3								6
1849	3	325								8
1850	3	450								4
1851	0	2,716								2
1852	0	20,026	293							4
1853	42	4,270	64							5
1854	13,100	16,084[e]	12							0
1855	3,526	3,329[e]	61							6
1856	4,733	4,807[e]	23							13
1857	5,944	5,924[e]	14							—
1858	5,128	5,427[e]	13							5
1859	3,457	3,175[e]	171							2

Table 3.1 (continued)

Year	China[d] US	China[d] SF	China[d] Hawaii	Japan US	Japan Hawaii	Philippines US	Philippines Hawaii	Korea US	Korea Hawaii	India[j]
1860	5,467	7,343[e]	21							5
1861	7,518	8,433[e]	2	1						6
1862	3,633	8,188[e]	13	0						5
1863	7,214	6,435[e]	8	0						1
1864	2,975	2,969[e]	9	0						6
1865	2,942	3,097[e]	615	0						5
1866[b]	2,385	2,242[e]	117	7						17
1867	3,863	4,794[e]	210	67						2
1868	5,157	11,085[e]	51	0	148					0
1869	12,874	14,994[e]	78	63	0					3
1870	15,740	10,869[e]	305	48	0					24
1871	7,135	5,542[e]	223	78	0					14
1872	7,788	9,773[e]	61	17	0					12
1873	20,292	17,075[e]	48	9	0					15
1874	13,776	16,085[e]	62	21	0					17
1875	16,437	18,021[e]	151	3	0					19
1876	22,781		1,283	4	0					25
1877	10,594		557	7	0					17
1878	8,992		2,464	2	0					8
1879	9,604		3,812	4	0					15
1880	5,802		2,505	4	0					21
1881	11,890		3,924	11	0					33

Table 3.1 (continued)

Year	China[d]			Japan		Philippines		Korea		India[j]
	US	SF	Hawaii	US	Hawaii	US	Hawaii	US	Hawaii	
1882	39,579		1,362	5	0					10
1883	8,031		4,243	27	0					9
1884	279		2,708	20	0					12
1885	22		3,108	49	1,946					34
1886	40		1,766	194	979					17
1887	10		1,546	229	1,429					32
1888	26		1,526	404	4,211					20
1889	118		439	640	2,035					59
1890	1,716		654	691	3,764					43
1891	2,836		1,386	1,136	5,793					42
1892[c]	—		1,802	—	3,129					0
1893	472		981	1,380	4,063					0
1894	1,170		1,459	1,931	3,647					0
1895	539		2,734	1,150	2,203					0
1896	1,441		5,280	1,110	4,516					0
1897	3,363		4,481	1,526	758					0
1898	2,071		3,100	2,230	9,888					0
1899	1,660		975	2,844	9,908				22	17
1900	1,247			12,635					71	9
1901	2,459			5,269					47	22
1902	1,649			14,270					28	93
1903	2,209			19,968					564	94

Table 3.1 (continued)

Year	China[d]			Japan		Philippines		Korea		India
	US	SF	Hawaii	US	Hawaii	US	Hawaii	US	Hawaii	
1904	4,309			14,264					1,907	261
1905	2,166			10,331					4,929	190
1906	1,544			13,835					127	216
1907	961			30,226			210		39	898
1908	1,397			15,803			819[g]		26	1,040
1909	1,943			3,111					11	203
1910	1,968			2,720			3,349		19	1,696
1911	1,460			4,520			801[h]			524
1912	1,765			6,114			3,038			175
1913	2,105			8,281			5,746			179
1914	2,502			8,929			3,184			221
1915	2,660			8,613			1,232			161
1916	2,460			8,680			1,744			112
1917	2,237			8,991			2,930			109
1918	1,795			10,213			2,669			130
1919	1,964			10,064			2,727			171
1920	2,330			9,432			3,504			300
1921	4,009			7,878			3,294			511
1922	4,406			6,712			8,675			360
1923	4,986			5,809			7,336			257
1924	6,992			8,801			6,417			183
1925	1,937			723			10,369			65

Table 3.1 (continued)

Year	China[d]			Japan		Philippines		Korea		India[i]
	US	SF	Hawaii	US	Hawaii	US	Hawaii	US	Hawaii	
1926	1,751			654			4,995			93
1927	1,471			723			6,875			102
1928	1,320			550			12,572			102
1929	1,446			771			9,593			103
1930	1,589			837			7,372			110
1931	1,150			653			6,014			123
1932	750			526			1,226			87
1933	148			75			41			44
1934	187			86		3	107			28
1935	229			88		63				32
1936	273			91		72				13
1937	293			132		84				47
1938	613			93		116				34
1939	642			102		119				36
1940	643			102		137				52
1941	1,003			289		170				94
1942	179			44		51				36
1943	65			20		8				71
1944	50			4		4				41
1945	71			1		19				103
1946	252			14		475				425
1947	3,191			131		910				432

Table 3.1 (continued)

Year	China[d]			Japan		Philippines		Korea		India[i]
	US	SF	Hawaii	US	Hawaii	US	Hawaii	US	Hawaii	
1948	7,203			423		1,168		44		263
1949	3,415			529		1,157		39		175
1950	1,280			100		729		24		121
1951	335			271		3,228		21		109
1952	263			3,814		1,179		47		123
1953	528			2,579		1,074		75		104
1954	254			3,846		1,234		175		144
1955	568			4,150		1,598		263		194
1956	1,386			5,967		1,792		579		185
1957	2,098			6,829		1,874		577		196
1958	1,143			6,847		2,034		1,470		323
1959	1,702			6,248		2,503		1,614		351
1960	1,380			5,699		2,791		1,410		244
1961	900			4,955		2,628		1,442		292
1962	1,356			4,519		3,354		1,463		390
1963	1,605			4,605		3,483		2,560		965
1964	2,684			4,367		2,862		2,329		488
1965	1,611			4,119		2,963		2,139		467
Total	**416,694**	**27,790[f]**	**56,720**	**347,957**	**68,417**	**39,882**	**116,839**	**16,271**	**7,790**	**16,209**

Table 3.1 (continued)

Notes: Year referred to fiscal year, which varied as follows: 1820–32, 1843–50, year ending September 30; 1833–42, 1851–65, year ending December 31; 1866–1965, year ending June 30. Data relate to country of last permanent residence. The numbers represent alien passengers arrived for 1820–67; immigrant aliens arrived for 1868–91 and 1895–7; immigrant aliens admitted for 1892–4 and 1898–1965.

For Filipino migration to Hawaii, the numbers included steerage passengers only for 1907–24 and passengers of all classes for 1925–9; year referred to calendar year for 1907–10 and fiscal year ending June 30 for 1912–19.

a   Three quarters ending September 30.
b   Six months ending June 30.
c   Data included in the category of "other or unknown" and cannot be separated.
d   Including Formosa/Taiwan from 1957.
e   Not included in the calculation of the column total because it very much overlapped with the number in column 2 for the same year.
f   Not included the figures from 1854 to 1875. See note e.
g   Including 1908.
h   First half of calendar year.
i   Including Pakistan and Bangladesh until 1947.

Sources: Asian arrivals on the US mainland: Carter et al. (2006), table Ad136-148; Chinese arrivals at San Francisco Custom House: Coolidge ([1909] 1969), Appendix part I; Chinese arrivals in Hawaii: Glick (1980), table 1; Japanese arrivals in Hawaii: Carter et al. (2006), table Ad82-89; Korean arrivals in Hawaii: US Immigration Commission (1911), table 11; 1906–29: Lasker (1969), Appendix B; Filipino arrivals 1930–4: Hawaii Sugar Planters Association, in Nordyke (1977), table 12.

wave of Chinese immigration, the Chinese came much earlier than that. The first documented arrival of Chinese on the East Coast occurred in 1785, when a ship named *Pallas* sailed into Baltimore harbor from Canton. Three Chinese seamen on board – Ah Sing, Ah Chuan, and Ah Cun – were abandoned, together with some East Indian sailors, when the captain of the ship took off to get married (Chen 1980). They lived in Maryland and Philadelphia under the sponsorship of a merchant named Levi Hollingsworth for almost a year. According to church records, in 1793, a Chinese from Macao was in Monterey with a Western name, Jose Augustin de los Reyes. In 1796, a Dutchman, Van Braam Houckgeest, a Canton agent for the Dutch East India Company, came to settle in the United States near Philadelphia bringing five Chinese servants with him (ibid.). In 1815, Ah Nam, from Chinshan in Guangdong Province, was employed as a cook for the Spanish governor Pablo de Sola. His was the first Chinese name on record in California (Monterey). The US government did not collect immigration statistics until 1819, when the Immigration Commission was established, and only began to publish the data in 1820. As seen in Table 3.1, only forty Chinese arrived before 1848.

The Gold Rush

However, these early sporadic arrivals did not constitute a wave of immigration. That first wave started after gold was discovered in John Sutter's mill northeast of Sacramento on January 24, 1848, nine days before California was ceded by Mexico to the United States. Column 2 of table 3.1, based on the records of the Immigration Commission, shows only a few Chinese arrivals from 1848 to 1852. The figures are certainly inaccurate. Data of Chinese arrivals at the San Francisco Custom House (column 3) reported by Coolidge ([1909] 1969) better captured the reality. In February 1848, three Chinese – two men and a woman – were brought by Charles Gillespie, an American missionary, from China to San Francisco (Chen 1980), and the men worked in the mines shortly after arrival (Speer 1853). The number of Chinese increased significantly after 1848, and in particular 20,026 came in 1852. The fever of the Gold Rush calmed down a bit after 1854 because miners had to dig deeper in order to find gold, and surface mines were exhausted by the 1860s. But a large number of Chinese kept coming every year.

As the locomotive was imported to the United States in 1829, railroads were constructed rapidly in the eastern states up to the Mississippi River. The Central Pacific Railway Company began the construction of the first transcontinental railroad in January 1863, but only 50 miles of track had been laid after the first two years, largely because of a lack of cheap and dependable workers (Griswold 1962). The company's leadership initially opposed the employment of Chinese on account of their race, but facing no better alternatives it finally decided to hire fifty Chinese for a trial in February 1865 at a salary of $28 a month for twenty-six working days. Their dependability, patience, industriousness, quietness, and cheapness led to the hiring of fifty more, then 15,000 more, and many more later. These were reflected in the immigrant statistics in column 3 of table 3.1, especially after 1867. The number of Chinese immigrants rose significantly to almost 12,000 in 1881 and to nearly 40,000 in 1882. These numbers reflected the last-minute rushes for admission before the imminent passage of the Chinese Exclusion Act of 1882.

The total number of Chinese arrivals from 1848 to the enactment of the first Chinese Exclusion Act in 1882 was 308,163. Close to half of these early Chinese immigrants (about 48 percent) returned to China (Yang 2000b). Hence, there were many sojourners during that period of time.

The "bachelor's society"

In the first two years of the Gold Rush, most Chinese immigrants were merchants and craftsmen plus some servants and cooks. However, the majority of later immigrants were so-called coolies or manual laborers. In addition to working in gold mines and for railroad construction, some were also employed in agriculture, fishing, and manufacturing (e.g., the cigar, shoe, and garment industries). Most of these were men, usually married, who left their families behind and came to America to dig for gold, hoping to get rich quickly and then return home. Very few Chinese immigrants were women. For instance, in 1860 there were 1,858 Chinese men for every 100 Chinese women, a sex imbalance that was a very serious problem until 1920 and the reason why the early Chinese community was called a "bachelor's society." This shortage of women was the outcome of the growers' and labor recruiters' preferences for unattached male workers, a lower cost to sustain migrants' families in their homelands, a sojourner mentality of early Chinese migrants, restrictions for daughters-in-law in the emigrant communities in China, a hostile and unsafe environment for women and children in the American West, and, most importantly, the US immigration policy of restricting the entry of Asian women (Chan 1991: 104; Espiritu 2008: 20; Ling 1998).

Geographic origins

The overwhelming majority of the early Chinese immigrants to the United States and Hawaii hailed from a few areas in the Pearl River Delta of Guangdong Province (Mei 1984). About 60 percent originated from Siyi (Sze-Yup), or four counties – Taishan (Toishan), Xinhui, Kaiping, and Enping. Approximately 20 percent came from Sanyi (Sam-Yup), or three counties – Panyu, Nanhai, and Shunde. Another 20 percent came from Zhongshan (previously Xiangshan) and from the Hakka areas of Chixi and Baoan.

Settlement in Hawaii

While the majority of Chinese immigrants settled on the US mainland, a small proportion of them migrated to Hawaii. The first group of 293 Chinese arrived in Hawaii as indentured plantation workers in 1852 (table 3.1). The annual number was small in early years, but increased significantly after 1864 and especially after 1875. A total of 56,720 Chinese had arrived by 1899, one year after Hawaii was annexed to the United States. Like those to the mainland, most of the Chinese immigrants to Hawaii hailed from the Pearl River Delta.

Why they came

An important question is: What caused early Chinese immigration? Culture has been used to explain many phenomena, but this is not a viable explanation in this case because emigration to a foreign country was not part of Chinese cultural tradition. Emigration was discouraged. The Chinese were expected to return to their homeland, as reflected in the Chinese idiom *luoyeguigen* ("Fallen leaves return to their roots"), which suggests that an individual should retire or die in his or her native land. This idiom reflects a strong Chinese homeward and nostalgic norm.

To understand the determination process of early Chinese immigration, one must consider the conditions of both China and the United States, the international contexts that linked the two countries together, and the migration policies of both countries. In the mid- to late nineteenth century, China was facing several domestic crises that put pressure on people to emigrate, and Guangdong Province was affected the most. One of these was an economic crisis. As discussed later, the agricultural economy almost collapsed, leading to starvation and destitution, and urban employment opportunities decreased. This situation was aggravated by natural disasters (e.g., the collapse of a dam causing floods along the Yangtze River, droughts), corruption (e.g., the embezzlement of funds for repairing dykes and dams by venal officials), and heavy taxes. A number of political uprisings also threw China into turmoil. The Taiping Rebellion (1851–64), led by Hong Xiuquan, spread through southern and central China, causing an estimated 25 million deaths. The Red Turban Revolt (1854–5) occurred in five of the main emigrant counties.[1] There was also prolonged ethnic warfare (1855–68) between the Hakka (guest people) and the "Punti" (local people) in the Pearl River Delta, especially the Siyi area (Mei 1984). Villages were ruined, lives were lost, and thousands became homeless. The declining government of the Qing Dynasty (1644–1911) was unable to cope with these economic, political, and social challenges. People suffered. They wanted to find alternatives. Emigration to a foreign land became an option (ibid.).

In contrast, conditions in America were much better. As a result of the Mexican–American War in 1846–8, the United States expanded its territories towards the Southwest. The newly acquired lands offered plenty of unexplored resources and job opportunities. In particular, the discovery of gold in California attracted many adventurers, who hoped to make instant fortunes. The hearsay that gold could be picked up in the streets in San Francisco fascinated gold diggers. Salaries in the United States were much higher than those in China. Although the Civil War took place in 1861–5, it did not have much impact on the West. These sharp disparities in economic, political, and social conditions naturally created pushes away from China and pulls to America.

However, the disparities between China and the United States only laid the necessary conditions to motivate Chinese emigration. Interactions between the two countries were required to turn emigration into action. In the 1840s the Western industrialized and imperialist powers began aggressively to invade China and bring it into the world capitalist system through trade.

Britain was the first Western power to open up China. It provoked the Opium War (1840–1), in which China was defeated and forced to sign the Nanjing Treaty. This treaty required China to pay a ransom of $6 million for Canton and an indemnity of $33 million; to open Guangzhou (Canton), Shanghai, Xiamen (Amoy), Ningbo (Ningpo), and Fuzhou (Foochow) to foreign trade; and to cede Hong Kong. It also exempted British nationals from Chinese law, limited China's tariffs to 5 percent on imported goods, and allowed opium to flood into China. Following Britain's lead, other Western powers signed similar treaties with China. For instance, the Treaty of Wangxia (1844) granted the United States most-favored-nation status in trade and other matters. US citizens were exempt from Chinese law and would be tried in US consular courts. As a result of its defeat in the Second Opium War (1856–60), China signed the Treaty of Tianjing. In addition to further indemnities of 666,666 pounds of silver, China had to allow foreigners to live in Peking, to accept missionary activities, and to open additional ports to foreign trade. The foreign invasions turned the country into a semi-feudal and semi-colonial country and "the sick man of East Asia."

These Western involvements weakened the imperial power of the Qing Dynasty. The influx of cheap foreign goods disrupted China's traditional agricultural and handicraft economy, worsening the economic crisis and displacing workers from the agriculture and cottage industries. Chinese peasants did not want to work in traditional agriculture and left their villages for urban areas to look for jobs and businesses. They became potential emigrants. Moreover, foreign missionaries and trade contacts opened Chinese eyes to Western lifestyles, values, ideas, and opportunities and encouraged emigration. Some missionaries helped the emigration of Chinese. Because the development of capitalism in the United States demanded cheap and dependable labor, some US companies and their agents went to China to recruit men to work on plantations in Hawaii and in gold mines and railroad construction in California. During the Second Opium War, Canton was occupied by the British and the French. This made the recruitment of peasants aboard foreign ships much easier, thereby undermining the government's emigration ban. All of these contributed to massive Chinese immigration in the pre-Exclusion era.

Migrants' social networks played an important role in the production and reproduction of early Chinese immigration. While the earliest Chinese immigrants did not have any prior social networks in America, they lived together in Chinese quarters or "Chinatowns," and normally worked together. Later they brought their brothers, fathers, uncles, sons, and fellow villagers to the Gold Mountain. Three types of ethnic organizations kept them together.

1 Clan (*zu*) is a family association or kinship association with membership based on lineage. In China one village was normally one clan. However, in America people with the same last name were eligible for membership, regardless of lineage. Clans provide protection and services for their members, such as organizing meetings, handling mail to and from home villages, sponsoring Chinese New Year banquets, returning

remains of the deceased to China, and building altars for worship.

2 *Huiguan* is a district association. Its members hailed from the same district, area, or region of China and normally spoke the same dialect. This was a higher-level association than the clan association. It provided protection, arbitration, and social and charitable services for members; acted as spokesman for the Chinese community; and served as the Chinese Chamber of Commerce until 1910.

3 *Tong* or secret society is a fraternal association. Its membership is based on common interest, regardless of lineage or locality. It was particularly attractive to those without power, money, or the support of major clan associations. Examples included the Triad Society and the Heaven and Earth Society. *Tong* engaged in political activities in China; organized protest against oppression; and became involved in criminal activities such as dealing in opium, gambling, and prostitution.

The emigrant community in their home villages also helped reproduce emigration generation by generation. Normally, Chinese emigrant men got married before their departure or returned to get married and then went back to America. They regularly sent remittances back to support their families, and their wives took care of the elderly and the children. Parents-in-law and the clan closely watched and controlled women, especially their chastity. The families then sent grown-up sons or adopted sons to America, and they in turn got married before they left or returned to get married later. The whole cycle was repeated again and again.

Chinese emigrant men returned to their home villages from time to time for a visit or to resettle. Usually, they carried a success story. Those who failed either could not afford to return or did not want to do so in fear of losing face; nor did they pass on bad news back home. Consequently, village Chinese saw only the bright side of the emigration story. This encouraged more men to pursue their dreams in America and created a culture of emigration.

US open-door immigration policy in the pre-Exclusion era certainly made Chinese immigration possible. However, US immigration policy treated Chinese men and women differently. While Chinese men were allowed to enter in order to meet the labor needs, Chinese women were barred by the Page Law of 1875, which forbade the entry of Chinese, Japanese, and "Mongolian" prostitutes, felons, and contract laborers (Chan 1991; Peffer 1986). Virtually all Chinese women were suspected of being prostitutes (Chan 1991: 105). On the other side of the Pacific Ocean, the Qing Dynasty prohibited emigration until 1860. Emigrants were considered as rebels, traitors, or human trash, and emigration was a crime subject to the death penalty. But the lax enforcement of this law by the Qing government emboldened some adventurous migrants. Later, under US pressure, the Qing government relaxed its emigration policy as a result of the Burlingame Treaty in 1868 and finally abolished the death penalty in 1894 (Chen 1980).

The anti-Chinese movement and Chinese Exclusion

The anti-Chinese movement got started soon after the arrivals of significant numbers of Chinese. The first anti-Chinese riot occurred in the fall of 1849 in Tuolumne County, near the southern limit of the Mother Lodge (Chen 1980: 47), and the movement intensified after the number of Chinese arrivals increased substantially in 1852. Some white miners organized to deny Chinese mining rights, and the Chinese encountered physical attacks and property damage. Anti-Chinese riots escalated and increased in the 1870s and 1880s. The local and state governments also enacted a series of ordinances or policies restricting Chinese immigration; imposing extra taxes; and barring the Chinese from working for government, owning land, and testifying against whites in court. The Workingmen's Party of California was formed in 1877, with the slogan "The Chinese must go!"

The "Chinese issue" became a national issue in the 1876 presidential debate, and congressional hearings and debate began in 1879. During this period, anti-Chinese riots spread to other parts of the nation. Finally, Congress passed the Chinese Exclusion Act, and President Chester Arthur signed the bill into law on May 6,

1882. Among other provisions, this Act suspended the immigration of Chinese laborers, both unskilled and skilled, for ten years and prohibited Chinese immigrants already in the United States from naturalization. The Chinese became the first ethnic group excluded from immigration in US history. Note that some were exempted from exclusion, among them diplomats, merchants, teachers, students, and tourists. However, immigration authorities had discretionary power to decide who could enter. Some exempted Chinese found the humiliation too much to endure.

The 1884 amendments to the Chinese Exclusion Act of 1882 broadened the ban of "Chinese laborers" to encompass all ethnic Chinese, regardless of their country of origin (McClain 1994). The Scott Act of 1888 prohibited Chinese reentry after temporary departure unless they already had family or property in the United States. The Geary Act of 1892 extended the ban on immigration of Chinese laborers for ten years. The 1893 McCreary amendment to the Geary Act further expanded the definition of "laborer" to incorporate merchants, laundry owners, miners, and fishers (Hall 1999); it also increased restrictions on Chinese businessmen (Chen 1980). In 1894, the Chinese Exclusion Act was extended to Hawaii. The General Deficiency Appropriations Act of 1904 extended the Chinese Exclusion laws indefinitely.[2]

As table 3.1 demonstrates, the Chinese Exclusion Act of 1882 effectively shut down Chinese immigration for the remainder of the 1880s, and the numbers of Chinese immigrants dwindled to a trickle. Nonetheless, Chinese exclusion was never total because non-laborers were not among the excluded class. Significant numbers of Chinese continued to arrive, and the number of immigrants between 1883 and 1943 totaled 103,006. But one thing is clear: the level was significantly lower than that of the pre-Exclusion era. It is worth mentioning the "paper sons" phenomenon after the San Francisco earthquake and fire in April 1906 destroyed the Federal Building that housed all of the US government official records, including immigration records and most of the birth and citizenship records of the city. Many Chinese fraudulently claimed to be US-born citizens and subsequently brought their sons, nephews, cousins, or others as their "paper sons" to

America, creating "paper families" (Lau 2006). An estimated 175,000 Chinese, including both legal immigrants and paper sons, were detained and examined at Angel Island Immigration Station between 1910 and 1940 (Angel Island Association 2009; Lai, Lim, and Yung 1999). About 10 percent of them were deported and sent back to China (Takaki 1989: 238). Those admitted as immigrants are reflected in the statistics of table 3.1. Separated from their husbands and sons, some Chinese female detainees were depressed and committed suicide, but others protested their ill treatment by the immigration authorities and fought for their rights (Ling 1998).

The repeal of Chinese Exclusion laws

All the Chinese Exclusion laws were finally repealed in 1943 by the Magnuson Act, in order to counter Japanese propaganda that the United States was anti-Asian by barring members of allied countries and treating the Chinese as an inferior people. The repeal was a political decision to deal with the embarrassment and win World War II. The Magnuson Act assigned an annual quota of 105 immigrants of Chinese descent, regardless of country of origin, and granted Chinese immigrants the right to become US citizens. The status of Chinese Americans improved significantly during and after the war. For example, they could work for the government and in some industries from which they were previously banned (e.g., the defense industry), own real estate, and in some states intermarry with whites.

Post-World War II immigration

As can be calculated from table 3.1, in the period 1944–65, 33,275 Chinese immigrated to the United States. This was not on account of the repeal bill with the nominal annual quota of 105, but mainly because of several special laws or executive orders.

1 The War Brides Act of December 28, 1945, allowed the spouses and children of members of the US armed forces to

immigrate to America. A total of 5,132 adult Chinese women came within three years under this Act (Zhao 2002: 80).

2 The Alien Fiancées and Fiancés Act of June 29, 1946, permitted members of US armed forces who served during World War II to bring their foreign-born fiancées into America as non-immigrant temporary visitors.

3 The Chinese Alien Wives of American Citizens Act of August 9, 1946, placed Chinese wives of US citizens in the non-quota category. It permitted the entry of 2,317 Chinese women between July 1947 and June 1950 (ibid.).

4 The Displaced Persons Act of 1948 was intended to help European refugees to enter the United States, but many non-immigrant Chinese were eligible to apply for permanent residency under this Act. A total of 3,654 Chinese students, visitors, and seamen were granted permanent residence because of the Chinese Civil War.

5 The Immigration and Nationality Act of 1952, also known as the McCarran–Walter Act, favored family reunification. Chinese women were allowed to join their husbands in the United States.

6 The Refugee Relief Act of 1953 allowed 4,777 Chinese refugees to enter over a period of three years.

7 The Refugee-Escapee Act of September 11, 1957, granted permanent resident status to 2,000 persons from China. It also waived deportation requirements for those who confessed to illegal entry and passport fraud if they were the spouses, parents, or children of US citizens or permanent residents.

8 The Executive Order of May, 1962, made by President John Kennedy permitted Hong Kong refugees to enter the United States. About 15,000 came. The entry of a large number of Chinese women, as well as other educated, middle-class Chinese immigrants, helped "remake Chinese America" by transforming the "bachelor's society" into a family-centered ethnic community (Zhao 2002).

To summarize, significant Chinese immigration to America commenced in 1848. More than 300,000 Chinese, mostly male laborers from the Pearl River Delta region of Guangdong Province, had immigrated to the United States before the Chinese Exclusion in 1882. The bulk of these migrants stayed on the West Coast, especially in California, but close to one-sixth of them settled in Hawaii. The contrast between the economic and political crises, exacerbated by the natural disasters in China, on the one hand, and the economic opportunities to get rich in America, on the other, generated potential pushes to leave China and pulls to America. Western invasions, starting in 1840, brought cheap foreign goods to China, hit the traditional agricultural economy hard, displaced Chinese peasants from the lands, and created a pool of potential emigrants. The demand for cheap labor on the West Coast of the United States and in Hawaii drove the recruitment of Chinese laborers, especially for the construction of the transcontinental railroads and for the plantations in Hawaii. The emigrant community in the home villages and the immigrant community in the United States helped produce and reproduce Chinese immigration. America's open-door immigration policy before 1882 set no obstacles to early Chinese immigration apart from the restrictions on the entry of Chinese women. Furthermore, the anti-emigration policy of the Qing Dynasty up to 1894 was loosely enforced and had little effect in deterring Chinese emigrants. All of these forces worked cumulatively and interactively to engender early Chinese immigration to the United States. The anti-Chinese movement and Chinese exclusion were largely the result of economic competition between the Chinese workers and white workers and racism, among other factors. All the Chinese Exclusion laws were eventually abolished in 1943, in the US effort to defeat the Japanese in World War II. The postwar period witnessed the entry of many Chinese women, stranded students, political refugees, and professionals, which had profoundly transformed the Chinese American community.

Japanese Immigration and Exclusion

The Japanese were the second group of Asians to immigrate to America in large numbers. Unlike the Chinese, many more

Japanese came to Hawaii than to the US mainland in the nineteenth century before this was reversed in the twentieth century. This section follows the chronological order of Japanese immigration, first to Hawaii and then to the US mainland.

Western influences

As an island nation, Japan had been relatively secluded from foreign intervention throughout its history. During the Tokugawa period (1600–1868), the shogun (military rulers) sealed off the borders from 1636 to 1853, and emigration was illegal until 1885 (Spickard 2009). However, the arrival of US navy Commodore Matthew Perry at Edo (later renamed Tokyo) Bay in 1853 forced Japan to open up to foreign trade and contact with the outside world. In 1854, Japan and the United States signed a treaty that gave the latter similar privileges acquired by those Western nations from China. Japan signed several additional similar treaties with Western imperial powers in the next few years.

Western influences induced great social transformations in Japan. A revolution in 1868 known as the Meiji Restoration brought down the Tokugawa government and began sweeping reforms of national life. The new leadership created new governmental institutions, a new social structure, a new economy, and a new unified national identity (Spickard 2009). The Japanese government actively pursued modernization and Westernization by sending the brightest young students to the United States and Europe to learn Western science, technology, government, law, education, and culture and by permitting the entry of the English language, foreign products, Christian missionaries, and foreign ways of life. Japan was rapidly undergoing industrialization through building textile, steel, and shipbuilding industries. Its economy became an integral part of the world market. Rapid urbanization followed. Profound social changes were accompanied by huge social cost, as industrialization and urbanization led to great agricultural decline and social disruption. Many farmers lost their land for failing to pay taxes because a new system taxed them on the appraisal value of their land rather than the amount of their harvest (Chan 1991: 9). Foreign competition left many workers unemployed. Wages also plummeted. Word of the booming economy and higher wages in Hawaii and the United States made the lure of the other side of the Pacific Ocean hard to resist. Restriction on emigration also began to loosen. The Japanese government became interested in emigration.

To Hawaii from Southwestern Japan

In 1868, a pioneer group of 148 Japanese landed in Hawaii (table 3.1).[3] They were among several hundred Japanese illegally hired and shipped to Hawaii, Guam, and California. These pioneer contract laborers were secretly recruited and sneaked to Hawaii by Eugene Van Reed, an American businessman in Japan and the Hawaiian consul general (Conroy 1953). They were mistreated by their supervisors and soon left for Honolulu. Having learned of their treatment, the Japanese government pressed them to return and banned all emigration, but although forty of them did return home in late 1869 the majority chose to stay. That was the reason why Japanese immigration stopped for the next seventeen years.

However, Hawaii needed labor badly. In 1881, during his world tour, Hawaii's King Kalakaua tried but failed to persuade Japan to permit emigration to Hawaii (Chan 1991). His two envoys dispatched to Japan in the next two years also came back empty-handed. The Japanese government finally lifted the ban on emigration in 1885. Robert Irvin, the American consul general and special agent of the Board of Immigration for Hawaii Kingdom, started to recruit Japanese laborers. His close relationship with the Japanese foreign minister, Inouye Kaoru, and the president of a Japanese import-export company, Masuda Takashi, greatly facilitated his recruiting efforts. Following the recommendation of Inouye and Masuda, both natives of Yamaguchi, Irvin chose Southwestern Japan as the recruiting site. Masuda even dispatched his employees to help sign up prospective workers village by village. Thus, the majority of Japanese migrants came from Southwestern Japan, including Yamaguchi, Hiroshima, Okayama, and Wakayama prefectures on Honshu Island, and Fukuoka, Nagasaki, Kumamoto, Saga, and Kagoshima prefectures on Kyushu Island. The recruitment was relatively easy given the attraction of higher salaries and opportunities in Hawaii and the pushes in Japan. Because of these changes, large immigration to Hawaii restarted in 1885 and continued unabated (see table 3.1). More than 68,000 arrived in the nineteenth century.

To the Pacific Coast

Before 1885, small numbers of Japanese also arrived on the US mainland. However, the numbers increased significantly and almost steadily from 1885 until 1899, albeit not as great as the numbers to Hawaii. Some came from Hawaii, and more came directly from Japan. These early arrivals settled down along the Pacific Coast, forming small communities within small towns and large cities. They normally found employment as farm workers, but some also worked in lumber mills and mining camps. The large increases in immigration to Hawaii and the US mainland were not accidental. They happened shortly after the 1882 Chinese Exclusion. When the supply of cheap Chinese labor was cut off, the Japanese were brought in to fill the gaps.

In the first nine years of the 1900s, the numbers of Japanese immigrants increased substantially. The total of 136,601 included almost 34,000 Japanese who left Hawaii for Pacific Coast ports from 1902 to 1906 (Chan 1991). In 1908, Executive Order 589, signed by President Theodore Roosevelt, prohibited the remigration of Japanese holding passports from Hawaii, Mexico, or Canada to the US mainland, reducing the Japanese exodus from Hawaii to the continental United States to a trickle. Unlike the Chinese, however, many more Japanese women migrated to America because the Japanese government promoted female migration in order to deal with problems of prostitution, alcoholism, and gambling.

The Gentlemen's Agreement

As with the Chinese, the increase of Japanese immigration and racism led to an anti-Japanese movement. White workers feared the competition of Japanese, and so the unions refused to accept Japanese workers. They resented the presence of the Japanese, whom they saw as "unassimilable," "pagan," "strangers," and "a menace." In San Francisco, around 1901, white workers started a political campaign for Japanese exclusion, and they urged Congress to extend the Chinese Exclusion to the Japanese. The California legislature also requested Congress to legislate for Japanese exclusion. Joining the anti-Japanese exclusionist hullabaloo, newspapers such as the *San Francisco Chronicle* and organizations such as the Native Sons of the Golden West demanded the segregation of whites and Asians in the public schools. On October 11, 1906, the San Francisco Board of Education ordered principals to send "all Chinese, Japanese and Korean children to the Oriental School." The Japanese government quickly protested to Washington, charging the action as violating a treaty provision that safeguarded the equal educational opportunities of Japanese children in the United States. In response to this international crisis, President Theodore Roosevelt later met with Mayor Eugene Schmitz and San Francisco school board members in the White House. The meeting revealed the real purpose and larger agenda of the school board's segregation order: Japanese exclusion. A compromise was reached whereby the schools would be desegregated, but President Roosevelt would ensure the cessation of Japanese immigration. The result was the Gentlemen's Agreement of 1907–8.

The Gentlemen's Agreement was not a single document but consisted of six diplomatic notes exchanged between the US and Japanese governments in late 1907 and early 1908 after more than eighteen months of negotiations (Daniels 1988).[4] The Japanese government agreed not to issue passports to Japanese laborers, skilled or unskilled, to the continental United States. In return, Japanese laborers already in the United States could bring over their wives, children, and parents. The agreement took effect in

1908. As the provisions leaked out during the process of nego-tiations, large numbers of Japanese laborers tried to rush in, as reflected in the numbers of admissions in 1907 (30,226) and 1908 (15,803).

"Picture brides" and the "Ladies' Agreement"

In terms of its intention, the Gentlemen's Agreement amounted to Japanese exclusion. Nonetheless, this was not the effect. From 1909 to 1924, a total of 118,868 Japanese – the wives, children, and parents of Japanese laborers residing in the United States – immigrated to the US mainland. About 20,000 of them were "picture brides," whose marriages were arranged through the exchange of photos (Takaki 1989: 47; also see Uchida 1987). These women held wedding ceremonies without the presence of their husbands, registered their new married names, applied for passports, and then sailed to America to meet their husbands for the first time. Many single men could not return to Japan to get married because of travel costs and the possibility of losing their deferred military draft status if they stayed in Japan for more than thirty days (Chan 1991).

Up to 1908, Japanese immigrants were predominantly male, but starting in 1909 there were more women than men. Consequently, anti-Japanese groups stepped up their attacks. They stirred up public sentiment concerning the high fertility of Japanese women and complained that the arrival of picture brides was a violation of the Gentlemen's Agreement. To ease tension, the Japanese gov-ernment put a stop to picture brides in the "Ladies' Agreement" in 1920 and, in spite of raucous protests, ceased to issue passports to them after March 1920 (Chan 1991: 108).

The Japanese government's promotion of female migration and the influx of picture brides produced a more balanced sex ratio in the Japanese community and allowed the formation of families, in contrast to the "bachelor's society" and "mutilated families" of the Chinese community. For example, in 1900, 22.3 percent of the total Japanese population in Hawaii (47,503) was female, and this ratio rose to 31.2 percent in 1910 and 42.7 percent in 1920.

In California, the sex ratio increased from 5.4 percent in 1900 to 15.1 percent in 1910 and 36.9 percent in 1920. By 1920, more than half (about 58 percent) of the Japanese female population on the US mainland was married.

Institutional discrimination and Japanese exclusion

The Japanese suffered a lot of institutional discrimination. The Alien Land Act passed by the California legislature in 1913 prohibited the Japanese, as well as other "aliens not eligible for citizenship" (i.e., other Asians), from owning land and also barred them from leasing the land for more than three years in a row (Takaki 1989). By 1920, twelve other states had passed alien land acts. To circumvent this law, Japanese farmers purchased land under the names of their American-born children or a corporation. But the Alien Land Act of 1920 in California imposed further restrictions by banning aliens ineligible for citizenship from holding land in guardianship for their children who were citizens. The Supreme Court ruling on the Ozawa case in November 1922 prohibited Japanese from becoming naturalized citizens because they were "not Caucasian" (ibid.).

Immigration after World War II

The Immigration Act of 1924, often known as the National Origins Act of 1924, replaced the stopover Emergency Quota Act of 1921 and introduced the permanent "national origins quota system," which set an annual immigration quota for each country based on its population residing in the United States in 1890.[5] Western and Northern European countries received large quotas. For instance, for fiscal year 1924–5 the annual quotas for the United Kingdom, Germany, Ireland, and Sweden were 34,007, 51,227, 28,567, and 9,561 respectively. Southern and Eastern European countries received smaller quotas. For example, for the same period the quotas for Italy, Russia, and Poland were 3,845, 2,248, and 5,982 respectively. The quota for each of the Asian countries was only 100. However, spearheaded by California's governor, Hiram Johnson, and helped by Senator Henry Cabot Lodge of Massachusetts, the Act inserted a special anti-Japanese provision that "No alien ineligible to citizenship shall be admitted to the United States."[6] Albeit not named, Japanese were excluded from immigration because of the Supreme Court ruling on the Ozawa case.[7] This 1924 Act effectively ended Japanese immigration until 1952, as evidenced in the diminishing and small numbers of Japanese immigrants admitted during that period (table 3.1). In so doing, it also cut off the most important source of growth for the Japanese community and froze the Issei (first-generation) community.

The Immigration and Nationality Act of 1952, also known as the McCarran–Walter Act, lifted the ban on immigration from the "Asia-Pacific Triangle" and annulled naturalization exclusions against Asians, although this law still retained most of the discriminatory features of the 1924 National Origins Act.[8] The Japanese American Citizenship League also won a significant victory by including a clause in the Act that permitted Issei to become naturalized citizens and an immigration quota of 185 for Japan. As a result, significant Japanese immigration resumed in 1952, and a total of 68,544 Japanese (most of them non-quota immigrants) arrived in America in the period 1952–65. The main reason that the actual number of Japanese immigrants each year was much greater than 185 was a result of a combination of the new eligibility of all Asians to become US citizens and the family reunification provision of the Act, which made the immediate relatives of US citizens non-quota immigrants. Also note that a large majority of Japanese immigrants during this period were women (see Daniels 1988: Table 7.4; Chan 1991; Glenn 1986), approximately three-quarters of whom were wives of US servicemen (Kim 1977).[9]

In sum, Japanese immigration formed part of the migration movement from Asia to meet the labor needs of the United States. Shortly after the Chinese Exclusion Act of 1882, substantial numbers of Japanese laborers, mostly from the southwestern prefectures of Japan, were brought to Hawaii and the Pacific Coast of the mainland. The numbers of migrants to the continental United States grew even greater at the beginning of the twentieth century. Foreign intrusion, starting in the mid-nineteenth century, opened Japan to the West and brought political, economic, and social transformation during the Meiji era. Industrialization, urbanization, and Westernization disrupted the traditional agricultural economy, dislocated farmers from their lands, and left many jobless, thus creating a pool of potential emigrants. Western influences also heightened the prospective Japanese migrants' understanding of the disparities in job opportunities and salaries between the United States and their homeland, which had existed even before the arrival of Westerners. The US demand for cheap labor was the driving force behind the Japanese immigration. More concretely, American labor recruiters played a crucial role in luring Japanese laborers to Hawaii and the US mainland, attracting them with promises of greater opportunities and higher wages. This deliberate recruitment also explains why the majority of early Japanese immigrants came from a few prefectures in Southwestern Japan. The social networks linking the emigrant communities and the immigrant community sustained the continuous migration through family and community connections before the Gentlemen's Agreement and through *yobiyose* (summoning families) and picture brides thereafter. The early non-exclusionist and active recruitment policies of Hawaii and the US government permitted the entry of Japanese, including women, and the policy of the Japanese government both supported emigration after the initial failed experiment and promoted female migration. Because of the stronger international position of Japan, the Gentlemen's Agreement did not exclude the Japanese because of the deal that allowed the arrival of wives, children, and parents of Japanese laborers already in the United States. However, the Immigration Act of 1924 basically excluded all Japanese, including the wives of US citizens (Ichioka 1988) until the removal of the discriminatory clause of the 1924 Act by the McCarran–Walter Act allowed significant Japanese immigration to resume in 1952. US military bases in Japan in the period 1952–65 played a crucial role in the influx of a large number of Japanese women as "war brides." The Japanese in America in the pre-1965 period experienced racism, prejudice, discrimination, and exclusion. It is also worth mentioning that, during World War II, 112,581 Japanese Americans on the US mainland (i.e., about 89 percent) were sent to the concentration camps, one-third of them being Issei immigrants and two-thirds US-born American citizens. This internment ruined many Japanese American communities and wreaked havoc on Japanese Americans.

Korean immigration and exclusion

In 2003, Korean Americans celebrated the 100th anniversary of Korean immigration to the United States. Nevertheless, the history of Korean immigration can be traced back earlier. In 1885, Philip Jaisohn (So Chae-p'il) came to the United States as a political exile (Choy 1979). He became the first naturalized US citizen of Korean descent and the first Korean American medical doctor. After his return to Korea in 1896, he became an influential political reformer. Based on the data of ethnicity rather than country of origin from the US Immigration Commission (1911), table 3.1 also shows that a total of 168 Korean immigrants arrived between 1899 and 1902, albeit in small annual numbers. However, it is probably safe to claim that the first *wave* of Korean immigration took place in 1903–5, when 7,400 Koreans arrived.

Foreign interference

Foreign interference in the late nineteenth century preceded the departure of these early Korean migrants. From the 1860s on, Western ships began to enter Korean waters. In 1876, Korea and Japan signed the Treaty of Kanghwa. This treaty declared the independence of Korea from China's suzerainty, which had lasted for over 200 years. Moreover, it opened three ports to Japan for trade, allowed Japan to control Korea's foreign trade, and granted the Japanese extraterritorial rights of immunity from Korean laws (Choy 1979). Korea signed a similar treaty with the United States in 1882 and treaties with Britain, Germany, Russia, Italy, and France shortly after that.

Foreign involvement intensified the already worsening economic and political conditions and disrupted normal life. In the late 1880s, poverty became prevalent. Because of persecution, in 1894 the Tonghak ("Learning of the East"), a secret organization whose doctrines were embodied in a collection of tenets based on Confucianism, Buddhism, and Taoism, rebelled against the government. This rebellion was suppressed with the help of Chinese troops, as China still claimed suzerainty over Korea. As Japan sent more troops into the Korean peninsula to counter the Chinese troops, the Sino-Japanese War (1894–5) erupted. Japan eventually won the war and increased its control of Korea. Japanese imperialism and oppression aggravated Korean lives. The Sino-Japanese War led to new forms of imperial expansion, including foreign financial control, the sale of land to foreigners, concessions awarded to foreign industrialists, and increasing missionary influence (Pomerantz 1984). Adding to this turmoil and oppression were the severe famine years before the first Korean exodus.

As Korea gradually opened to the outside world, Christian missionaries started to pour in. American medical missionary Horace Allen arrived in Korea in 1884 and won the trust of King Kojong (reigned 1864–1907) after saving the life of an injured minister (Patterson 1988). He further consolidated his relationship with the king by helping him escape from the Japanese to the Russian legation. Allen was appointed secretary of the American legation in Seoul in 1890 and then the American minister to Korea from 1897 to 1905. In these capacities he played a crucial role in recruiting Koreans to Hawaii.

Labor migrants to Hawaii

At the turn of the twentieth century, Hawaii relied heavily on cheap labor for its sugar plantation economy. As Hawaii was certain to be annexed to the United States in the mid-1890s, Chinese laborers fell out of favor because Chinese Exclusion would soon apply to them. Japanese laborers had become the dominant force on the island and grew more militant. Laborers of other ethnic groups were sought by planters to control workers through the "divide and conquer" strategy. Koreans became one of the groups tar-geted for recruitment. In 1902, representatives of the Hawaiian Sugar Planters' Association had a meeting with Horace Allen in Honolulu when he stopped there on his way back from the United States to Seoul. After returning to Korea, he convinced King Kojong to permit the emigration of Koreans to Hawaii, thus laying the groundwork for labor recruitment (Choy 1979). From 1868 emigration had technically been illegal (Patterson 1988), but now control began to be relaxed.

The work of recruiting Korean workers fell to Allen's friend David Deshler, who had businesses in Korea and Japan. He set up an office and opened a bank that lent money to Koreans for their trips. His recruiters and interpreters published advertisements, distributed posters, and visited Christian congregations. Although large disparities between Korea and Hawaii existed before the recruitment, they were not understood until the arrival of labor recruiters, who portrayed Hawaii as a land of opportunity, a "land of gold," and a "land of dreams." Prospective Korean migrants learned through newspaper advertisements and posters that as plantation workers they would receive free housing, medical care, and $16 (about 64 won – Korean dollars) a month for working sixty hours per week. Compared to the economic hardship, political turmoil, Japanese oppression, and lack of opportunity in Korea, emigration to Hawaii became very appeal-ing. However, at the beginning no one signed up because Koreans were suspicious and feared the unknown and leaving their rela-tives. The initial snag was overcome when Rev. George Jones of the Methodist Episcopal Church of Inch'on, a personal friend of Allen, intervened and encouraged members of his church to go to Hawaii. Many more followed (Patterson 1988).

It is evident that Korean Christian churches played an impor-tant role in the first wave of Korean emigration, as churchgoers spread the information and grouped together for the adventure. Christian converts constituted 40 percent of these early immi-grants (Chan 1991; Choy 1979; Patterson 1988; Takaki 1989). Since the churches were located in urban areas, the majority of these immigrants originated from different cities, in contrast to a few selected rural areas in early Chinese and Japanese immigration. Some 70 percent were literate (Takaki 1989). Among their various occupations were farmers, miners, urban laborers, domestic servants, artisans, policemen, ex-soldiers, government workers, and monks (Patterson 1988; Takaki 1989). Less than 10 percent of them were women (Takaki 1989: 56).

"Picture brides"

The first wave of Korean immigration was short lived. After Japan's victory in the Russo-Japanese War (1904–5), Korea formally became its "protectorate." In order to prevent the competition between Korean workers and Japanese workers in Hawaii and to counter the Korean independence movement in the United States, Japan pressed the Korean government to ban emigration. As a result, only very small numbers of Koreans arrived from 1906 to 1910 (see table 3.1). In 1910, Korea was annexed by Japan, and so Korean immigrants disappeared from the official US immigration record as they were lumped together with Japanese immigrants. However, this did not mean there were no Korean entrants. Some 1,000 Korean women arrived in America as "picture brides" between 1907 and 1920, since Koreans were treated as subjects of Japan and carried Japanese passports under the terms of the Gentlemen's Agreement (Takaki 1989). About 500 Koreans also came as political refugees with no passports between 1910 and 1924 (Choy 1979). Since Korea remained a Japanese colony until the end of World War II, the Immigration Act of 1924 that excluded Japanese from immigration applied to them, and there was no official record of Korean immigration during that period. Thus, Korean exclusion was disguised and co-opted by Japanese exclusion.

Moving to the US mainland

As Korean plantation workers in Hawaii discovered the hardships and limited opportunities, some decided to leave, and approximately 1,000 of them eventually returned to Korea (Chan 1991).

From 1905 to 1910, 1,015 Koreans remigrated to the US mainland (Takaki 1989). Most of them moved to California, but some also settled in Utah, Colorado, Wyoming, Arizona, and Alaska to work in mines, on the railroads, and in fisheries.

During the early period of immigration, Korean religious and ethnic organizations helped bond the Korean immigrant community in Hawaii and keep contact with the homeland. Soon after their arrival they established churches, which served both their religious and their political needs (for Korean independence). They also formed a *Tong-hoe* (village council) on each plantation of ten or more families. An umbrella organization for all *Tong-hoe*s, called *Hanin Hapsong Hyop-hoe* (United Korean Society), was founded in 1907, and a *Sinmin-hoe* was established in 1903 to support the independence movement. As some Koreans remigrated to the US mainland, they set up a *Chin'mok-hoe* (Friendship Society) in 1903 and a *Kongnip Hyop-hoe* (Mutual Assistance Society) in 1905 (Choy 1979). In 1909, the *Taehan Kookmin-hoe* (Korean National Association) was formed through the merger of the Hawaii United Korean Society and the California Mutual Assistance Society. It became the official spokesman of all Koreans in the United States and had chapters in Hawaii and on the mainland.

Experiences of discrimination and exclusion

Like the Chinese and Japanese, Korean immigrants during the early period became targets of anti-Asian violence and institutional discrimination. For instance, in the early 1910s Korean farm laborers were attacked in a number of places in California. Their employment was restricted to a few occupations, such as farm laborers, railroad workers, gardeners, janitors, restaurant workers, and house servants, although a small number of them gradually became farmers, hotel owners, and small business entrepreneurs, running laundries, barbershops, groceries, bakeries, tobacco shops, and photo shops. In the mid-1900s, the anti-Asian groups demanded the extension of Chinese Exclusion to the Japanese and Koreans, and in 1906 the San Francisco Board of

Education required Korean students to attend segregated school with the Chinese. The Alien Land Act of 1913 also prohibited Koreans from owning land and leasing land for more than three years. Koreans encountered housing segregation.

Korean War brides and orphans

Pending its independence after World War II, Korea, a colony of Japan since 1910, was divided at the 38th parallel: the north was occupied by the Soviet Union and the south was controlled by the US military administration under the direction of General Douglas MacArthur from its headquarters in Tokyo. In August 1948, the Republic of Korea was founded in the south with Syngman Rhee as its first president. A month later, Kim Il-Sung established his Democratic People's Republic of Korea in the north. The United States supported South Korea, while China backed North Korea. The Korean War broke out in June 1950, and ended in 1953 after a truce agreement was signed between the United States and South Korea on the one side and China and North Korea on the other. More than half a million American soldiers fought in this war.

Since 1948, US troops have been stationed in South Korea. Today there are still about 40,000 US soldiers in thirteen army and air force bases throughout the country, including Wonju, Munsan, Taegu, Chunchon, Pyongtaek, Pusan, Kunsan City, Osan, and Seoul. The US military presence in Korea certainly had effects on post-World War II Korean immigration to the United States. Starting in 1948, small numbers of Korean immigrants were admitted, but significant increases took place after the end of the Korean War. A total of 16,271 Koreans arrived in the United States between 1948 and 1965. The majority of them were either war brides who married US servicemen stationed in South Korea (about 40 percent) or orphans whose parents had died during the war (30 percent). In 1955, a special act of Congress allowed Bertha and Harry Holt, an evangelical couple from rural Oregon, to adopt eight war orphans from Korea. The Holts inspired many Americans to adopt, and the Holt Agency evolved from a family project to an international adoption agency, taking in not only war orphans and Amerasians (children of Korean women and US soldiers),[10] but also children of unmarried women and poor families.

The US military presence in South Korea also indirectly influenced Korean immigration during this period. Because of the economic opportunities, information flow, and cultural impact, more Koreans came to the United States as non-immigrants, mostly studying at American colleges and universities, and later adjusted their status.

In brief, the first wave of early Korean immigrants, who were largely laborers from urban areas, first arrived in Hawaii and then spilled over to the Pacific Coast of the US mainland. In the late nineteenth and the early twentieth century, foreign interference opened Korea to the outside world and exacerbated the deteriorating economic and political conditions there, as famines, poverty, the Tonghak rebellion, and the Sino-Japanese War plagued the country. Meanwhile, capitalist development in Hawaii and the US West Coast demanded cheap, reliable labor. Through American minister Horace Allen, labor recruiters deliberately recruited Koreans for Hawaii. The portrayal of improved conditions and salary as well as greater opportunities helped Koreans understand the existing disparities and motivated them to leave their homeland for Hawaii. Korean Christian churches also played a critical role in the recruitment. The relaxation of emigration controls in Korea and the facilitation of immigration to Hawaii made this immigration possible. Korean churches and ethnic institutions in both the immigrant and the emigrant communities helped sustain the migration and the survival of immigrants. However, the colonization of Korea by Japan, Japan's restriction of Korean immigration, and the Immigration Act of 1924 largely stopped early Korean immigration, although on the whole it was concealed and absorbed by Japanese exclusion. US military involvement in the Korean War and its presence in South Korea led to the large influx of Korean women and war orphans. Exclusion and racial discrimination also characterized the experience of early Korean immigrants.

Asian Indian immigration and exclusion

India is one of the oldest civilizations in the world, with a history dating back to 2500 BC. Historically, India was invaded by the Europeans, the Muslims, and the Moguls before being colonized by Britain. Before its independence, India included Pakistan and Bangladesh. On partition in 1947, Pakistan, dominated by Muslims, became an independent country, the eastern part of Bengal joining it as a province which was later renamed East Pakistan. It gained its independence in 1971 after a war of liberation and took the name Bangladesh. Hence, Asian Indian immigration before 1947 naturally included those immigrants from Pakistan and Bangladesh. In the past, people of Indian origin were called "East Indians," but in the last two decades the term "South Asians" has gained growing popularity among the communities originating from the Indian subcontinent (including India, Pakistan, Bangladesh, Sri Lanka, and Nepal).

Early Indian immigration

The first Indians arrived in the United States in 1785, when some East Indian sailors, together with three Chinese seamen, were left in Baltimore as the captain of *Pallas* disappeared to get married (Chen 1980). In 1790, an Indian from Madras visited Salem, Massachusetts. In the following decade, a few young Asian Indians who served their English captains in the two largest shipowners in India, Crowninshield and Derby, returned to Salem for a visit as the town developed its Indian trade. While it is unclear whether all of these settled in Salem permanently, a small number evidently did around 1851 (Jensen 1988). Some Indians also accompanied their English captains to other parts of the East Coast. The data from the US Bureau of Immigration in table 3.1 do show small numbers of Indian arrivals from 1820 to 1901 and modest increases from 1902 to 1906, totaling 1,525 in the period 1820–1906. Asian Indian immigration reached its peak during 1907–10, with a total of 3,837 immigrants in just four years. This was not fortuitous, as it happened around the time when the Gentlemen's Agreement that excluded Japanese laborers went into effect. Asian Indians, together with Koreans and Filipinos, became an alternative source of cheap labor. Asian Indian immigration then dipped sharply after 1910. Most of these earliest immigrants originated in the Punjab, though some came from the United Provinces (Uttar Pradesh), Bengal, and Gujarat. In particular, the majority were from the Punjab districts of Amritsar, Hoshiarpur, Jullundar, Ludhiana, Ferozepore, and Lahore (Chan 1991: 20). In the 1947 partition, all of these districts remained part of India, except for Lahore, which was under the jurisdiction of Pakistan. Chan hypothesized that the Punjab's convenient location to many transportation routes, social networks, access to credit, and recruitment efforts might offer some explanations for this geographic concentration. Most of these immigrants were adherents of Sikhism, a syncretization of Hinduism and Islam. The overwhelming majority were male laborers.

Causes of early Indian immigration

The causes of early Indian immigration can be sought from the interplay among the impact of British colonization, conditions in India, conditions and demand for cheap labor in America, and migration regulations. British involvement in India began in 1608, when the ships of the East India Company (EIC) arrived at the western port of Surat. At that time, India was controlled by the Mogul Empire. With the permission of Emperor Jahan-gir (reigned 1605–27), the EIC established a trading post in Surat in 1615. It exported sugar, tea, indigo dye, spies, cotton, and textiles. With the decline of the Mogul Empire in the early eighteenth century, the country was torn apart as many regional states emerged and warred to create their own empires. To protect its own interests, the EIC established its own private army and police force and recruited Indian soldiers and policemen, called sepoys. The sepoys were not only deployed within India, but also sent to other British colonies such as Hong Kong. The EIC expanded its settlements elsewhere and built commercial ports in Bombay, Madras, and Calcutta. Indian merchants and workers flocked to these locations to work for the company.

As the export of cotton clothes boomed in the first half of the eighteenth century, the profits of the EIC rose. France, Britain's main rival for world domination at the time, also wanted a share of the benefits, and in 1719 the French India Company (the Compagnie Perpétuelle des Indes) was formed from various rival trading companies. The competition and conflict between the French and the British led to wars in southern India in the 1750s. The victory of the British over the French at the Battle of Plassey in 1757 firmly established British domination in India and is often considered the beginning of formal British colonization. The British instituted the political, legal, and educational systems in India, and all schools began to teach pupils in English. English also replaced Persian and Hindi as the language used by public administrators.

Despite harsh British rule and bleak economic conditions, few Indians migrated to other countries before the mid-nineteenth century. This was partly on account of a Hindu belief that an Indian should not cross the "black water" – the ocean. Another reason was that a British law enacted in the early 1800s banned Indians from leaving their native provinces in order to prevent any unified resistance to British rule. However, in the mid-nineteenth century, following the abolition of slavery, the British Empire needed plantation workers to work in its colonies in the Western hemisphere and Africa. An indentured worker system was established to replace the slavery system, and Indians signed a contract to work for a period of time, usually five years, in one of the British colonies for pay, food, and housing. By the 1840s, many had left India for Trinidad in the Caribbean, Guyana in South America, and Mauritius off the coast of Africa (Ingram and Girod 2004). By the 1860s, Indians had worked in the British colony of Natal in South Africa. Later, Indian indentured workers were sent to Malaya and Fiji in the Pacific Ocean. This indentured worker system set off the Indian diaspora movement, of which immigration to the United States was just a part.

The indentured workers left India for British colonies because of deteriorating economic conditions at home. In the second half of the eighteenth century, the British introduced a capitalist agricultural economy to replace the traditional Indian land tenure system.

Many small landowners were forced to borrow money from money lenders who charged exorbitant interest rates or to sell their land in the case of late payments. Because of this change, the land had largely come under the control of the EIC, which constructed roads and canals to irrigate fields but failed to maintain them. This negligence resulted in a lack of irrigation, which caused famine. As a result, in the first half of the nineteenth century more than 1.5 million Indians died of starvation, and poverty spread across the country (Ingram and Girod 2004). Moreover, as the Indian traditions, religions, and ways of life were destroyed or eroded, discontent and resentment grew to an unbearable degree. The outcome was the 1857 Sepoy Mutiny, which represented the first battle for Indian independence. The revolt almost toppled the British but was eventually suppressed in mid-1858. After this war, India was no longer controlled by the EIC, but governed directly from England. The opening of the Suez Canal in 1869 led to a great trade imbalance between Britain and India, changing the latter's entire economic structure. Millions of spinners, weavers, potters, and other artisans lost their livelihood. By the end of the nineteenth century, about 90 percent of Indians became landless agricultural workers.

In the late nineteenth century, the British Empire started to lose control of the colonies that produced grain and other agricultural products. To make up the shortfall, the British government relied increasingly on India, the remaining largest colony, to produce rice, wheat, and other food products. British landlords, who controlled much of the land in Punjab and Bengal, exported a large amount of grain to Britain. Prolonged drought also struck huge agricultural areas of India four times between 1876 and 1891. The cruel colonial policies and prolonged drought led to a total of eighteen famines between 1876 and 1900, resulting in more than 20 million deaths. These, coupled with disastrous economic crises, rendered the Indian independence movement more animated. The leaders of the movement organized a nationwide boycott of foreign goods in 1905 and other protests against British rule. The Punjab region in particular was devastated by famines and anti-British protests. There was also a plague there in 1907 that caused half a million deaths (Jensen 1988).

Deteriorating economic conditions and social unrest pushed many Punjabis to leave their homeland for better opportunities elsewhere. In addition to other British colonies, the Pacific Northwest of the United States and Canada became highly attractive destinations for the first wave of Indian immigrants. This was partly because of the demand for cheap laborers in the lumber and agriculture industries as well as in railroad construction. Moreover, Punjabis learned from letters coming back from the Pacific Coast that workers made $2 to $5 a day – albeit misinformation – which was much greater than their meager income at home of ¢5 to ¢15 a day.

Labor recruitment also played an important role. A significant proportion of Indians were lured initially to British Columbia in Canada before moving to the United States. Several Canadian companies in railroad and some small businesses owned by Asian Indians actively recruited Indians from 1905. They sent agents to India and disseminated the flyers that exaggerated the economic opportunities in British Columbia. Canadian Pacific steamship companies also tried to lure Indians in order to increase ticket sales. Such recruitment by agents and subagents of some steamship companies in Punjab was also evident in Indian immigration to the United States (Melendy 1977: 203).

Available data indicate that more than 5,000 Asian Indians migrated to Canada, mostly Vancouver, in the period 1905–18 (Jain 1975). In particular, over 2,000 arrived per year in both 1907 and 1908. However, they met with strong resistance, including discrimination and riots. Finally in 1908 the Canadian government essentially shut the door to Indian immigration by denying entry to those who did not arrive in Canada from their country of origin or citizenship via "continuous journey," a requirement impossible for Asian Indians to meet because there was no direct steamship service between India and Canada. In addition, Canada raised the amount of money each arriving immigrant had to possess from $25 to $200 (Melendy 1977). Because of these measures, immigration to Canada virtually stopped after 1908. Many Indians in Canada moved south to Washington, Oregon, and California.

Some (e.g., Chan 1991; Mazumdar 1984) view early Indian

immigration to the United States as a spillover from Canada. Nonetheless, available data suggest that this was not the case. The data from US Immigration Commission (1911) show that, from 1901 to 1910, only 15 percent of Indians came from Canada while 73 percent hailed directly from India (see Mazumdar 1984: table 16.1). In fact, immigration to the United States ran parallel with the movement to Canada, although most Indian immigrants to US Pacific coastal states "came via British Columbia" as part of the journey by ship.[11] Some worked in lumber mills in Washington and Oregon. Others worked on the construction of the Western Pacific Railroad near San Francisco. But the majority of them were drawn to the farming areas in California. California became a magnet because it offered a landscape similar to Punjab, farming jobs with which Indians were familiar in their homeland, and the possibility of owning land. In California, Indian migrants followed crops from place to place all the year round, starting in the Sacramento Valley, working in orchards, vineyards, and sugar beet fields. They then moved south to the San Joaquin Valley in Central California to pick grapes and citrus, and finally ended up in the cantaloupe and cotton fields in the Imperial Valley in the south.

Asian Indian exclusion

Before 1910, there was no federal legislation or policy against the immigration of Indians, partly because of the labor shortage in some industries and partly because of the relatively small number of Indian admissions. As more immigrants arrived, and as the economic competition between white workers and Indians increased, the reaction took a negative turn. Indians had become a threat to white labor and society, and many white workers demanded an end to Indian immigration. In 1907, the Oregon legislature enacted a law that prohibited Indians from becoming permanent residents of the state. An anti-Hindu riot took place on September 5 in the port city of Bellingham, Washington, as some 500 white men attacked the lumber mills, broke into bund houses, and attempted to drive the "Hindus" out of town. As a result, some Indians were hospitalized, and 750 fled to Canada. Similar incidents occurred in

Everett, Washington, in 1907 and in the town of Live Oak and the Fair Oaks area of California in 1908. On March 21, 1910, white lumbermen at Saint John, Oregon, led the entire community in expelling Hindu workers (Melendy 1977). The Asiatic Exclusion League (AEL) and major newspapers in San Francisco were quite vocal about their fear of the "Hindu invasion."

In response to pressure from the AEL and the newspapers, Daniel Keefe, US commissioner general of immigration and naturalization, issued a directive to Hart North, commissioner of immigration in San Francisco, on April 27, 1910, with the following guidelines: (1) there was no federal law barring the admission of "Hindus," and the Bureau of Immigration "will not inject race as the basis of rejection"; (2) "Hindus" were required to go through an "exact physical examination"; (3) "no public charge will be admitted"; and (4) immigrants must have a source of immediate employment, otherwise "the Hindu might be rejected." The implementation of this directive led to a sharp increase in the number of rejections. In 1910, nearly half of the potential immigrants were refused admission and returned to India. This directive remained in effect for the remainder of the Taft administration. During Woodrow Wilson's administration, tight control of Indian immigration lingered on; this strict control explains why it declined markedly after 1910 (see table 3.1). In certain years, the majority of immigrants were debarred. For example, the rejection rate was 62.5 percent in 1911, 55.5 percent in 1913, and 78.5 percent in 1915. The total rejection rate from 1911 to 1916 was 58.5 percent. In this case, the rigid implementation of immigration policy rather than legislation was used to curb Indian immigration.

Eventually, Congress passed the Immigration Act of 1917, overriding the earlier veto by President Wilson. This Act established the "Asiatic Barred Zone" and basically prohibited all Asian laborers from immigration – except for Filipinos, who were US wards, and Japanese, who were governed by the Gentlemen's Agreement. This exclusion Act accounted for the continuous low level of Indian immigration after 1917. Note that some Indians continued to arrive after 1917 as non-laborers, though the numbers were generally small. From 1918 to 1947, a total of 4,185 Indians immigrated. Indian immigrants were also made ineligible for US citizenship by a 1923 US Supreme Court ruling, in *United States* v. *Bhagat Singh Thind*, because they were not "free white persons." They did not regain their right to citizenship until 1946, when President Harry Truman signed the Luce–Celler Act into law.

Immigration after India's independence

After India gained independence from Britain in 1947, Indian immigration remained at a low level but increased somewhat in the late 1950s and the first half of the 1960s. More than 5,000 Indians immigrated between 1948 and 1965 (see table 3.1). Data from the INS reveal that about one-third or more in later years of these migrants were professional, technical, managerial, and kindred workers. If their spouses and children were included, these educated and skilled immigrants and their families constituted a large majority of the Indian arrivals during 1948–65. The sex ratio was much more balanced, with slightly more males than females. Their geographic origins were more diverse than those of the early immigrants, dominated by Punjabis. Most of the new arrivals originated from large cities such as Bombay and Calcutta.

In short, Indians were among the earliest Asian arrivals in the United States, but the level of immigration was relatively low compared with that of Chinese, Japanese, Filipinos, and Koreans. The peak of Indian immigration occurred during 1907–10, right after the Gentlemen's Agreement, as employers searched for alternative sources of cheap labor. Most of these immigrants were male laborers who originated from several districts in the Punjab region. Many came directly to America while a significant proportion arrived indirectly from Canada, as they encountered exclusion there. British colonization of India laid the foundation for an Indian diaspora and early emigration to the United States, as it displaced Indians from their traditional agricultural economy and turned them into landless laborers; a large number traveled to British colonies around the world as plantation workers, soldiers, and policemen. Furthermore, British colonial policies exacerbated the economic crises in India and led to revolts and the Indian independence movement (Ghadr). The poor economic conditions and social unrest motivated early immigrants to find opportunities elsewhere. The demand for cheap labor, job opportunities, and much higher wages in the United States and Canada offered an alternative for a better life that Indian migrants found hard to resist. Deliberate recruitment of Indians by the agents of some steamship companies also played a significant role. Since there was no restriction on emigration in India during that period and the early US immigration exclusion legislation did not target Indians, immigrants could come in significant numbers before 1910, but this situation was short lived. With the growing numbers of Indian immigrants came the Indian exclusion movement. As a result, the US government took action to place strict limits on the entry of Indians in the form of a policy directive – the 1910 directive of the commissioner general of immigration and naturalization. Finally, the Immigration Act of 1917 excluded Indian laborers.

Filipino immigration and exclusion

Spanish colonization

Filipinos immigrated to America in a very different context. Western influences in the Philippines began in the sixteenth century. Ferdinand Magellan landed on the island of Cebu and claimed it for Spain in 1521, and the Philippines, named after King Philip II of Spain, formally became a Spanish colony in 1571 and remained so until 1898. The Spaniards established their political, economic, and educational systems, and Catholicism became the dominant religion. Manila, the capital, formed a hub of the Spanish galleon trade, linking the Philippines with Europe and the New World.

US colonization

With the aid of Filipino rebels led by Emilio Aguinaldo, US troops defeated Spain in the Spanish–American War in 1898. Aguinaldo declared the independence of the Philippines on June 12, 1898. In the Treaty of Paris signed on December 10 of that year, Spain ceded the Philippines, Guam, and Puerto Rico to the United States (Cuba was granted independence), with a US payment to Spain of $20 million. The Philippines became a US colony. This was followed by the Philippine–American War, also called the Philippine Insurrection, from 1899 to 1902, as the rebels resisted American colonization but eventually failed. The total casualties included 4,234 American soldiers, 16,000 Filipino soldiers, and 200,000 civilians due to famine and diseases.

Following the American model, the Philippines established its government, but real power remained in the hands of the colonial administrators. English became an official language. US businesses soon dominated the economy, and the Philippines was rendered a supplier of cane sugar, pineapples, and other raw materials to the US market. Americans created an extensive public school system. English was being taught from the first grade. Schools adopted the American curriculum and textbooks. George Washington and Abraham Lincoln became children's heroes (Lasker 1969), and American values were instilled in the young. As a result of US colonization, Filipinos became US nationals or wards and until 1934 could freely immigrate to America.

The Manilamen

It should be noted that the earliest Filipino settlement in the United States dates back to 1763, with the Manilamen at Saint Malo in the bayou of Louisiana, near New Orleans (Bautista 1998). The Manilamen were Filipino sailors who jumped from the Spanish galleons plying between Manila and Acapulco, Mexico, and then traveled east to Vera Cruz, where they boarded another ship or traveled by land to Louisiana. The Saint Malo village consisted of about thirteen to fourteen large houses populated by men only who depended on fishing for their living. The Manila village, the second and largest Manilamen settlement, was built on Barataria Bay in the Mississippi Delta by the Gulf of Mexico, and the fishermen there started the shrimp-drying industry (Espina 1988). The

Saint Malo village was ruined by a strong hurricane in 1915, and the Manila village was destroyed by Hurricane Betsy in 1965. Other Malinamen settlements in Louisiana were Alombro Canal and Camp Dewey in Plaquemines Parish and Leon Rojas, Bayou Cholas, and Bassa Bassa in Jefferson Parish.

The *Pensionados*

However, it was the American colonization of the Philippines that set the stage for the exodus of Filipinos to the United States. After the American takeover, the US Congress passed the *Pensionado* Act in 1903 in order to train qualified and highly educated civil servants embodying American ideals. Under the *Pensionado* program (1903–38), an estimated 14,000 Filipino students were sent to US schools such as the University of Illinois, the University of California, Purdue, Columbia, Harvard, Stanford, Cornell, Yale, Northwestern, and the University of Southern California to study in various programs – education, engineering, medicine, business, government, and agriculture (Melendy 1977). They were called *Pensionados* because they studied at the expense of the colonial government. Early on, most of them returned to the Philippines to become provincial and national leaders. Nevertheless, not all Filipino students in the United States were *Pensionados*, especially from the 1920s. These students were supported by their families, and many stayed in the United States permanently after adjusting their status to that of immigrants; however, *Pensionados* were not immigrants.

Labor migrants to Hawaii

Unlike *Pensionados*, most of the Filipino immigrants to America before Philippine independence were laborers. They first arrived in Hawaii, and some later moved to the mainland. Table 3.1 shows only 210 Filipino arrivals in Hawaii in 1907. Later increases did not transpire by chance, as the Gentlemen's Agreement took effect in 1908, and Filipinos were brought in to replace Japanese workers. From 1907 to 1924, the total number of admissions was

57,675. After the Immigration Act of 1924, Filipino immigration to Hawaii escalated to 10,369 in 1925 and continued at a high level thereafter. A total of 44,404 Filipinos came between 1925 and 1929. The data from Lasker (1969) end in 1929, but the data from the Hawaiian Sugar Planters' Association (HSPA) made available by Nordyke (1977) indicate that, even as the Great Depression (1929–39) hit Hawaii, large numbers of Filipinos still arrived between 1930 and 1932, though the numbers dwindled to a trickle in the next two years. The total number of Filipino immigrants to Hawaii from 1907 to 1934 was 116,839. In the 1930s, Filipinos replaced the Japanese as the largest ethnic group of plantation workers.

Several factors contributed to the large immigration of Filipinos to Hawaii in the early period. The situation at home was poor, and economic conditions along the coast of Ilocos and parts of the Visayan Islands were particularly miserable. Landholdings were small; capital was difficult to come by; steady employment in urban centers was lacking; industrial jobs were scarce; and wages were low. In other rural areas, poverty was growing (Melendy 1977). Tenants could not make end meet. After American colonization, many Filipino farmers gradually lost their land and became laborers. Living conditions were rudimentary and opportunities were very limited. Because of the high fertility rate, children were underfed and lived in an unsanitary environment. Nonetheless, people do not move just because conditions at home are bad: there must be a better alternative available. In comparison, in Hawaii, labor was scarce, jobs were abundant, and wages were high. Through labor recruiting advertisements, the contrast between the homeland and America induced the pushes and pulls.

Nevertheless, had there been no demand for, and active recruitment of, Filipino labor, these pushes and pulls would not have been activated. In the first half of the twentieth century, the agricultural economy of Hawaii required a constant supply of cheap migrant labor. To meet this demand, the HSPA organized systematic recruitment of Filipino workers. It advertised Hawaii as "a land of opportunity," "a paradise of happiness and prosperity," and a glorious adventure and normally offered Filipino workers a three-year contract that included free transportation to Hawaii, housing, water, fuel, and medical care. Agents showed a free movie of life in Hawaii. In 1906, the HSPA sent an attorney, Albert Judd, to Manila to recruit 300 Filipino families, but he was able to bring only fifteen Filipino workers, all male Ilocanos from Northern Luzon (Melendy 1977). George Wagner, a former resident of Hawaii assigned by Judd to continue his recruiting effort in the Philippines, signed up 150 Filipinos during 1907. The recruitment was halted after that and did not resume until 1909, when the effect of the Gentlemen's Agreement was felt by the planters in Hawaii. Hawaii's Territorial Board of Immigration determined that Filipinos were the only viable source of replacement for the earlier Asian plantation laborers because the Chinese, the Japanese, and Koreans were barred from immigration and most of them left plantations for towns, moved to the West Coast, or returned to their homelands. Steamship travel agents also actively recruited Filipinos to Hawaii and the US mainland (Lasker 1969).

US colonization played a dual role. For one thing, it turned Filipinos into US nationals who were not constrained by US immigration policy. For another, US economic penetration into the Philippine economy created opportunities for contacts, and Americanization in education and culture brought Filipinos closer to Western ideals and the pursuit of better opportunities.

Once the immigrant community in Hawaii and the channels of communication with their relatives and friends at home were established, Filipino migration to America gradually became self-sustaining. Those who failed did not write home, but success stories and remittances were sent back, encouraging more migrants. By 1925, the sugar planters no longer needed actively to recruit laborers and instead relied on voluntary application (Lasker 1969; Melendy 1977). Starting in 1926 they no longer paid for the transportation of Filipino laborers.

According to Lasker's (1969: appendix C) data from the Philippines Islands Bureau of Labor, the majority (65.5 percent) of these Filipino laborers in Hawaii hailed from the northwestern provinces of Ilocos Norte, Ilocos Sur, Abra, La Union, Pangasinan, and Tarlac. Ilocos Norte and Ilocos Sur alone accounted for about 47 percent of the total. It is not surprising that this densely populated coastal region became the main area of emigration. Arable land along the mountainous coast was very limited, and there was continuous economic hardship. There had been a tradition of permanent and seasonal migration in the region. Ilocos was also the main target of labor recruiters because the people were perceived as "stalwart, mild mannered, energetic and saving" and the "best workers" (Melendy 1977). Approximately 29 percent came from the middle provinces of Cebu, Bohol, Oriental Negros, and Leyte. Residents in the Cebuano provinces were no strangers to sugar plantations because the Spaniards and Americans had established plantations there (Chan 1991). The rest of the laborers were from other provinces.

Like the Chinese and Koreans, a large majority of the Filipino laborers to Hawaii were male. Based on my calculation of the data from Lasker (1969: appendix B), between 1907 and 1924 the sex ratio of the Filipino immigrants was 6.5 men to one woman, plus a significant number of children; in the period 1925–9, the imbalance worsened to 28.7 to one. Many of these migrants were sojourners who planned to save enough money to return home to buy their own house or lot, till a small farm, or get married. Melendy (1977) reported that 38,946 Filipinos returned to the Philippines between 1909 and 1931. Again according to my calculation of the data from Lasker (1969: appendix B), the return rate of Filipino migrants in Hawaii, including children who returned with their parents, was 21.7 percent during 1907–24, 40.5 percent during 1925–9, and 30 percent in the whole period from 1907 to 1929.

Life at the plantation was difficult. Filipino laborers worked at least ten hours a day, six days a week, and twenty-six days a month. Work involved planting, hoeing, and carrying sugar cane. The wage of men was 40 pesos ($20) a month, or ¢90 per day, but working wives earned 28 pesos ($14) a month (Melendy 1977). They complained about the low wages, poor housing, abusive *luna* (plantation foreman), strict plantation police, and isolation.

Migration to the US mainland

As Filipino migrants in Hawaii discovered new opportunities on the US mainland and elsewhere, they remigrated. On the mainland, laborers had a better chance to lease land as tenant farmers and eventually to buy land as farmers if they could save enough money. Available data from Lasker (1969: appendix B) indicated that, from 1907 to 1922, almost every year a relatively small number of Filipinos (mostly men) moved from Hawaii to the continental USA. In 1923, the number jumped to 1,098 because of the imminent passage of the Immigration Act of 1924. Since this Act excluded Japanese, Koreans, and other Asians ineligible for US citizenship, Filipinos who were US nationals became the favorite source of replacement labor. Furthermore, the growers in California and other western coastal states preferred Filipinos because they were hardworking, docile, ununionized and could serve as strike breakers. With the soaring new demand for Filipino laborers on the West Coast, particularly California, remigration of Filipinos increased to usually more than 2,000 each year after 1923. In addition, hundreds came directly to the mainland per annum. The majority of these laborers were farm workers, moving from farm to farm. Many worked in the San Joaquin Valley of California and elsewhere, picking asparagus, lettuce, tomatoes, celery, onions, peas, beets, carrots, cotton, grapes, oranges, and melons. They were perceived as ideal "stoop labor" because they were shorter and worked faster than white men. Normally they worked ten hours a day, twenty-six days a month. The sex ratio was fourteen men to one woman.

Filipinos also migrated to other parts of the United States. Some farm workers moved to Arizona, Utah, Colorado, Montana, and North Dakota. Out of the agricultural season, Filipinos often worked in the 1920s and 1930s as gardeners, dishwashers, and domestic servants in such cities as Chicago, Detroit, New York, and Philadelphia. A significant number also found jobs in the Merchant Marine (Melendy 1977; Mangiafico 1988). Through labor contractors, thousands of Filipinos found their way to the Alaska fishing and canning industries.

The experiences of Filipinos on the US mainland were very different from those of their counterparts in Hawaii. In Hawaii, they competed with the Japanese, Chinese, and Korean plantation workers, but on the mainland they competed with and were confronted by whites. As more Filipinos arrived on the mainland in the 1920s, an anti-Filipino exclusionist movement began, especially in California. Pressures for exclusion came from two main fronts. Firstly, white workers resented the economic competition of Filipino laborers, since they were willing to do the same jobs at a much lower wage, and they were considered "a menace to white labor." Tensions intensified as the United States entered the Great Depression in 1929 and jobs became increasingly scarce. Secondly, there was an outcry from white racists against interracial relationships between Filipino men and white women. Many young single Filipino men danced with white girls in dance halls or clubs after work, and some even dated and married white women. This clashed with California's anti-miscegenation law banning marriage between the Malay race and whites and threatened white racial purity. As a result of these conflicts, between 1926 and 1928 there were a number of small incidents of individual violence and riots against Filipinos in California and Washington. In California large-scale riots against Filipinos erupted in the San Joaquin Valley town of Exeter in October 1929, near Watsonville in January 1930, at Escalon in August 1933, and elsewhere (Melendy 1977).

The Tydings–McDuffie Act of 1934

Coupled with violence, there were a number of legislative attempts to exclude Filipinos from immigration. In 1929, the California legislature passed a resolution calling for a congressional enactment to restrict Filipino immigration. But the US national status of Filipinos precluded this from happening. Then San Francisco Congressman Richard Welch introduced a repatriation bill, but it did not go through before 1934. No existing law could be applied to Filipinos for the purpose of exclusion. Granting independence to the Philippines became the only solution to the Filipino "problem" (Takaki 1989).

Finally, because of the joint force of the exclusionists and the independence advocates, in 1934 Congress passed the Tydings–McDuffie Act. This allowed the independence of the Philippines in two stages: a self-governing commonwealth state under US tutelage in 1935, and a fully independent country in 1946. However, the Act also made Filipinos foreigners for immigration purposes. They were no longer US nationals and could no longer freely enter the United States. The Philippines was allocated an annual immigration quota of fifty persons, practically amounting to nil immigration. However, because of lobbying by the HSPA Section 8 of the bill allowed unlimited Filipino immigration to Hawaii whenever there was a demonstrated labor shortage, to be determined by the Department of Interior. Remigration of Filipinos from Hawaii to the mainland was prohibited.

In fact, the exclusion legislation was largely unnecessary, because as a result of the Great Depression Filipinos were already coming in diminishing and small numbers right before 1934. But still the exclusionists managed to pass the Filipino Repatriation Act of 1935. This Act provided transportation at federal expense to Filipinos who wanted to return to the Philippines, on the condition of losing their right of immediate reentry and being able to return in the future as part of the annual quota of fifty. But only 2,190 of the 45,000 Filipinos in the United States took advantage of this Act (Melendy 1977).

World War II and postwar immigration

After the Tydings–McDuffie Act, Filipino immigration came to a virtual halt. During World War II, Japan occupied the Philippines, and Filipino immigration was suspended apart from the small number serving in the US military (see table 3.1). The Selective Service Act allowed Filipinos to serve in the US military, and many served in the navy and army, forming the First and Second Filipino Infantry Regiments. In 1946, the Philippines achieved independence, and the annual immigration quota doubled to 100 – the same as the quota for other Asian countries – and Filipinos became eligible for US citizenship. The number of immigrants rose to 475 in 1946 and quickly to thousands in the next two decades. Between 1946 and 1965, the total number was 39,036, among whom the large majority were women and children. The largest source – around half of the immigrants admitted – was war brides of Filipino veterans and American servicemen who were stationed in the US naval and air bases in the Philippines or visited the country on leave. If their children were counted, they constituted 70 to 90 percent. A second source was nurses (6 to 18 percent). The Exchange Visitor Program (EVP) of the State Department, beginning in 1948, offered foreign nursing graduates an opportunity for two-year postgraduate study and clinical training in US hospitals on the condition that they return to their homeland after their training. Filipinas soon became an important and preferred source for the EVP because of the past US–Philippines colonial tie, the English-language schooling of Filipino nurses, and the adoption of the American model in Philippine nursing schools (Posadas 1999). The US Mutual Educational and Cultural Exchange Act of 1961 required exchange visitors to return to their home country for two years before applying for a US immigrant visa, but many Filipino exchange nurses used multiple strategies to avoid returning to the Philippines, including marrying US citizens, immigrating to Canada, exiting the United States through Canada or Mexico and then reentering as students, and petitioning for a waiver (Choy 2003). Many who failed to stay managed to migrate back to the United States in the 1950s and 1960s after the passing of the McCarran–Walter Act. US military, educational, and cultural involvements in the country certainly contributed significantly to the postwar Filipino immigration.

To sum up, Filipino immigration to America commenced in the early twentieth century. The bulk of Filipino laborers came to Hawaii from the northwestern parts of the Philippines and some remigrated to the continental USA. While three centuries of Spanish colonization changed the foundation and culture of the country, it was US colonization of the Philippines in 1898 that set immigration in motion. Poor economic conditions in the Philippines and the bright economic prospects and opportunities in Hawaii formed a marked contrast and resulted in pushes from the homeland and pulls to the destination. However, the pushes and pulls were not realized until the representatives of the HSPA began active recruitment of Filipino laborers. Behind this recruitment was the urgent demand for cheap labor to replace the Japanese and Korean plantation workers after the Gentlemen's Agreement and to break strikes among the existing Asian plantation labor forces. Because of the demand for labor, and because of the status of Filipino US nationals, there was no legal barrier to Filipino immigration; nor did the Philippines government impose any restrictions on emigration. As increasing number of Filipinos migrated to the US mainland, an anti-Filipino exclusion movement followed, especially in California. The outcome was the Tydings–McDuffie Act of 1934, which brought Filipino immigration to a virtual halt through to the independence of the Philippines. Because of US military, educational, and cultural involvement, significant Filipino immigration resumed after World War II, as many women came first as war brides of either Filipino or American soldiers and later as nurses.

Summary

In the pre-1965 period, five Asian groups immigrated to America in large numbers: Chinese, Japanese, Filipinos, Koreans, and Asian Indians (in the order of the number of immigrants). The Chinese flocked to the Pacific Coast, especially California, with a much smaller number to Hawaii. The Japanese, Koreans, and Filipinos initially came to Hawaii through labor recruitment by sugar planters and then spilled over to the US mainland. Indians arrived in some Pacific coastal states either directly or indirectly via Canada. Normally, these immigrants originated from a few rural areas, though Koreans were mainly urban residents. With the exception of some later arrivals after World War II, they were largely laborers. All of these groups were dominated by males during the initial periods. The sex ratio imbalance among the Japanese was significantly alleviated after the Gentlemen's Agreement, which allowed Japanese wives, as well as children, to join their laborer husbands already in the United States. The skewed sex ratio boosted the social values of Asian immigrant women in these "bachelor" communities because unmarried women were highly sought after as sexual and marital partners (Espiritu 2008). However, in the period of after the war until 1965, a large majority of immigrants from these groups were women, mostly "separated" wives and war brides, and children. Their arrivals transformed these Asian immigrant communities into gender-balanced and family-oriented ones and injected an important source of natural population growth. As a result of these demographic transformations and changing employment opportunities for men and women, gender roles and gender relations became more egalitarian in these communities.

There were some common determinants of these migration movements. Western intervention or colonization preceded large emigration in all cases, as foreign involvement changed the traditional economies; displaced farmers or peasants from their lands; exacerbated economic, political, and social conditions; established cultural and ideological linkages between migrants and the host country; and created opportunities for contacts and even international marriages. Homeland conditions in the sending countries were unfavorable on account of economic crises or distress (e.g., famine, starvation, unemployment, low wages), political turmoil (e.g., war, ethnic fighting), and social unrest (e.g., social movements). In comparison, conditions on the US mainland and in Hawaii were much better in terms of jobs, wages, and political stability. These disparities generated pushes from the homeland and pulls to the destination. The demand for cheap labor in America was an underlying engine driving the migration, as the Asian groups were all alternative sources of cheap labor. In almost every case, deliberate labor recruitment was involved. Because of the demands for cheap labor, US immigration policies initially imposed few restrictions on the entry of these groups, except for the women. The social networks of the migrants, both at home and at their destination, kept the migration flows going.

However, along with large increases in immigration, the anti-Asian exclusion movements began because of economic competition with white workers and anti-Asian racism. All of these groups were treated badly, suffering prejudice, riots, and institutional discrimination. Laborers from all Asian groups were eventually excluded from immigration by the Chinese Exclusion laws, the Gentlemen's Agreement, the 1910 Directive of Commissioner General of Immigration, the Immigration Act of 1917, the Immigration Act of 1924, and the Tydings–McDuffie Act of 1934.

4

Post-1965 Asian Immigration

The Immigration and Nationality Act of 1965 marked a new era in Asian immigration to the United States. This chapter highlights important changes in immigration legislation since then; analyzes the trends in post-1965 Asian immigration, settlement patterns of new Asian immigrants, and types of immigrants; and applies the macro–micro interactive and cumulative causation theory developed in chapter 2 to explain this new immigration. Additionally, it discusses Asian immigrant transnationalism and undocumented immigration.

The immigration reform since 1965

The ineffective national origins quota system, Americans' growing rejection of the discriminatory national origins quota system that favored immigration from Northwestern Europe, the increasingly tolerant attitudes of Americans towards ethnic minorities, and the decreasing opposition to immigration owing to continuing postwar prosperity led to the passage of the Immigration and Nationality Act of 1965, which was signed into law by President Lyndon Johnson on October 3, 1965 (Yang 1995). This Act repealed the national origins quota system in operation since 1924 while seeking to control immigration to a manageable level. It established an annual ceiling of 170,000 for the Eastern hemisphere and a quota of 20,000 for each country. It also imposed for the first time an annual ceiling of 120,000 for the Western hemisphere, but with no per country quota. The total annual worldwide ceiling was set at 290,000. To determine the eligibility of applicants from the Eastern hemisphere, the law established a seven-category preference system, including a seventh category for refugees, but this system did not apply to the Western hemisphere. In addition to these quota immigrants, there was no hemispheric or per country limit for immediate relatives (i.e., spouses, minor children, and parents of US citizens over twenty-one years old) or non-quota immigrants. Family reunification became the cornerstone of US immigration policy. Only a small number of visas were allotted to refugees from both hemispheres. This Act formally took effect on July 1, 1968.

The 1976 amendment to the Immigration and Nationality Act of 1965 extended the seven-category preference system and 20,000 per country quota to all Western hemisphere countries. This amendment reinforced the notion that people of all countries should be treated equally as far as immigration was concerned. The 1978 amendment established a unified system by merging the two hemispheric ceilings into a single worldwide ceiling of 290,000 visas each year. It retained the seven-category preference system with only minor modifications.

The Refugee Act of 1980 established a separate policy for refugee admissions. It removed the seventh preference category for refugees and decreased the annual worldwide ceiling to 270,000. It also broadened the definition of "refugee" and set an annual worldwide ceiling of 50,000 refugees through 1982.

The Immigration Reform and Control Act (IRCA) of 1986 was designed to control and deter undocumented immigration. Under this Act, all undocumented immigrants who were in the United States on or before January 1, 1982, and had lived in the country continuously since then were granted amnesty and were eligible to apply for permanent residency after two years. The Act also imposed penalties on employers who knowingly hired undocumented immigrants, created a Special Agricultural Worker program to deal with possible shortages caused by employer sanctions, and beefed up border inspection and enforcement.

The Immigration Act of 1990 modified and expanded the immigration system since 1965 and created the current immigration system (see table 4.1). It increased the total level of legal immigration to 700,000 for fiscal years 1992–4 and 675,000 in fiscal year 1995 and thereafter. It set an annual cap on total immigration, including both numerically limited and numerically exempt categories. It kept family reunification as the main avenue of admission but increased employment-based immigration. As part of the latter, it created a new "investor immigrants" category to attract those who would invest $1 million or more in urban areas and $500,000 or more in rural areas to create ten or more jobs. "Special immigrants" is a new employment-based category for certain religious workers. The Act further created a new category termed "diversity immigrants" or lottery immigrants to diversify the sources of immigration and provide opportunities for some countries adversely affected by the 1965 Act.[1] It changed the per country annual limit from 20,000 to 7 percent of the total family and employment limits for each independent country and from 5,000 to 2 percent of the total family and employment limits for each dependent area beginning in fiscal year 1992. Although Congress has been working on a new comprehensive immigration reform, no new bill on legal immigration or comprehensive immigration reform has been approved as of this writing.

Trends

What are the trends in post-1965 Asian immigration? Data from the CIS (before 2001, the INS) include countries of the Middle East located on the continent of Asia in the calculation of the total number of Asian immigrants. The existing analyses of Asian immigration normally use just the data from the CIS. However, I have made a special effort in this study to remove the Middle Eastern countries from Asia in accord with the concept of Asian Americans used by the US government (see chapter 1). Figure 4.1 shows the trends in immigration to the United States by region. It is clear that Asian immigration, without counting the Middle

Table 4.1 Current immigration system created by the Immigration Act of 1990

Category	Description	Limit
Family-sponsored immigrants		480,000
Family-sponsored preferences		226,000[a]
First	Unmarried sons and daughters of US citizens and their children	23,400[b]
Second	Spouses, children, and unmarried sons and daughters of permanent resident aliens	114,200[c]
Third	Married sons and daughters of US citizens	23,400[c]
Fourth	Brothers and sisters of US citizens aged 21 or older	65,000[c]
Immediate relatives of adult US citizens (spouses, children, and parents) and children born abroad to alien residents		Not limited
Employment-based preferences		140,000
First	Priority workers (i.e., persons of extraordinary ability, outstanding professors and researchers, and certain multinational executives and managers)	40,040[d]
Second	Professionals with advanced degrees or aliens of exceptional ability	40,040[c]
Third	Skilled workers, professionals (without advanced degrees), and needed unskilled workers (limited to 10,000)	40,040[c]
Fourth	Special immigrants	9,940
Fifth	Employment creation ("investors")	9,940
Diversity immigrants		55,000
Per-country limits		
Independent country		7%[e]
Dependent area		2%[e]
Total		**675,000**

Notes: The limits of family-sponsored and employment-based immigrants are adjusted annually based on visa usage in the previous year. The annual limit of diversity immigrants is also adjusted, if necessary. Family third and fourth preferences and all categories of employment-based preferences include the spouses and children of immigrants in the categories.

Table 4.1 (continued)

---

^a The limit of family-sponsored preferences cannot go below a minimum of 226,000.
^b plus unused family fourth preference visas.
^c Numbers not used in higher preferences may be used in these categories.
^d Plus unused employment fourth and fifth preference visas.
^e Of the total family and employments limits.

Source: DHS, *Yearbook of Immigration Statistics* (1991–2003).

Eastern countries, has increased continuously, with fluctuations, in the post-1965 period. From 1966 to 2009, the number of Asian immigrants totaled 9,552,207.[2] Figure 4.1 also indicates that Asia and Latin America have become the main sources of immigration since 1965. The level of European immigration was highest before 1965, but then steadily decreased until 1988, when it began to rebound. African immigration was at a very low level but has increased significantly since the end of the 1980s. Immigration from North America and Oceania has remained stable at a very low level.

Figure 4.2 displays trends in immigration by major Asian sending countries. Several patterns emerge. First, immigration from China, the Philippines, and India has increased at high levels with fluctuations since 1965, and these three countries have become the largest suppliers of Asian immigrants. The Philippines had maintained the highest level of immigration in Asia between 1968 and 1992. However, Filipino immigration declined after 1992 before increasing again in 2006–7. Since 1993, except for the years 1995–7, the Philippines has yielded the position of the leading country to either China or India. The closure of the last two large military bases in 1992 may largely explain the temporary declines in Filipino immigration after 1992 in absolute and relative terms, because there was no longer the opportunity for international marriages between US soldiers and Filipinos.

China's immigration has been growing incessantly since 1965. Notice that the data based on country of birth for China before 1982 included Taiwan. Nearly half of the Chinese immigrants

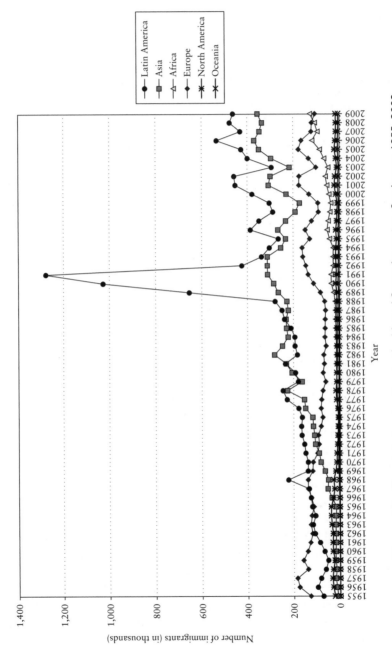

Figure 4.1   Trends in immigration to the United States by region, fiscal years 1955–2009

Post-1965 Asian Immigration

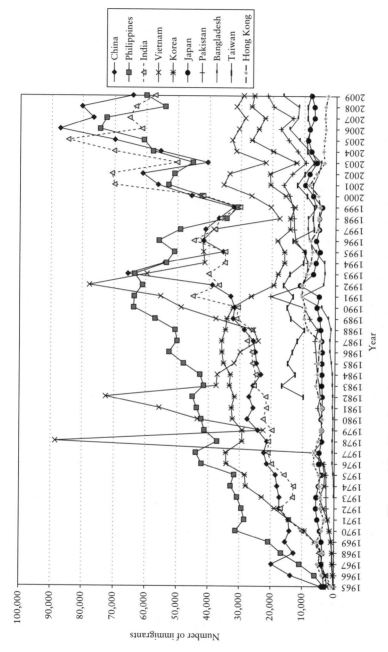

Figure 4.2 Trends in Asian immigration by country of birth, 1965–2009

before 1979 came from Taiwan following the relocation of the Nationalist government there in 1949, even though they were born on the mainland. After China and the United States established diplomatic relations on January 1, 1979, immigration from China has been on the rise. The peak in 1993 and 1994 was a result of the Chinese Student Protection Act (CSPA) of 1992 in response to the Tiananmen Square incident in 1989.[3] The use of some employment-based immigration quotas by the CSPA partly explains the small declines in the number of Chinese immigrants in the subsequent few years. China became the largest sending country in Asia in the periods 1998–2000 and 2006–9. The surge in Chinese immigration since 2005 has been consistent with the surge in total US immigration in the same period. Much of this was the result of an increase in the adjustment of status to permanent legal resident, which was a likely outcome of the CIS's efforts to accelerate the processing of immigration applications in order to eliminate the backlog of applications pending for at least six months.

Indian immigration resembles Chinese immigration in patterns and levels. In the early years, the majority of Indian immigrants were highly educated professionals, especially physicians, engineers, scientists, and computer specialists; many were students who completed their graduate studies at an American university, obtained a job, and became permanent residents. Since 1991, Indian immigration has accelerated, since many Indian professionals and technicians have entered as employment-based immigrants under the Immigration Act of 1990. India surpassed all Asian countries in the number of immigrants between 2001 and 2005, and it is likely that it could become the leading sending country in Asia in the years to come.

Second, the pattern of Korean immigration somewhat resembled a camel's hump. The number of Korean immigrants increased from 1965 to 1977 and then remained much at the same level in the late 1970s and through the 1980s before declining in the 1990s because of South Korea's rising living standard, democratization, and improved security following dialogue between North and South Korea. It rebounded significantly in the early twenty-first century, the result of a major economic crisis in Korea and several other Asian countries beginning in 1997 that again pushed many Koreans to the United States (Min 2006b).

Third, the tide of Vietnamese immigration ebbed and flowed considerably because of refugee influx. The first wave of immigrants, the former elite of South Vietnam, were political refugees who began to arrive in 1975 following the collapse of Saigon and who adjusted their status to permanent residents after a year of continuous residency in the United States. The second wave of refugees, the so-called boat people, started in 1979 and lasted for almost a decade; the apex in 1982, with more than 72,000 immigrants, reflected their adjustment of status to permanent residents after a year. The third wave reached its acme in 1992 and coincided with the normalization process of US–Vietnam relations that began in April 1991. The majority of these Vietnamese were regular immigrants rather than refugees.

Fourth, immigration from Japan had been quite stable at a low level relative to other major Asian donor countries up to the 1980s but has increased significantly since the 1990s. Since World War II, Japan has gradually emerged as a world economic power. Living standards in Japan have risen tremendously since the late 1960s. Japan surpassed the United States in per capita income between 1987 and 2000. These improved economic conditions explain why most Japanese were not motivated to leave their homeland for America. The INS data indicate that the majority of those who did immigrate were women in the period from 1965 to 1985 and very likely after 1985 if the data were available (Akiba 2006). Severe gender inequality in Japan in comparison with that in America – patriarchal attitudes and practices, traditional gender role expectations, unequal employment opportunity, and lower pay for women – apparently pushed Japanese women toward the United States; many married American men. Another major category, mostly men, consisted of representatives of Japanese companies working in their US subsidiaries on a three- to five-year rotational basis. A high proportion of these had permanent resident status, but had every intention of returning to Japan after service (Fang 1996; Yokoyama 1989). Nevertheless, since 1990

Japanese immigrant admissions have increased. It is not coinciden-
tal that Japan's prolonged economic recession since 1990 has gone
hand in hand with its increased immigration in the same period, as
some Japanese sought better employment and education opportunities in the United States.

Fifth, immigration from Hong Kong and Taiwan had also been
stable but has decreased in more recent years. Immigration from
Hong Kong had hovered in the range of 3,000 to 7,000 annually from 1966 to 1987. The IRCA of 1986 increased the annual
quota for immigrants admitted under the preference system for
all dependent areas (including Hong Kong) from 600 to 5,000
beginning in fiscal year 1988. The Immigration Act of 1990
further increased the quota for Hong Kong to 10,000 beginning
in fiscal year 1992 and then to 20,000 beginning in fiscal year
1995. Moreover, facing the uncertainty of Hong Kong's return
to Chinese rule from Britain in 1997, many Hong Kong Chinese
tried to find a safer and better alternative elsewhere – or at least
a backup place in the case of unwanted or unexpected changes.
The United States, Canada, and Australia became their favored
alternatives. These policy and social changes explain the significant increases in immigration from Hong Kong between 1988 and
1996. However, after the reversion to Chinese rule Hong Kong
remained largely unchanged, at least economically and in daily
life. Life elsewhere was difficult to adjust to for many Hong Kong
emigrants. The "emigration fever" cooled down, and hence there
has been an overall declining trend in immigration since 1997,
even with an increase of immigration quota to 20,000 per year.

Taiwan shared an annual quota of 20,000 with China and was
tallied under China before 1982. But since then it has received its
own quota of 20,000 per year and has been counted separately. As
shown in figure 4.2, immigration from Taiwan fluctuated between
1982 and 1996 but fell below 10,000 annually after 1996 except
for 2001. Rising living standards, democratization, and improved
social conditions, especially college education opportunities, contributed to the significant declines in Taiwanese immigration. Also
note that a combination of immigration from China, Taiwan, and
Hong Kong as well as some ethnic Chinese from Indo-China put

the level of Chinese immigration above the level of immigration from other Asian ethnic groups.

Finally, immigration from Pakistan and especially from Bangladesh was relatively low before the 1990s, but both have seen substantial increases since the 1990s. A couple of factors may have contributed to these significant increases. The decline in labor migration opportunities in the Middle East oil production countries in the early 1990s forced Pakistanis and Bangladeshis to look for economic opportunities elsewhere (Kibria 2006). Bangladeshis and Pakistanis became unexpected beneficiaries of the "Diversity Immigrants" program (commonly known as the "Green Card Lottery" program) instituted by the Immigration Act of 1990. In the period 1992–2009, 34,040 Bangladeshis and 12,836 Pakistanis were admitted as diversity immigrants. Pakistan and Bangladesh are very likely to emerge as big Asian sending countries in the near future. Together with India, Nepal, and Sri Lanka, they have boosted South Asian immigration to a level parallel with or sometimes even surpassing Chinese immigration. Countering the prediction that immigration from South Asia may decrease as a result of discrimination against South Asians in the aftermath of 9/11, the evidence in figure 4.2 appears to suggest that such an effect was only temporary; South Asian immigration rebounded after 2003.

In the years 1966–2009, the ten countries or political entities in figure 4.2 as the major countries of origin had sent 8,603,901 immigrants to the United States, accounting for 90.1 percent of all Asian immigrants in this period. The numbers and rankings of these top ten countries are straightforward, as shown in figure 4.3. If we sum China, Taiwan, and Hong Kong, the total number of Chinese immigrants was more than 2.1 million, slightly higher than the number of Filipinos. The total number of South Asian immigrants from India, Pakistan, and Bangladesh was nearly 2 million.

In chapter 3, we learned that the major Asian immigrant groups were dominated by males before World War II but saw some transformation in the postwar years. Has the pattern of sex composition changed in the post-1965 period? Figure 4.4 offers a clear

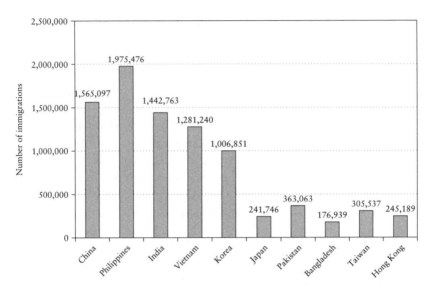

Figure 4.3 Total numbers of Asian immigrants by country of birth, 1966–2009

answer.[4] Available data on the sex ratio – the number of males per 100 females – of major Asian immigrant groups from the INS indicate that post-1965 Indian immigration was male dominated at least until the 1970s, almost equalized between 1982 and 1992 (except for 1991), and has become female dominated in more recent years (except for 2001). These trends are consistent with the fact that early Indian immigrants were mostly men, but family reunification has brought many Indian women to America since the 1980s and more women than men in recent years. Somewhat similar trends have transpired where Pakistani immigrants are concerned.

According to the available data, Pakistani immigration was dominated largely by men until 1992 before becoming more or less balanced, albeit still favoring rather more males. Before 1978, Vietnamese immigration was dominated by women who married US servicemen; since then the refugee adjustments appeared to bring about male dominance until 1989, followed by a return to female dominance after that point, reflecting the reunification of Vietnamese women with their refugee husbands. The sex ratios

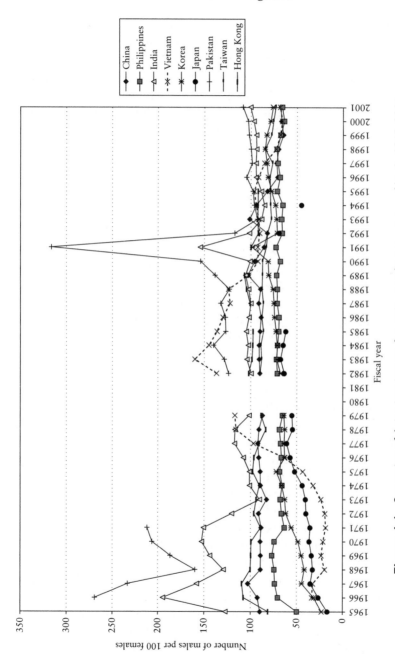

Figure 4.4 Sex ratios of Asian immigrants for major sending countries of birth, 1965–2001

of immigrants from Hong Kong were more or less equal. Except for a few years, the sex ratios of Chinese immigrants were below 100, often in the range of high 80s or 90s until 1994, indicating more female Chinese immigrants than their male counterparts. The immigration of Filipinos, Koreans, Japanese, and Taiwanese had consistently been female dominated, largely associated with the international marriages between Asian women of these groups and US servicemen.

Settlement patterns

In chapter 3, we also learned that, historically, most Asian immigrants settled on the West Coast and in Hawaii. Has this pattern changed since 1965, and where do post-1965 Asian immigrants settle after arrival in the United States? The INS published data on the states of immigrants' intended permanent residence for selected countries up to 2001 (except for 1980–1), but discontinued thereafter. Table 4.2 shows the top three states of intended residence for main Asian sending countries between 1966 and 2001. It is evident that Chinese immigrants largely preferred California and New York to other states. In particular, California was the no. 1 choice, except for 1971. The preexisting Chinese communities and the geographic/climatic and economic advantages in these two states acted as magnets, though these preferences tended to decrease over time as immigrants expanded their horizons to other states. More and more have moved to New Jersey, Massachusetts, Texas, Illinois, Pennsylvania, Maryland, Michigan, Virginia, Washington, Ohio, and Florida.

Following their predecessors, post-1965 Filipino immigrants continued to flock to Hawaii and especially California; Illinois was also a quite consistent destination. For Asian Indian immigrants, New York was the most favored destination in 1971, but in more recent decades California took the first place. The top three destinations for Korean immigrants had been consistently California, New York, and Illinois in 1971 and 1982, and California, New York, and New Jersey in 1991 and 2001. Virginia was another

Table 4.2 Top three states of intended permanent residence for major Asian sending countries, selected years (%)

Year	China		Philippines		India		Korea		Vietnam		Japan	
1966	CA	46.0	CA	39.4							CA	35.0
	NY	25.7	HI	22.2							HI	10.1
	MA	3.5	Guam	8.7							NY	6.2
1971	NY	28.0	CA	35.4	NY	21.8	CA	18.7				
	CA	23.9	HI	13.0	IL	10.2	NY	12.9				
	MA	3.4	IL	9.3	CA	9.4	IL	7.4				
1982	CA	38.4	CA	45.0	CA	15.4	CA	29.1	CA	41.4		
	NY	22.6	HI	10.5	NY	15.0	NY	9.2	TX	11.5		
	IL	3.0	IL	5.9	IL	10.3	IL	5.7	IL	4.8		
1991	CA	37.1	CA	51.4	CA	22.8	CA	27.5	CA	38.9		
	NY	29.3	HI	6.9	NY	20.3	NY	19.6	TX	9.5		
	IL	3.5	NY	6.4	NJ	11.0	NJ	5.4	NY	4.0		
2001	CA	30.7	CA	43.6	CA	23.5	CA	34.9	CA	36.7	CA	37.8
	NY	14.3	HI	6.3	NJ	13.0	NY	9.1	TX	10.6	NY	9.8
	NJ	5.8	IL	5.6	IL	7.1	NJ	7.9	WA	4.3	HI	6.1

Note: No data were available for 1980–1.

Source: The author's calculation based on data from INS (1966, 1971, 1982, 1991, 2001).

Table 4.3 Percentage distribution of immigrants settling in urban or metropolitan statistical areas by major Asian sending countries, selected years

Year	China	Philippines	India	Korea	Vietnam	Japan
1966	97.8	91.1				88.6
1971	98.7	98.5	97.9	98.0		
1982	99.7	99.4	99.5	99.7	99.3	
1991	97.5	90.7	95.7	92.8	97.6	
2001	96.9	91.2	97.3	95.7	97.5	93.8

Notes: Data refer to urban areas in 1966, 1971, and 1982, and metropolitan statistical areas in 1991 and 2001. No data were available for 1980–1.

Source: The author's calculation based on data from INS (1966, 1971, 1982, 1991, 2001).

popular destination in 1991 and 2001. California was also the most popular destination for Vietnamese immigrants, followed by Texas. For Japanese immigrants, California, Hawaii, and New York had remained the most popular destinations.

Post-1965 Asian immigrants are urban bound and metropolitanized. The INS published data on urban or rural settlement up to 1986, but switched to data on settlement in metropolitan statistical areas (MSAs) starting in 1987. Table 4.3 shows the rates of both urban and MSA settlement.[5] As evidenced in the table, unlike their pre-1965 counterparts, post-1965 Asian immigrants were uniformly urban-bound, with a rate of urban settlement close to 100 percent. They were also more metropolitanized compared with immigrants from Mexico and Canada, both with a rate of MSA settlement at about 90 percent.

New Asian immigrants cluster in urban centers for a number of reasons. First, urban centers represent a modern lifestyle; second, existing Asian communities are located there; and, third, employment and investment opportunities are greater in urban centers than in rural areas.

Another new development in settlement pattern associated with post-1965 Asian immigration is the emergence of what Wei Li (1998, 2009) dubbed "ethnoburb" – a suburban residential and commercial community with a significant concentration of an ethnic minority population. An ethnoburb is different from an ethnic enclave in location, scale, population density, resident class composition, economic function, and intergroup interaction (Li 2009). Most importantly, an ethnoburb is an amalgam of a multiethnic enclave and a middle-class suburb. Historically, ethnic enclaves (e.g., Chinatown, Little Tokyo, Little Italy) were concentrated in urban centers with a predominantly ethnic, lower-class, foreign-born population. Suburbia was associated with white, middle-class, native-born families. However, since the late 1970s ethnoburbs have been emerging in some Asian immigrant communities. Monterey Park in East Los Angeles is the first suburban Chinatown documented by Fong (1994).[6] Other suburban Chinatowns have been mushrooming in cities along the San Gabriel Valley east of Los Angeles (e.g., Arcadia, Alhambra, San Gabriel, Rosemead, Rowland Heights, Temple City, and Hacienda Heights) (Zhou, Tseng, and Kim 2008) and elsewhere (e.g., Flushing in New York, Cupertino in the Silicon Valley, Richardson near Dallas). Examples of suburban Koreatowns include Garden Grove in northern Orange County, California, and Fort Lee and Palisades Park, both in Bergen County, New Jersey, while examples of suburban Indiatowns are Edison and Iselin in central New Jersey (Min 2006c). Changes in US immigration policy, the global economy, geopolitics, and local city conditions have led to the influx of new middle-class Asian immigrants into these communities and therefore to the formation and growth of these ethnoburbs.

Types of immigrants

How do Asians immigrate to the United States, or through what channels do they gain admission? Asians immigrate to the United States under different categories. According to the current system established by the Immigration Act of 1990, these categories or types may be lumped together into family-sponsored immigrants, employment-based preferences, refugee and aslyee adjustments, diversity immigrants, and others. Alternatively, categories may be divided into new arrivals and adjustments or highly skilled migrants and non-highly skilled migrants. Some Asian children enter as adoptees. The patterns of these different types vary across Asian countries.

Family-sponsored immigrants

Currently, family-sponsored immigrants include family-sponsored preferences (subject to numerical limitation) and immediate relatives of US citizens (exempt from numerical limitation). In fiscal years 1992–4, spouses and children of Immigration Reform and Control Act amnesty recipients also fell into this category. Table 4.4 shows the percentage distributions of Asian immigrants by type of admission and major sending countries of birth for 1992, the first year in which data under the new system were published, and for 2007, the latest year data became available when analysis for this project was undertaken.[7] In both 1992 and 2007 the majority of Chinese from the mainland and Hong Kong, Filipinos, Indians, Pakistanis, and Bangladeshis, as well as Chinese from Taiwan in 2007 and Koreans in 1992, were admitted as family-sponsored immigrants. For instance, between 74 and 76 percent of Filipinos in 1992 and 2007 entered under this category – more than half of them as immediate relatives of US citizens. It appears that family reunification is the main path of immigration for these groups. Also note that immediate relatives emerged as the main immigrants among Japanese and Cambodians in 2007.

"Chain migration" is a term often used to describe how the number of immigrants multiplies through social networks. Chain migration is a very common phenomenon in post-1965 immigration to the United States, and this term is particularly applicable to the immigration of post-1965 Asians through family sponsorship. Oftentimes, one family member arrives first, either through kinship or employment or adjustment of status. That person then sponsors his or her spouse and children. Once both the husband and wife become US citizens, each further sponsors their parents

Table 4.4 Percentage distribution of Asian immigrants by type of admission and major countries of birth, 1992 and 2007

Country Year	Total number	Family-sponsored preferences	Employment-based preferences	Immediate relatives of US citizens	Refugee & asylee adjustments	Diversity	IRCA legalization & dependents	Other[a]
China								
1992	38,907	31.4	28.4	29.4	2.27	0.19	7.5	0.8
2007	76,655	19.9	18.1	35.4	26.15	0.03		0.03
Taiwan								
1992	16,344	28.2	51.2	17.2	0.06	0.20	2.8	0.3
2007	8,990	33.9	28.9	34.1	0.09	2.87		0.1
Hong Kong								
1992	10,452	54.6	26.8	11.9	1.85	0.55	1.8	2.5
2007	3,527	51.5	21.2	25.8	0.14	0.96		0.31
Philippines								
1992	61,022	23.7	15.9	50.1	0.36	0.02	4.1	5.8
2007	72,596	18.6	23.7	57.0	0.51	0.01		0.12
India								
1992	36,755	39.4	26.4	26.7	0.09	0.09	6.7	0.7
2007	65,353	28.8	43.9	27.9	4.10	0.09		0.24
Pakistan								
1992	10,214	42.4	12.2	26.6	1.26	0.06	15.2	2.3
2007	13,492	23.8	24.1	43.5	8.06	0.02		0.50
Bangladesh								
1992	3,740	33.6	13.6	24.7	0.27	0.13	17.6	10.1
2007	12,074	25.0	9.6	34.0	3.93	26.95		0.47

125

Table 4.4 (continued)

Country Year	Total number	Family-sponsored preferences	Employment-based preferences	Immediate relatives of US citizens	Refugee & asylee adjustments	Diversity	IRCA legalization & dependents	Other[a]
Korea								
1992	19,359	32.4	24.3	39.0	0	0.13	3.3	0.8
2007	22,405	9.9	50.5	39.5	D	D		0.07
Japan								
1992	11,028	2.6	29.0	23.1	0.05	43.88	0.7	0.6
2007	6,748	2.0	33.9	60.6	0.22	2.98		0.33
Vietnam								
1992	77,735	15.6	0.2	14.5	41.36	0.01	0.01	28.3
2007	28,691	43.3	D	48.7	6.16	D		1.1
Cambodia								
1992	2,573	5.2	0.8	16.7	65.88	0.04	0.16	11.2
2007	4,246	11.1	1.2	78.3	6.62	1.32		1.44
Laos								
1992	8,696	1.6	0.1	5.8	92.30	0	0.07	0.1
2007	2,575	4.6	D	37.0	57.17	D		0.12
Indonesia								
1992	2,916	7.7	15.0	13.3	0.45	51.34	1.75	10.5
2007	3,716	4.5	20.0	37.2	33.77	3.50		1.08

Notes: [a] Includes Amerasians, former H-1 registered nurses, and Indochinese parolees.
D = withheld by DHS for disclosure.

Source: The author's calculation based on data from INS (1992) and DHS (2007).

as immediate relatives and their siblings as family-sponsored preference immigrants. Parents and siblings then start the whole process again to bring in extended families. Through this chain migration, the snowball becomes ever bigger.

Employment-based preferences

Employment-based preferences are also an important path of post-1965 Asian immigration (for categories, see table 4.1). As seen in table 4.4, a significant proportion of Chinese, Filipino, South Asian, Korean, Japanese, and Indonesian immigrants entered as employment-based immigrants in 1992 and 2007. In particular, this category became the dominant mode of entry for Korean immigrants (50.5 percent) and Indian immigrants (43.9 percent) in 2007, as well as for around one-third of Japanese immigrants. Normally, the largest subcategory is second employment-based preference – advanced degree holders and workers with special skills – followed by third employment-based preference – skilled workers, professionals, and other unskilled workers. It is worth mentioning that the number of Asian investor immigrants (fifth employment-based preference) increased almost incrementally, from 30 in 1992 to 427 in 1993, 326 in 1994, 403 in 1995, 765 in 1996, and a high point of 1,212 in 1997, but then steadily declined to 629 in 1998, 170 in 1999, 127 in 2000, and 112 in 2001. Taiwan, China, Hong Kong, and Korea were among the largest sending countries of investor immigrants.

Refugee/asylee/parolee adjustment

Another important immigration route is through adjusting refugee or asylee or parolee status to that of permanent resident. A refugee is a person outside his or her country of nationality who is unable or unwilling to return to that country because of persecution or a well-founded fear of persecution. An asylee is an alien living in the United States or at a port of entry who is unable or unwilling to return to his or her country of nationality, or to seek the protection of that country, because of persecution or a well-founded fear of persecution. A parolee is an alien, appearing to be inadmissible to the inspecting officer, allowed to enter the United States under emergency (humanitarian) conditions or if that entry is determined to be in the public interest. Note that refugees and asylees are not immigrants when admitted, but are eligible to adjust their status to that of lawful permanent resident after one year of continuous presence in the United States. Parolees are not formally admitted to the United States, but are able to become permanent residents under some special circumstances. At least until the mid-1990s, the majority of Indochinese became permanent residents through the adjustment of refugee/asylee/parolee status. Table 4.4 shows that, for example, in 1992 close to 70 percent of Vietnamese (41.4 percent as refugee/asylee adjustments, plus 28.3 percent mostly as Indochinese parolee adjustments under the "other" category), about 66 percent of Cambodians, and 92 percent of Laotians received their green cards after adjusting their status. In 2007, refugee/asylee adjustment was still the main entry mode for Laotians, but not for Vietnamese and Cambodians. In more recent years, more Indochinese entered through family reunification than through refugee/asylee adjustment. Also note that the Indochinese are not the only Asian groups who benefit from refugee/asylee adjustment. For example, in 2007 a large percentage of Indonesians (34 percent), mainland Chinese (26 percent), and, to a lesser extent, Pakistanis (8 percent) obtained a green card via refugee/asylee adjustment.

Diversity immigrants

The diversity program was created by the Immigration Act of 1990 to diversify the sources of immigration through the lottery process. Only nationals of countries that have sent fewer than 50,000 immigrants to the United States in the preceding five years are eligible to enter the lottery, so many Asian countries are ineligible because they already exceed this number. However, countries such as Bangladesh, Pakistan, Japan, Nepal, and Indonesia have benefited greatly from this program. According to my calculation, based on the DHS data, from 1992 to 2009, 34,040 Bangladeshis,

12,836 Pakistanis, 10,958 Japanese, 12,055 Nepalese, and 5,329 Indonesians had entered under the diversity program. Most of the Pakistanis entered between 1996 and 2002, when Pakistan was qualified as a lottery recipient country, but Bangladeshis have continued to come under this program since 1996. Nepal has emerged as a large diversity program beneficiary since 2003.

New arrivals v. adjustments

Individuals can arrive in the United States as permanent residents (new arrivals) or as nonimmigrants but adjust their status to permanent residents (adjustments). Many Asians came as new arrivals. However, a high percentage, and in some groups the majority, of Asians first came as refugees, asylees, or parolees, visitors for business or pleasure, students, exchange scholars, or temporary workers and later changed their status to permanent residents. Figure 4.5 shows the rates of adjustment for major Asian groups from 1965 to 2002, the last year the DHS published data on adjustment by country. It is very clear that a large majority of Vietnamese adjusted from refugees or parolees to green card holders in the periods 1976–89 and 1993–6. Similar patterns occurred among Cambodians and Laotians (not shown). The proportion of Japanese status adjusters had been very high and on the rise over time. The adjustment rates of Indians were extremely high in the 1960s, declined in the 1970s and 1980s, but have risen again since the 1990s and especially in the early twenty-first century. A similar trend is detected for the mainland and Hong Kong Chinese, Koreans, and Filipinos. For all groups, there had been an increasing trend of adjustments, with very high levels of adjustment rates since 1990, mostly above 20 percent or much higher.

The brain flow

One salient feature of post-1965 Asian immigration is the high volume of the "brain flow," or migration of the highly skilled.[8] "Brain drain" is a term probably more familiar to the reader

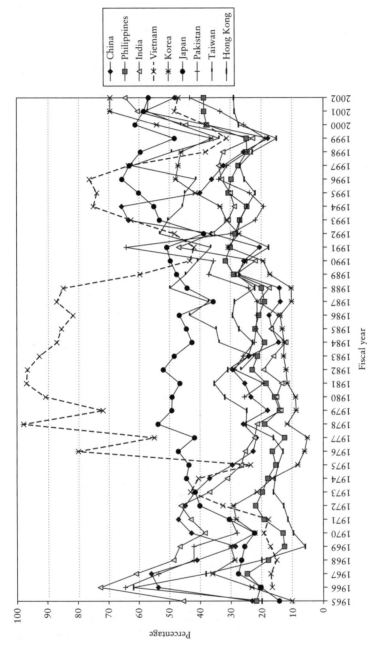

Figure 4.5 Percentage distribution of Asians who adjusted their status to permanent resident by country of birth, 1965–2002

because of the heated debate in the 1960s and 1970s. However, as I argued elsewhere (Yang 2001), the term "brain drain" reflects a sending-country perspective. Cheng and Yang (1998) suggested that "brain flow" is a more precise term because it reflects the perspective of both sending and receiving countries and because such migration involves both losses and gains to sending countries and possibly a two-way movement. Note that highly skilled immigrants could enter under the categories of employment-based preferences or family-sponsored immigrants and as either new arrivals or adjustments.

In the post-1965 period, Asia has become the largest supplier of highly skilled immigrants to the United States. As shown in table 4.5, Asia, again excluding the Middle East countries on the continent, sent the largest number of highly skilled immigrants in all years except for 1966. Asians accounted for more than half of all the highly skilled immigrants in both 1971 and 2001 and between 41 and 47 percent in 1991 and 1982, respectively. The total number has increased continuously, with India, China, the Philippines, Taiwan, and Korea among the major sending countries. China and Taiwan supply a large number of scientists, engineers, and other professionals, while India is the largest donor of engineers, scientists, and physicians, largely male (Yang 2001). The story of Ashok Shah reported in chapter 1 is just one of many examples. The Philippines is known as the biggest supplier of nurses and other health professionals, mostly female (Espiritu 2008; Ong and Azores 1994). The story of Diwata Lopez narrated in chapter 1 reflects this reality. The decline in numbers of both Indians and Filipinos in 1982 may be attributed to the Health Professions Educational Assistance Act of 1976, which restricted foreign medical graduates from entering into the United States as immigrants or as exchange visitors and from practicing or training in the US medical profession. The numbers of such immigrants from Pakistan, Hong Kong, Japan, and Bangladesh also showed a general upward movement.

To be sure, international students are not immigrants, but they are an important source of brain flow. The United States is the largest recipient of foreign students in the world, and Asian

Table 4.5 Numbers and percentages of highly skilled immigrants by region and major Asian sending countries, selected years

Region and country of birth	1966		1971		1982		1991		2001	
All countries	36,812	11.4	55,104	14.9	64,740	10.9	86,866	4.8	111,672	10.5
Europe	14,567	11.7	9,885	10.2	11,641	16.8	17,881	13.2	22,183	12.6
North America	4,419	15.6	2,125	16.2	2,521	23.4	3,407	25.2	4,512	20.6
Latin America	9,849	7.9	8,533	5.8	12,047	6.6	19,147	1.5	13,025	2.9
Africa	703	22.4	2,365	34.9	2,855	19.4	4,305	11.9	7,066	13.1
Oceania	323	17.7	604	20.7	747	19.5	818	13.1	1,101	18.0
Asia	5,764	16.7	28,714	32.0	30,272	10.7	35,281	11.3	58,773	19.1
China	1,715	12.5	4,566	31.7	4,662	17.2	4,815	14.6	12,565	22.3
Philippines	1,090	17.9	9,560	33.6	7,865	17.4	10,214	16.1	7,489	14.1
India	1,453	59.1	7,688	53.7	5,451	25.1	6,946	15.4	22,997	32.7
Korea	366	14.7	3,319	23.2	3,304	10.4	2,031	7.7	2,227	10.7
Vietnam	40	14.5	118	5.8	1,471	2.0	895	1.6	1,038	2.9
Japan	332	9.8	644	14.4	663	17.0	774	15.3	1,518	15.8
Taiwan[a]					3,131	31.7	3,244	24.4	3,204	26.3
Hong Kong	154	4.0	208	6.5	722	14.5	2,138	20.5	1,992	23.9
Pakistan	209	60.2	1,245	58.6	940	20.7	1,416	7.0	2,426	14.7
Bangladesh					140	21.9	568	5.3	736	10.3

Notes: Percentage refers to highly skilled immigrants as a percentage of the total immigrants from a region or country. No data were available for 1981 and after 2001.
[a] Included in China before 1982.

Source: The author's calculation based on data from INS (1966, 1971, 1982, 1991, 2001).

countries are the largest suppliers of foreign students. According to the latest data released by the Institute of International Education in *Open Doors*, in the academic year 2007–8 India topped the list of countries of origin for international students for the seventh consecutive time, with a total of 94,563 students, followed by China (81,127), South Korea (69,124), and Japan (33,974). Taiwan, Thailand, Nepal, Vietnam, Hong Kong, and Indonesia were also among the top twenty countries of origin. Students from just these ten Asian countries constituted 56 percent of all foreign students in the United States in that year. Many of these students become immigrants after completing their degree programs and securing a job.

Temporary workers with special skills under H1 visas (H1 workers) are another major source of brain flow. The H1 program was established by the Immigration and Nationality Act of 1952 to import temporary foreign "workers of distinguished merit and ability." Many Filipino registered nurses came to the United States under the H1 category (starting in 1970). However, Asia was not the leading supplier of such workers before the 1990s. The Immigration Act of 1990 created the H-1B visa program to bring in temporary foreign workers in "specialty occupations," including computer systems analysts and programmers, physicians, professors, engineers, managers, and accountants. H-1B workers are allowed to stay for up to three years initially, with extensions not exceeding three years. These workers must meet one of the following criteria:

1   hold a US bachelor's or higher degree required by the specialty occupation from an accredited college or university;
2   possess a foreign degree equivalent to a US bachelor's or higher degree required by the specialty occupation from an accredited college or university;
3   have any required license or other official permission to practice the occupation in the state to be employed; or
4   have the equivalent of the degree required by the specialty occupation through a combination of education, training, and/ or experience.

Since 1992, the first year in which data were collected on this program, Asia has become the leading region for H-1B workers, and the number has skyrocketed. India had commanded the lead, increasing from 8,246 in fiscal year 1992 to 157,613 in fiscal year 2007, a 1,811 percent increase. In the same period, the number of such workers rose continuously, from 2,731 to 16,628 for China,[9] from 11,502 to 14,435 for Japan, from 1,329 to 11,479 for Korea, from 4005 to 7,201 for the Philippines, and from 634 to 3,147 for Pakistan. The large increments were largely due to the American Competitiveness and Workforce Improvement Act of 1998, which increased the annual ceiling of H-1B visas for initial employment from 65,000 to 115,000 in fiscal years 1999 and 2000 and to 107,500 in 2001, and the American Competitiveness in the Twenty-First Century Act of 2000, which further raised the annual cap to 195,000 in fiscal years 2001–3. Each year, a large number of temporary workers, including those with H-1B visas, adjust their status to permanent residents.[10] For example, in 2002 (the latest year such data are available) 33,373 Indians, 13,501 Chinese, 4,225 Filipinos, 2,497 Koreans, and 1,615 Pakistanis adjusted their status. Nevertheless, some of these H-1B workers may spend many years as temporary migrants and remain "probationary Americans" or return to their home countries (Park and Park 2005). It should be mentioned that international students and H-1B workers combine to contribute to the brain flow. Many international students become H-1B workers after graduation and later take up permanent residency.

Adoptees

Some Asian children were adopted by American citizens and were therefore exempt from numerical limitation. Where do most Asian adoptees come from? What are the trends and levels in Asian adoption? Figure 4.6 presents the relevant data available since 1976. It shows that Korea was the dominant sending country before 1995, with a total of more than 90,000 adoptees between 1976 and 2009. Josh Shave, reported in chapter 1, was just one of the many Korean adoptees who came to America during that time. The

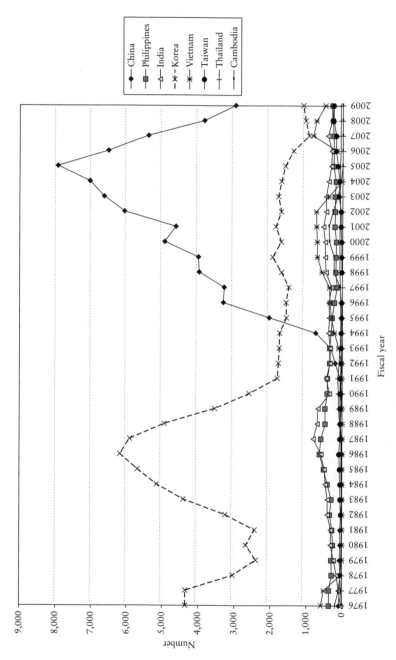

Figure 4.6 Numbers of Asian adoptees from major sending countries, 1976–2009

135

first-generation adult Korean adoptees held their first gathering in September 1999, with nearly 400 attendees. The decline in the number of Korean adoptees since the 1990s was due to increased internal adoption and the decreasing supply of adoptable orphans (Min 2006b). However, since 1995, China has replaced Korea as the leading adoption country. The number of Chinese adoptees rose continuously until 2005 and then decreased significantly. A total of 74,572 Chinese adoptees have arrived in the United States since 1976. The substantial increases can be attributed to the low prices of adoption, the availability of a large number of girls as a result of China's controversial one-child policy, and looser regulatory control by the Chinese authorities. But tighter control in recent years has led to a decline in Chinese adoption.

Causes

What conditions cause the substantial increases in post-1965 Asian immigration? The macro–micro interactive and cumulative causation theory of Asian immigration presented in chapter 2 can be very helpful in guiding our answer to this question. The following factors are important.

First, changes in US immigration policy made large Asian immigration possible. Recall that, before 1965, the annual immigration quota for most Asian countries was 100, and in the case of the Philippines between 1934 and 1946, it was fifty as a result of the Tydings–McDuffie Act. However, the Immigration and Nationality Act of 1965 abolished the discriminatory national origins quota system and gave people in all countries an equal opportunity to immigrate to the United States. It is worth emphasizing that this change in the law is crucial, because without it the substantial growth in Asian immigration would not have been possible.

Second, changes in the emigration policies of some Asian countries enabled many Asians (mainland Chinese in particular) to emigrate. After the communist takeover in 1949, China basically closed its doors to emigration, and before 1979 it was very difficult for people to obtain a passport. Since 1979, however, as part of the reform and open-door movement, the Chinese government has gradually slackened its hold over emigration, and it is now much easier to leave China (though there remain controls on political dissidents). South Korea used to impose certain restrictions (Light and Bonacich 1988), but many obstacles have been removed over time. Since 1987, the elected civilian government in South Korea has imposed no restriction on emigration.

Third, large disparities between many Asian sending countries and the United States in economic, political, social conditions push Asians to leave their homelands and pull them to America. Compared to the United States, all Asian sending countries (except for Japan) have offered a much lower income, a poorer quality of life, and less opportunity for college education, especially before the 1990s. Specifically, no Asian countries other than Japan have had a higher per capita gross national income (GNI) than the United States (see United Nations 2008). The per capita GNI of Japan had lagged behind that of the US until 1986, but overtook it between 1987 and 2000, and then fell behind again after 2001. Asian countries, save Japan, have also trailed behind the United States in quality of life as measured by the UN Human Development Index (HDI) (see United Nations 2009), which takes into account life expectancy, educational attainment, and adjusted real income. Even Japan did not outshine the United States until the early twenty-first century on this index. Until recent years, opportunity for college education in Asian countries was very limited. Only a small proportion of high-school graduates were able to attend college, and competition for admission through standardized examinations was very strong. In contrast, college is within reach of any student in America who really desires it, and so America becomes an alternative for college education for many Asian parents. Furthermore, there was a lack of democracy in many Asian countries at least until the mid-1980s. For example, Taiwan did not allow freedom of assembly or hold direct presidential elections until 1986. South Korea was under a military dictatorship and did not have a direct presidential election until 1987. Hong Kong is still not a functioning democracy, having had no elections for either its governor during British rule or its chief executive under Chinese rule. There are still tight political controls and no popular elections at the provincial or national level in China and Vietnam. The rule of man oftentimes overshadows the rule of law. Individual freedom is much limited. These disparities motivate Asians to leave their homelands for America. Many Asians immigrated to the United States because they wanted a better life and better opportunities for themselves and especially for their children. The stories of Yoshi Yamaguchi and Takae Jeong in chapter 1 lend credence to this point. The significantly narrowing gaps in per capita income, quality of life, and opportunities for college education in South Korea, Taiwan, Hong Kong, and Singapore in more recent decades also explain why fewer people have been motivated to come from these places than in earlier decades. The declines in income in Japan since 1990 as a result of its recession also explain why Japanese immigration to the United States has increased since then.

Fourth, military, political, economic, and cultural connections between the United States and Asian sending countries turn the immigration dreams of many Asians into reality. As mentioned earlier, because of US military bases in South Korea, the Philippines, Japan, and Taiwan, substantial numbers of women in these countries have come to the United States through marriage with US servicemen (Glenn 1986; Kim 1977; Min 2006b; Williams 1991; Yuh 2002). US involvement in the Vietnam War has brought more than a million of Vietnamese, more than 200,000 Cambodians, and close to 300,000 Laotians as refugee-turned immigrants. The normalization of diplomatic relations between China and the United States in 1979 and between Vietnam and the United States in 1994 has facilitated the immigration of many Chinese and Vietnamese. The very close economic ties between the United States and Japan, the Philippines, South Korea, Taiwan, and, more recently, China, India, and Vietnam through investment and trade have promoted Asian immigration by establishing the ideological linkages between prospective immigrants and the United States and creating opportunities for emigration. Continuing US cultural influences in Asian sending countries through a military presence,

TV programs, publications, exchanges of students and scholars, and other cultural activities have continued to motivate Asians to emigrate. In particular, the huge number of Asian students who have studied in the United States has become a very important source of post-1965 immigration. The role of US involvement in bringing in Asian immigrants to America is shown in a number of stories narrated in chapter 1 (e.g., Kazuko Miller, Diwata Lopez, Ashok Shah, and Dug Nguyen).

Finally, existing social networks sponsor many new Asian immigrants and sustain the continuation of post-1965 Asian immigration. Family reunification has become the major route, as the majority of immigrants come through the sponsorship of their families and relatives, though a significant proportion have arrived through employment opportunities created by their relatives, friends, ethnic firms, and ethnic communities or have found employment through their social networks. Moreover, the relatives, friends, ethnic firms, and ethnic communities of new Asian immigrants help the newcomers settle and adapt through assistance in housing, jobs, schooling, ethnic food and markets, language, information for naturalization, and so on. Chain migration has kept the numbers multiplying, leading to drastic increases in post-1965 Asian immigration. Several stories in chapter 1 (e.g., Takae Jeong and Dug Nguyen) shed light on the role of existing social networks in facilitating new Asian immigration.

Immigrant transnationalism

"Transnationalism" is a buzzword these days. But its meanings vary widely, from operations or activities of terrorists, rebels, clashing factions in civil wars, and members of criminal groups across nations (US Secretary of Defense 1996) to the operation of multinational corporations across national borders (economic transnationalism), global cooperation and coordination across nation-states in governance (political transnationalism), "multiple ties and interactions linking people or institutions across the borders of nation-states" (Vertovec 1999: 447), and many others.

In my view, as a general term "transnationalism" refers to the process that links people, groups, and institutions together across national borders. The emphasis is on the transcendence of social relations across boundaries of nations/states rather than cooperation between countries. Transnationalism has many dimensions, including but not limited to the economic, political, cultural, and environmental spheres. In international migration studies, our interest lies in "immigrant transnationalism." The classic definition of immigrant transnationalism is provided by anthropologists Basch, Glick Schiller, and Szanton Blanc (1994: 7): "the processes by which immigrants forge and sustain multi-stranded social relations that link together their societies of origin and settlement." However, the use of this definition tends to include all border-crossing activities by all immigrants as transnationalism, because immigrants have always maintained ties across national borders. In this book, I define immigrant transnationalism as the process by which immigrants as well as their social institutions engage in regular and sustained involvement in economic, political, social, cultural, or personal practices across national borders (Yang 2006a). Differing from the classic definition, this definition stresses the regularity and sustentation of cross-border activities or practices spanning economic, social, cultural, political, and even personal dimensions. While most immigrants engage to varying degrees in some kinds of transnational activities (e.g., phone calls, remittances, homeland visits), not all immigrants are transnationals (Portes 2003). The most salient feature of immigrant transnationalism is the emergence of a growing class of "transnational migrants," or "transmigrants," who live their lives across international borders (Yang 2006a). With their feet in two or more countries, these transnationals are "the hybrid of sojourners *and* settlers in both home and host countries, and they constantly sojourn and settle in pursuit of maximal opportunities" (Yang 2000b: 254).

As I discussed elsewhere (Yang 2006a), there are two broad types of Asian transnational immigrants: transnational entrepreneurs and transnational salaried workers. Transnational immigrant entrepreneurs are those who own a business or engage in self-employment across national borders. A widely known category is the *kongzhong feiren*, or "astronauts," who travel *frequently* between the host country and the home country or other countries for business. Some Asian astronauts own factories manufacturing apparel, shoes, furniture, electronics, and toys in their home countries and sell finished products to the host country and elsewhere. Some have companies headquartered in the host country but with branches in the home country. Some run import and export businesses. Others operate businesses that provide services for international travel, remittances, emigration, information on studying abroad, document translation, and banking and finance. Such international commuting is common and well known, especially in the Chinese immigrant communities in the United States (e.g., Chan 2002; Cheng and Yang 1996; Hu-DeHart 1999; Wong 1998, 2006). Nonetheless, astronauts are a minority among transnational entrepreneurs. The majority live mostly in one country but travel a few times a year while maintaining constant cross-country communication.

Transnational salaried workers are employed by companies or social institutions in both home and host countries. For instance, some migrants work as overseas representatives of host companies in the homeland or representatives of homeland companies in the host society, often in a position of great responsibility (e.g., branch CEO, manager, director). Some are representatives of international organizations in the United States (e.g., the UN, IMF, World Bank) but are stationed in their homeland for a few years. Some are double-loaded professionals employed by social institutions in both the home and host countries to teach, research, consult, train, and so on. Some are "second-career professionals" who have retired in the host country but keep their homes, institutional ties, and host country citizenship and then take on a new job in the homeland as politicians, administrators, managers, advisers, professors, etc. (Yang 2006b). A large number of transnational migrants are salary-based. Wong's (2006) research revealed that a large majority of the Chinese transnational migrants in Silicon Valley's high-tech industry are not entrepreneurs.

Of course, the above two types do not exhaust all kinds of

Asian transnational migrants, and their activities go beyond the economic domain. For example, some are transnational political activists who donate to homeland political parties or candidates, participate in homeland electoral campaigns and rallies, vote in homeland elections, and publish in homeland newspapers, magazines, or other publications. Others engage in sociocultural transnational activities in hometown associations or alumni associations and in homeland charity organizations; give donations to homeland community projects; and participate in periodical lecture tours, workshops, performances, and religious activities. More often, many transnationals are regularly involved in personal activities such as visiting family members and relatives in the homeland, sending remittances to relatives, and caring for the elderly or children across borders. However, without a regular job these political, sociocultural, and personal transnational practices cannot normally exist alone, and they are often an extension of economic activities or necessary engagements that enable transmigrants to participate fully in, and benefit from, their economic activities. It should be mentioned that, although stories of Asian transnational migrants based on qualitative studies cited above and elsewhere abound, reliable and generalizable statistics are few and far between. This is an area that cries out for future research.

Some recent studies (Koehn and Yin 2002; Laguerre 2009; Mishra 2009) demonstrate the transnational involvements of Chinese, Filipino, Vietnamese, Korean, and Indian immigrants in homeland politics and homeland–US relations. Levitt (2007) examined religious transnationalism among immigrants, including Indians from the state of Gujarat, who kept one foot in their homeland by taking part in religious institutions through communication technology and the ease of air transportation. Espiritu and Tran (2002) explored personal transnational practices of Vietnamese and their children in visiting the homeland, communicating with relatives and friends in Vietnam, sending remittances, participating in charitable causes, and investing in Vietnam. Nevertheless, by and large research on Asian immigrant transnationalism, especially among non-Chinese, remains scant and calls for more scholarly attention.

Undocumented immigration

Compared with undocumented immigration from Latin America, especially Mexico, undocumented Asian immigration receives less publicity. However, many Americans remember the *Golden Venture*, a rusty human cargo ship with 286 passengers that ran ashore off a beach at Queens, New York City, on June 6, 1993. Ten of the undocumented Chinese immigrants, mostly from Fujian Province, drowned fleeing the ship, six eluded capture after the grounding, and the rest were detained by the federal authorities. Since then, three books on undocumented Chinese immigration have been published. One, by Peter Kwong (1997), addresses the labor aspect of undocumented Chinese immigrant workers in New York. A second book, by Ko-Lin Chin (1999), studies the causes, methods, and social organization of undocumented immigration and the experiences of Chinese immigrants after arrival. The third volume, by Sheldon Zhang (2008), focuses on the social networks and organizations of undocumented Chinese immigration. Zhao's recent book (2010) also provides a significant amount of ethnographic data on the lives of undocumented Chinese immigrants. In fact, undocumented Asian immigration is a larger problem than has been recognized and is an issue of significant magnitude that requires some discussion. How many undocumented immigrants are from Asia? What is the level of undocumented immigration from Asia compared with that from other regions of the world? What is the trend in undocumented Asian immigration? Which countries do such immigrants come from? Where do they stay? How do they come? Why do they come? These questions will be briefly addressed below.

According to the latest estimates produced by the DHS (Hoefer, Rytina, and Baker 2008), in January 2008, 1.2 million of the total 11.6 million undocumented immigrants were Asians (including those from the Middle East), ranking second after the total for North America (8.8 million), covering Canada, Mexico, Central America, and the Caribbean. Asians made up about 10 percent of the total undocumented, while 76 percent came from North America, 7 percent (0.8 million) from South America, 3 percent (0.4 million) from Europe, and 3 percent (0.4 million) from other

Table 4.6 Numbers (in 1,000s) of unauthorized immigrants from major Asian sending countries, 1990, 2000, and 2008

Country	1990 (INS)	2000 (INS)	2000 (DHS)	2008 (DHS)
All countries	3,500	7,000	8,460	11,600
Asia	311	500	1,200	1,200
Bangladesh	5	17		
China	70	115	190	220
India	28	70	120	160
Japan	6	14		
Korea	24	55	180	240
Malaysia	4	9		
Pakistan	17	26		
Philippines	70	85	200	300
Sri Lanka	2	3		

Sources: INS Office of Policy and Planning (2003) and Hoefer, Rytina, and Baker (2008).

regions. The total number of undocumented Asian immigrants has remained constant since 2000.

The Philippines, Korea, China, and India are the major sending countries of the undocumented from Asia. Based on the data from the DHS, between 2000 and 2008 the number from the Philippines had increased by 50 percent, the fastest in Asia (table 4.6), followed by Korea and India, each with a growth rate of 33 percent, and by China (about 16 percent). According to the 1990 and 2000 data from the INS (2003), Pakistan, Bangladesh, Japan, Malaysia, and Sri Lanka also sent significant numbers of undocumented immigrants to this country. The numbers of undocumented immigrants apprehended by the DHS shed some light on the sending countries. According to the data from the DHS (2002–7), from 2002 (the first fiscal year after 9/11) to 2007, China ranked no. 1, with 12,003 individuals apprehended, followed by Pakistan (8,335), India (4,965), Indonesia (4,613), the Philippines (3,790), Korea (3,091), and Vietnam (2,298). Reinforcing the data on undocumented immigrant population estimates, these figures suggest that Pakistan, Indonesia, and Vietnam were also emerging as major sending countries in recent years.

There is a lack of statistical evidence about the geographic distribution of undocumented Asian immigrants. Nevertheless, it may be assumed that it resembles that of the legal Asian immigrant population, with a concentration in California, New York, New Jersey, Illinois, and Texas.

People become undocumented immigrants through two broad channels: they either cross a border illegally without inspection or they arrive legally and overstay their visas. How do the Asian undocumented come? According to my calculation, based on the latest apprehensions data from the DHS (2002),[11] in fiscal year 2002 a large majority (about 81 percent) of the undocumented immigrants from mainland China were illegal border crossers, as opposed to some 19 percent of visa overstayers. Among Chinese illegal border crossers, many left China by sea or overland and then flew to the United States; a large proportion of them made the first leg to Hong Kong or Myanmar (Burma) overland and the second leg to Mexico or Canada by air, and finally crossed the US border by land. A smaller percentage sailed normally across the Pacific Ocean to reach the US West Coast, although a few ships (e.g., the *Golden Venture*) routed across the Atlantic Ocean to reach the US East Coast (Chin 1999). However, other Asian groups were mainly visa overstayers, among them approximately 55 percent of Indians, 69 percent of Koreans, 77 percent of Pakistanis, 83 percent of Filipinos, 84 percent of Vietnamese, and 86 percent of Indonesians. The largest category of overstayers in these groups consisted of temporary visitors who failed to return home after the expiration of their visas, except for Vietnamese, who were mostly "other temporary migrants." Note that apprehension data may undercount visa overstayers because, on account of a lack of resources for the DHS to track down these people, many of them go uncaught. Thus, the overstay rates of Asians are likely to be much higher.

In general, the very reasons that motivate legal Asian immigration also underlie undocumented Asian immigration. The goals are the same but the means are different. There is little analysis of motivations for undocumented Asian immigrants apart from the Chinese. According to Chin's (1999) survey of 300 Fujianese illegal border crossers in New York's Chinatown, "to make money" dominated the reasons for their coming to the United States (61 per cent); "to make money" in combination with "to avoid the one-child policy," "to enjoy freedom," "to reunite with a spouse," "to escape from personal problems," "being under pressure to migrate," or "other reasons" constituted another 25 percent; "political freedom" and "religious freedom" motivated 5 percent and 1 percent, respectively; and other reasons explained the remaining 9 percent.[12] Although they are not generalizable to the undocumented Chinese population due to the non-random nature of the survey, the results suggest that economic reasons were most important, but political considerations were also significant.

Summary

Asian immigration to the United States has soared since 1965. About 9.6 million Asians immigrated to America between 1966 and 2009. Together with Latin America, Asia has become one of the two main sources of immigration. Major Asian sending countries or political entities include China, the Philippines, India, Vietnam, Korea, and, at a lower level, Pakistan, Taiwan, Hong Kong, Japan, and Bangladesh. The trends in immigration from these countries vary greatly. California, New York, Hawaii, Illinois, New Jersey, Massachusetts, and Texas are among the favored states for settlement. Unlike their pre-1965 counterparts, the majority of post-1965 Asian immigrants settle in urban areas. The emergence of suburban ethnic towns, called "ethnoburbs," among some Asian immigrant communities is a new development.

The majority of Asian immigrants came to the United States through family sponsorship, and chain migration characterizes such migration. Sponsorship via employment is another important channel. Adjustment of refugee/asylee status is the main path of immigration for Indochinese immigrants. Bangladesh, Pakistan, Indonesia, and Japan have benefited greatly from the Diversity Immigrants program. Brain flow or migration of the highly skilled is another important characteristic of post-1965 Asian immigration. Asian students studying in America and workers of the H-1 program (especially the H-1B program since 1990) are the main sources of Asian brain flow. Adoption from Asian countries has also contributed significantly to post-1965 Asian immigration, with Korea before 1995 and China since 1995 being the largest suppliers of Asian adoptees.

Many factors together explain the substantial increases in post-1965 Asian immigration to the United States. Changes in US immigration policy since 1965; changes in some Asian countries' emigration policies; pushes and pulls generated by the large disparities between Asian sending countries and the United States in economic, political, social conditions; military, political, economic, and cultural linkages between the United States and the Asian homelands; and Asian immigrants' social networks have together caused the large growth in immigration.

Immigrant transnationalism is a growing phenomenon in the Asian immigrant community. Of particular salience is the emergence of a transnational migrant class whose members live their lives across national borders. Transnational entrepreneurs and transnational salaried workers are the two main types of Asian transnational migrants.

Although Asia is not the largest source of undocumented immigration to the United States, undocumented Asian immigration is significant, currently ranking second after that of Latin America. The Philippines, Korea, China, and India supply the majority of undocumented immigrants from Asia, while Pakistan, Indonesia, and Vietnam are emerging as significant contributors in more recent years. While the majority of Chinese undocumented immigrants enter through crossing borders illegally, the main avenue of entry for other Asian groups is overstaying visas. Economic reasons appear to be the dominant motivation for undocumented Asian immigration, but political reasons are also significant.

5

Impacts of Asian Immigration on US Society

The existing literature is replete with material concerning the adaptation of new Asian immigrants, but thin on theories that explain Asian immigration and even thinner on the effects of post-1965 Asian immigration on American society. However, its impact is an issue that concerns the American public and policy-makers and ought to be addressed. How has post-1965 Asian immigration impacted the population, race and ethnic relations, the economy, social and cultural institutions, and the politics of the United States? This is the central question of this chapter.

Demographic impact

How has Asian immigration impacted the Asian population in America and the US population as a whole? As shown in table 5.1, the Asian population has grown rapidly, from 980,337 in 1960 to 15.5 million in 2008 (including Asians of two or more racial backgrounds). It is normally assumed that this growth is largely due to immigration. While the claim may be true, the contribution made by Asian immigration to Asian population growth has not been documented. Has there been any change in the contribution of Asian immigration to Asian population growth over time? Are there differences in such contribution across major Asian groups? These questions have not been answered but deserve to be looked at. Using the census data on both the

Table 5.1 Asian population, total and by ethnicity, 1860–2008

Year	Total	Chinese	Japanese	Filipinos	Koreans	Indians	Vietnamese	Other
1860	34,933	34,933						
1870	63,254	63,199	55					
1880	105,613	105,465	148					
1890	109,527	107,488	2,039					
1900	114,189	89,863	24,326					
1910	146,863	71,531	72,157	160				
1920	182,137	61,639	111,010	5,603				
1930	264,766	74,954	138,834	45,208				
1940	254,918	77,504	126,947	45,563				
1950	321,033	117,629	141,768	61,636				
1960	980,337	237,292	464,332	176,310				
1970	1,439,562	435,062	591,290	343,060	69,150			
1980	3,309,519	806,040	700,974	774,652	354,593	361,531	261,729	50,000
1990	6,908,638	1,645,472	847,562	1,406,770	798,849	815,447	614,547	779,991
2000 (alone)	10,242,998	2,432,585	796,700	1,850,314	1,076,872	1,678,765	1,122,528	1,285,234
2000 (total)	11,898,828	2,879,636	1,148,932	2,364,815	1,228,427	1,899,599	1,223,736	1,153,683
2008 (alone)	13,735,764	3,067,548	762,585	2,500,881	1,386,906	2,531,306	1,441,771	2,044,767
2008 (total)	15,500,000	3,620,000	1,300,000	3,090,000	1,610,000	2,730,000	1,730,000	1,420,000

Sources: Data for 1860–1960 from Carter et al. (2006), table Ad145-184; data for 1970–2000 from the US Bureau of the Census. Estimates of Asians alone (one race) in 2008 calculated by the author using the 2008 ACS; rough figures for Asians total in 2008 from the US Bureau of the Census (2010).

149

total population and foreign-born population of all Asians and major Asian groups, I calculated the percentage contributions of immigration to the growth of the total Asian population and for major Asian groups in the period 1960–2000.[1] Figure 5.1 shows the results. For the Asian population as a whole, immigration has been the major contributor to population growth, but the contribution has changed over time, peaking in the period 1970–80 (88.3 percent). For these six major Asian groups, immigration contributed most to population growth in the 1970s, retained a major role in the 1980s (the Japanese excepted), and had a mixed effect in the 1990s.

Post-1965 immigration has transformed the Asian population from one that is largely native born (i.e., US born) into one that is largely foreign born. As shown in table 5.2, foreign-born Asians constituted only approximately 37 percent of the Asian population in 1960, but with the large increase in immigration since 1965 they have become the great majority since 1980. A similar transformation has occurred among the Chinese population. The Filipino population was already mainly foreign born before 1965, and this was even more the case after 1970. Koreans and Vietnamese have remained largely foreign born, and foreign-born Indians have always been in the majority. Only the Japanese population has remained largely US born, although the percentage of the foreign born has increased since 1970.

As a result of the entry of more women, the sex ratio of the Asian population is now tilted more toward females. According to the 2000 census data, for Asians either alone or alone plus a combination with one or more other races, there were about 94 men for every 100 women – lower than the ratio of 96:100 for the total US population. The latest data from the American Community Survey confirm that on July 1, 2007, the sex ratio for Asians remained basically the same (Asians alone = 94.2, and Asians alone plus a combination with one or more other races = 94.8). Since young people are more likely to move, immigration also rendered the Asian population younger than the total US population. In 2000, the median age of Asians (including those of two or more races) was thirty-one, in comparison with thirty-five for the total

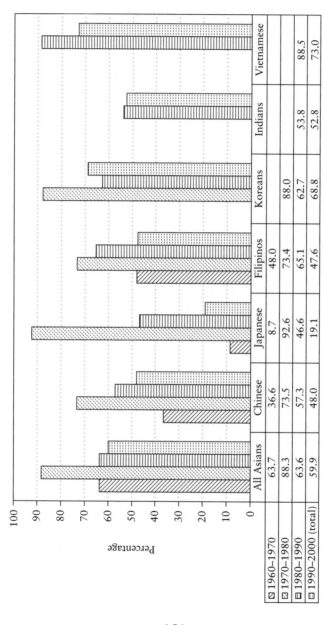

Figure 5.1 Contribution of immigration to Asian population growth, all Asians and major groups, 1960–2000

	All Asians	Chinese	Japanese	Filipinos	Koreans	Indians	Vietnamese
1960–1970	63.7	36.6	8.7	48.0	88.0		
1970–1980	88.3	73.5	92.6	73.4	62.7	53.8	88.5
1980–1990	63.6	57.3	46.6	65.1	68.8	52.8	73.0
1990–2000 (total)	59.9	48.0	19.1	47.6			

Table 5.2 The foreign born as a percentage of the total population, all Asians and major Asian groups, 1960–2000

Group	1960	1970	1980	1990	2000 (alone)	2000 (total)
All Asians	36.5	45.2	69.3	66.8	73.9	63.6
Chinese	42.0	39.6	55.2	56.3	62.4	52.7
Japanese	23.5	20.3	31.6	34.2	43.6	30.2
Filipinos	59.5	53.9	64.7	64.9	74.0	57.9
Koreans		56.0	81.8	71.2	80.2	70.3
Indians			57.0	55.2	60.9	53.8
Vietnamese			88.3	88.4	88.0	80.8

Sources: Author's calculation based on data from Carter et al. (2006), table Ad145-184, and US Bureau of the Census.

US population; the percentage aged sixty-five or older was only 7.2 percent for Asians compared with 12.4 percent for the total US population (12 percent is the cutoff point for an old population).

As discussed in chapter 4, Asian sending countries have added 9.6 million immigrants to the total US population since 1965 and, in relative terms, Asian immigration has played an increasing role in US population growth. Based on my calculation and using the US census data, figure 5.2 shows that the contribution of Asian immigration to US population growth increased significantly from the 1960s to the 1980s and then dipped modestly in the 1990s. The demographic impact would be small if Asian immigrants were evenly distributed across the country. However, since they are highly concentrated in California, New York, Hawaii, Texas, New Jersey, Illinois, Washington, and Massachusetts, and especially in some major metropolitan areas of those states (see chapter 4), the impact is felt more in these places than in others.

Impact on race and ethnic relations

While the impact of post-1965 Asian immigration on the total US population may be limited, its impact on the transformation of

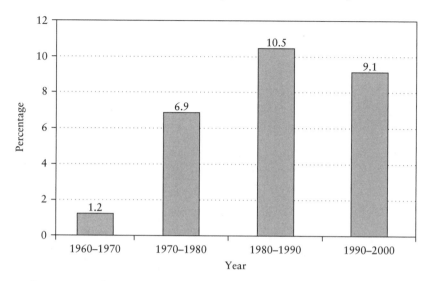

Figure 5.2   Contribution of Asian immigration to US population growth, 1960–2000

race and ethnic composition and relations is substantial. Figure 5.3 shows the percentage distributions of US population by race/ethnicity from 1960 to 2000, based on the decennial census data, and the latest projections for 2010–50 released by the US Bureau of the Census in 2008. It is evident that in 1960 the United States was still largely a black–white society, with nearly 89 percent whites,[2] about 11 percent blacks, and tiny percentages of other racial/ethnic groups. However, post-1965 immigration has fueled the phenomenal growth of Asians and Latinos and the corresponding proportional declines of non-Hispanic whites. Since 1970, the United States has been transformed into a multiracial and multiethnic society. According to the projections of the US Bureau of the Census, this racial and ethnic diversity will continue in the next four decades. By 2050, the United States is expected to be a "majority-minority" nation, with only 49 percent non-Hispanic whites.[3] In light of the Census Bureau's earlier projections, by the end of the twenty-first century, non-Hispanic whites will decline further, to 40 percent, but Hispanics, blacks, and Asians will increase, to 33 percent, 15 percent, and

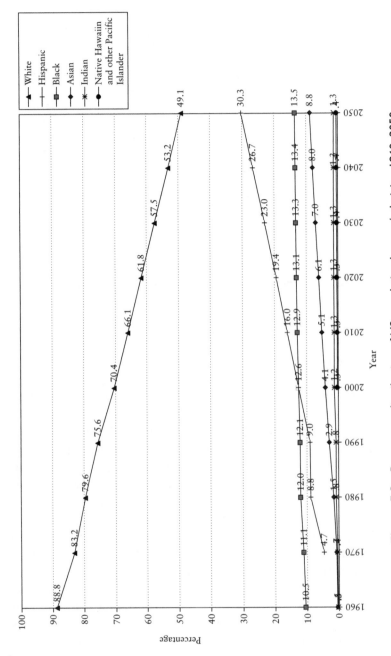

Figure 5.3 Percentage distribution of US population by race/ethnicity, 1960–2050

13 percent, respectively (see Yang 2006b). In 2004, several states, including Hawaii, New Mexico, California, and Texas, along with the District of Columbia, were already "majority-minority" states; with about 40 percent minority populations, Maryland, Mississippi, Georgia, New York, and Arizona were next in line (US Bureau of the Census 2005). In 2006, about 10 percent of the 3,141 US counties were majority-minority counties (US Bureau of the Census 2007).

These changes in racial and ethnic composition have transformed racial and ethnic relations. Today, it is grossly inadequate just to talk about black–white relations; rather, it behooves us to consider multiracial and multiethnic relations. Some scholars (e.g., Bonilla-Silva 2004; Gans 1999; Gold 2004) have argued that the US racial hierarchy is shifting. Gans (1999) speculated that the country is moving from its current white–non-white dichotomy toward a new dual racial hierarchy consisting of "non-black" and "black," with a third or residual category. The non-black category would include whites and "quasi-whites," such as an affluent segment of Asians and white Hispanics. The black category would encompass "African-Americans, as well as Caribbean and other blacks, dark-skinned or black Hispanics, Native Americans," and other dark-skinned peoples. The residual category would take in "the less affluent members" of Asian, Hispanic, Central and South American Indian, and the mixed Indian–Latino population. Apparently, both race and class were used to shape these categories. Drawing on the same race–class approach, but taking a somewhat different angle, Bonilla-Silva (2004) contended that the United States is moving from the current bi-racial black–white system to a tri-racial system consisting of whites, honorable whites, and the collective blacks. According to Bonilla-Silva, a few people of Asian origin are placed in the white category; Japanese, Koreans, Chinese, Indians, and Filipinos become honorable whites; and Vietnamese, Hmongs, and Laotians are put into the collective black category. Latinos are in all three categories. Native Americans are placed in the white and collective white categories, depending on their class and pigment. Regardless of the differences in categorization, there appears to be a consensus that a multiple racial hierarchy model is needed to better understand racial stratification and relations.

Given the changing racial hierarchy and relations, racial/ethnic regrouping and realliance are inevitable. It is in this context that a discourse has emerged on the position of Asian Americans in the American racial system in the foreseeable future. Referencing the experiences of becoming white for Germans, the Irish, and other northwestern European groups before the twentieth century and Italians, Jews, and other southeastern European groups in the twentieth century (e.g., Brodkin 1999; Ignative 1995; Jacobson 1999; Roediger 1991), some researchers (Hecker 1992: 16; Lee and Bean 2004; see also Zhou 2004 for a discussion) suggested that Asian Americans are next in line to become whites or honorable whites. Their greater socioeconomic attainment, residential integration with whites, and high interracial marriage rate with whites have been used to support such a claim. However, as I argued elsewhere (Yang 2006b), this scenario of "becoming white" is not very probable any time soon for a number of reasons. Most importantly, the white racial boundary is not likely to stretch to visible non-whites such as Asians, despite their high degree of assimilation (Alba and Nee 2003: 288). High socioeconomic status and residential assimilation do not automatically translate into a redefinition of the racial minority status of all Asian Americans as a group or a boundary crossing of Asian Americans into the dominant group. Secondly, although intermarriage can obscure the boundary between the two groups, the interracial marriage rate has yet to reach the point that will break down the boundary between whites and Asians. In fact, estimates based on the 5 percent Public Use Microdata Sample (PUMS) data from the 1980, 1990, and 2000 US censuses indicate that the Asian–white intermarriage rate decreased from 18 percent in 1980 to 15.3 percent in 1990 and 12.7 percent in 2000 (Yang 2006b). On the other hand, from 1980 to 1990, while interracial marriages between Asians and other racial groups had declined nationally, interethnic marriages among Asian groups had increased (Lee and Fernandez 1998), though there was a slight decline in the following decade. This trend could continue in the near future. Thirdly, continuing new Asian immigration will reinforce the Asian ethnic and panethnic boundaries. Fourthly, Asian Americans have not been fully accepted as Americans, as reflected in discrimination and the prevailing stereotype of "perpetual foreigners." Lastly, there is no indication that Asian Americans will be inclined to "whiten" themselves.

Another scenario for Asian Americans is to join the ranks of the non-black, a new category laid out by Gans (1999). Nevertheless, becoming non-black, which indicates racial boundary shifting, is also less likely to happen, because quasi-whites (a category of non-black) differ significantly from whites in their positions and experiences. Hence, the non-black label may not be very meaningful in real life.

Joining the non-white or Third World coalition is a possible third scenario. Although it is necessary for Asian Americans to join a non-white coalition, the feasibility of such an alliance remains questionable. A significant segment of the Asian American population is reluctant to ally with, or ambivalent about supporting, the people of color coalition, mainly because of self-interest, on account of the gap between Asian Americans and other minority groups in socioeconomic status. Quite a few Asians share more economic interest with whites. While blacks and Latinos (apart from Cubans) lean toward the Democratic Party (DP), Asian Americans were more or less evenly divided between the DP and the Republican Party (RP) – at least until recently. Furthermore, serious conflicts between minority groups, documented in research in the last two or three decades (Chang and Leong 1994; Johnson and Oliver 1989; Kim 2000; Min 1996; Oliver and Johnson 1984), further add to the difficulty of building a Third World coalition.

The most likely scenario for Asian Americans in the twenty-first century is to occupy an intermediate position in the US racial hierarchy. That is, they will not be subsumed under the categories of white, non-black, non-white, or black and instead are likely to remain in a middle position between whites and other minorities. They will not be fully accepted as equal to whites, but they will be perceived and treated differently from whites and from blacks, American Indians, and Latinos – viewed as a more "deserving" race (to use Gans's language) than other minority groups, the so-called model minority. On the other hand, they will not be promoted or assisted by government and social programs as much as other minorities. They will be somewhere in the middle of the racial hierarchy, remaining a separate minority group not fully fused into white society.

Economic impact

The economic impact of immigration is of paramount importance to the general public and government. The central question of this section is: How has post-1965 Asian immigration impacted the US economy? Specifically, has it degraded or enhanced the quality of the US labor force? How has it affected the US labor market? Do Asian immigrants contribute more in tax revenue or cost more in social services?

Impact on the quality of the US labor force

The impact of Asian immigration on the quality of the US labor force can be more meaningfully understood in the general context of a debate over whether post-1965 immigration lowers the quality of the US labor force. In the early 1990s, the economist George Borjas (1990, 1992) claimed that, compared with native-born citizens and immigrants admitted earlier, those immigrants admitted in the past two to three decades showed a declining labor market quality and on average had less schooling. Other scholars (e.g., Portes and Rumbaut 1990, 1996; Simon and Akbari 1995) discredited this argument and found higher levels of schooling and occupational skills and a general trend of increasing or stable education among new immigrants. However, these previous studies tend to focus on the overall average of all immigrants while neglecting or sidetracking the diversity across groups from different regions and countries of origin. As I argued then, the reliance on an overall average approach to the labor market quality of immigrants could generate misleading information and biased

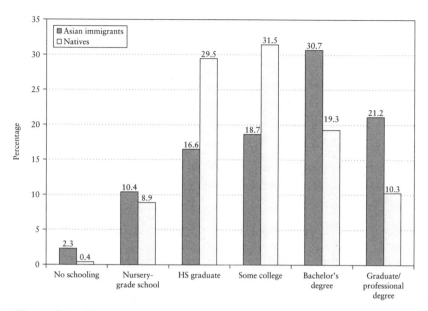

Figure 5.4 Educational attainment of natives and post-1965 Asian immigrants aged twenty-five to sixty-four, 2006–8

policy recommendations, and that much insight can be gained via a diversity approach (P. Yang 1999). Using the 5 percent PUMS data from the 1990 US census, I found that, unlike their Latin American counterparts, post-1965 Asian immigrants were generally more educated and skilled than natives.

Using the latest 2006–8 ACS data to update my earlier analysis, I found that the patterns remain basically unchanged. Figure 5.4 compares US-born citizens (natives) and post-1965 Asian immigrants aged twenty-five to sixty-four in educational attainment in 2006–8.[4] It is evident that post-1965 Asian immigrants outperformed native-born citizens in terms of bachelor's and graduate/professional degrees. Overall, some 71 percent of the total post-1965 Asian immigrants attained some college or higher education as opposed to 61 percent of the natives. Note that at the lower end of the spectrum – those with no formal education – post-1965 Asian immigrants lagged behind natives by almost 2 percent. This reflects the diversity of Asian immigrants, because

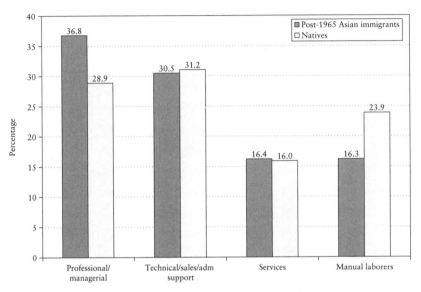

Figure 5.5 Occupational distribution of natives and post-1965 Asian immigrants aged sixteen to sixty-four, 2006–8

a small proportion, in particular the Indochinese, had a level of education much lower than that of the general US population. However, this fact should not detract from the generally higher educational level of post-1965 Asian immigrants. Post-1965 Asian immigrants also had the edge on natives in occupational attainment (figure 5.5). They were more likely to be professional and managerial workers and less likely to be manual laborers than natives. Both groups were about the same in the technical, sales, and administrative support category and the service category. In addition, in 2006–8 the occupational income score of post-1965 Asian immigrants (29.7) was higher than that of the natives (27.8), and the Duncan Socioeconomic Index score was 49.1 as opposed to 44.7, both indicating the slightly higher occupational standing of the post-1965 Asian immigrants over the natives. Hence, the argument that the labor market quality of post-1965 immigrants is lower than that of natives is invalid. Post-1965 Asian immigration has enhanced rather than degraded the quality of the US labor force.

Impact on the US labor market

What is the impact of post-1965 Asian immigration on the US labor market? Specifically, has it had an adverse effect on the employment and wages of native workers? Do new Asian immigrants take jobs away from native-born citizens or create jobs?

In the literature, there is no study that singles out the effect of Asian immigration on the US labor market. Its impact is normally subsumed under the impact of immigration in general. The American public widely shares beliefs that immigrants take jobs away from native workers and drive down wages (Espendshade and Hempstead 1996). However, empirical evidence provided by scholarly research offers little support for such beliefs. The counter-argument is that immigrants complement the native-born labor force for unwanted or less desirable jobs and lower the prices of goods and services. The most complete, unbiased report on this issue was provided by a National Research Council (NRC) panel consisting of twelve prestigious immigration experts appointed by a bipartisan US Commission on Immigration Reform (see Smith and Edmonston 1997).

The NRC panel report drew the following conclusions. First, immigrants provide a critical labor force for many businesses, in particular the agricultural and textile industries and the service sector, such as restaurants, hotels, and janitorial service. Second, at the national level, immigrants do not significantly decrease the job opportunities of competing native-born groups, who can move out of areas where immigrants move in. Third, immigrants do compete with some low-skilled, native-born workers and earlier immigrants in immigrant-concentrated areas. The report rejected the often-asserted assumption that African Americans suffer disproportionally from the inflow of low-skilled immigrants, because the majority of native-born blacks do not live in areas where immigrants are concentrated.

With regard to wage depression, the NRC report, based on many typical local labor market studies, concluded that immigration has only a weak effect (either positive or negative) on the wages of native workers. The group that suffers significant negative effects from new immigrants is actually earlier immigrants. For certain groups of native workers, such as high-school dropouts, immigrant competition had depressed their wages by about 5 percent since the 1980s. Moreover, immigrants lower prices for most domestic consumers, and especially for households with high levels of education and wealth.

Concerns about competition for jobs center on rivalry between immigrants and less-educated, less-skilled African Americans. However, empirical evidence is inconclusive and subject to different interpretations. While the NRC report (Smith and Edmonston 1997) rebutted the black–immigrant competition claim, Hamermesh and Bean (1998: 12) contended that "recent immigration to the United States appears to have exerted small negative effects on the economic situations of African Americans." Waldinger (1997) also found evidence of immigrant–black competition and the exclusion of blacks in the restaurant, hotel, printing, and furniture manufacturing industries in Los Angeles. Lim (2001) suggested that black–immigrant competition may force blacks to move up the socioeconomic ladder rather than out of the labor market, but there is little evidence of such competition. Lee (2000) detected little direct competition between blacks and Jewish and Korean immigrants in the retail and personal services industries because of their distinctive niches. Since new Asian immigrants are on average more educated and more skilled, they are less likely to pose much direct competition to the lower-class segment of the African American population. By and large, more empirical research is needed on this issue.

Furthermore, Asian immigrants create jobs through investment and the operation of businesses. One piece of direct hard evidence comes from the INS data on the investor immigrants program initiated by the Immigration Act of 1990. Available data indicate that 4,201 Asian investor immigrants were admitted between 1992 and 2001 (see chapter 4 for annual numbers).[5] Recall that an investor immigrant must invest at least $1 million in an urban area or at least $500,000 in a rural area and create ten or more jobs in order to qualify for admission. Assuming that, of these 4,201 investor immigrants, 90 percent invested in urban areas and 10 percent in rural areas in the exact amount of $1 million or $500,000 and created exactly ten jobs each, at least $5.9 billion had been invested and at least 42,010 jobs created during this period.[6] The actual amount of investment and the actual number of jobs created should be significantly greater than these conservative estimates. If data for the years after 2001 were available, these numbers would be even greater.

A piece of indirect evidence stems from the 2002 Survey of Business Owners (SBO), which is part of the 2002 economic census and combines data from a sample of more than 2.4 million businesses with administrative data. As shown in table 5.3, in 2002 there were more than 1.1 million Asian-owned firms, with over 2.2 million employees, generating more than $326.7 billion in revenue.[7] Note that such firms may be owned by US-born Asians rather than by immigrants. Nevertheless, foreign-born Asians are much more likely to be entrepreneurial or self-employed than US-born Asians. According to the 5 percent PUMS data from the 2000 census (either one race or two or more races), immigrants made up about 85 percent of all the Asian self-employed while US-born Asians accounted for only 15 percent. Hence, it is safe to say that a large majority of those 1.1 million firms were owned by Asian immigrants. The results of the SBO also found that 46.6 percent of the business revenues came from wholesale trade (26.7 percent) and retail trade (19.9 percent). This suggests that trade plays a very large part in Asian-owned businesses. Many of these transactions are carried out by Asian immigrants who help sell US products in their home countries and introduce the products of their homeland to America. Accommodation and food services contributed 10.1 percent to the revenues, while health care and social assistance, professional, scientific, and technical services, and manufacturing accounted for 25.6 percent. As is well known, many Asians in the hotel business and restaurants are immigrants. It should also be noted that businesses with paid employees accounted for 28.9 percent of the total Asian-owned firms and 89.1 percent of the gross revenues. This means that 71.1 percent of Asian-owned firms were small businesses with no employees and contributed to 11 percent of the revenues. Only 1,866 Asian-owned firms had 100 or more employees.

Table 5.3 The number and business revenues of Asian-owned firms, 2002

| | All firms[a] | | Firms with paid employees | | | |
	Number	Receipts ($ millions)	Number	Receipts ($ millions)	Number of employees	Annual payroll ($ millions)
Asian-owned firms[b]	1,103,587	326,663	319,468	291,163	2,213,948	56,045
Chinese	286,041	105,052	—	—	—	—
Indian	223,212	88,128	—	—	—	—
Korean	157,688	46,961	—	—	—	—
Vietnamese	147,036	15,512	—	—	—	—
Filipino	125,146	14,155	—	—	—	—
Japanese	86,910	30,623	—	—	—	—
Other Asian	89,118	24,276	—	—	—	—

Notes: [a] Includes firms with paid employees and firms with no paid employees.
[b] The estimates for the totals of Asian-owned firms are based on counts revised August 29, 2006. The sums of the figures for detailed Asian groups may not add up to the totals because an Asian-owned firm may be tabulated in more than one detailed group.

Sources: US Bureau of the Census and the 2002 Survey of Business Owners.

In particular, Asian immigrants have had a great impact on the high-tech industry in America. For example, in Silicon Valley, the symbol of the US high-tech industry, IC used to mean "integrated circuit," but now it means "Indians and Chinese," since in 1998 Chinese and Indian immigrants were CEOs of 24 percent of the Valley's high-tech companies, with 58,282 employees and total sales of $16.8 billion (Saxenian 1999). Jerry Yang created Yahoo!, and Sabeer Bhatia founded the free email provider Hotmail Corp. Saxenian also documented how Asian immigrant engineers and entrepreneurs contributed to the Valley's economy and how they acted as traders and middlemen to build social and economic networks back to their home countries that further enhanced entrepreneurial opportunities within the Valley.

Fiscal impact

The fiscal impact of immigration is another touching aspect of the debate. The essential question is: Are post-1965 Asian immigrants a financial plus or a financial burden? Put differently, do they pay more in taxes to government or do they receive more in public assistance? Again, the literature does not single out Asian immigrants in addressing this issue, but treats them as part of the immigrant total. Before the NRC panel report, a number of studies offered conflicting results on account of differences in assumptions, data, and methodology. For instance, North and Houston (1976) concluded that immigrants did not have an adverse effect on the public coffers of the United States. Using the 1976 Survey of Income and Education, Julian Simon (1981) found that immigrants admitted between 1950 and 1974 generated a total net benefit of $300 to $1,000 per family or $1,000 to $1,700 per family (if service usage benefit was included) in 1975, depending on the year of entry. Jeffrey Passel (1994) found that immigrants admitted into the United States between 1970 and 1992 produced a surplus of $25 billion to $30 billion. However, Rice University economist Donald Huddle (1993) estimated that in 1992 the net cost for roughly 20 million legal, undocumented, and amnestied aliens accepted into the United States since 1970 was $30.6 billion – an annual social welfare price tag of $1,585 per immigrant. George Borjas (1995) estimated that immigrant households imposed on native taxpayers a fiscal burden of $18.7 billion, $16.2 billion, or $13.7 billion, assuming a tax rate of 20 percent, 30 percent, or 40 percent, respectively. Compromising the arguments and findings on both sides of the debate, the NRC panel (Smith and Edmonston 1997) concluded that, at the national level, immigrants contribute up to $10 billion each year, benefiting the majority of the American people, since immigrants are concentrated in six states and their taxes go mostly to the federal government. However, the report estimated that, in California, services (especially education and health care) for new legal and undocumented immigrants cost each household headed by a native-born American $1,178 each year, because immigrant-headed households on average have more school-age children, are poorer, have lower incomes, and own less property than native households. Their taxes paid to the state and local governments are not enough to cover the cost of providing services to them.

While there is no study of the complete fiscal impact of Asian immigration, there are a few studies that address partly or completely the welfare use of Asian immigrants.[8] For instance, using the 1 percent PUMS from the 1980 census, Marta Tienda and Leif Jensen (1986) found that Asian as well as Hispanic immigrants were somewhat more likely to use a public assistance program (including AFDC, SSI, and General Assistance) than their native counterparts, while white and black immigrants were less likely to do so. But their study does not address whether Asian immigrants were more or less likely than *all* US natives to use public assistance income. Borjas (1995: table 2) showed that, in 1990, for the foreign-born welfare participation rates were very low among Japanese (2.3 per cent), Indians (3.4 percent), and Taiwanese (3.3 percent); moderate among Chinese (10.4 percent), Filipinos (9.8 percent), and Koreans (8.1 percent); but extremely high among Cambodians (48.8 percent), Laotians (46.3 percent), and Vietnamese (25.8 percent). Using the 1999 CPS data, a recent study (Lim and Resko 2003) reported that 7.9 percent of Asian/Pacific Islander immigrants used a cash assistance program compared with 3.3 percent of white immigrants, 7.6 percent of Hispanic immigrants, and 9.6 percent of black immigrants, and that 16 percent of Asian/Pacific Islander immigrants used one of the four welfare programs (AFDC/TANF, SSI, Medicaid, and food stamp) as opposed to 8.2 percent of white immigrants, 23 percent of Hispanic immigrants, and 20 percent of black immigrants. However, this study does not compare Asian immigrants with natives and combines Asian and Pacific Islander immigrants.

Using the 5 percent PUMS data from the 2000 census that asked respondents about their participation in public assistance programs in the previous year, I calculated the welfare participation rates of all post-1965 Asian immigrants, as well as by immigration cohort and country of origin, in comparison with all US natives in 1999. The analysis is restricted to householders who were eighteen years of age or older, and the results are shown in table 5.4. In 1999, the average welfare participation rate of all native householders was 2.2 percent. Asian householders who had immigrated since 1965 had a slightly higher rate, at 2.6 percent. However, this result was largely skewed by the inclusion of refugee groups, who are well known to have high welfare participation rates. Excluding Indochinese groups (i.e., Vietnamese, Laotians, and Cambodians) lowered the average rate of Asian immigrants to 1.4 percent – 0.8 percent lower than that of the native average. Table 5.4 also shows that, excluding the refugee groups from Indochina, none of the post-1965 Asian immigrant cohort had a higher welfare participation rate than the natives. The higher rates of the 1975–94 cohorts can be attributed largely to the influx of Indochinese refugees during that period. One can also see large variation in participation of cash assistance programs across national origin groups. While the majority of Asian groups (e.g., Japanese, Indian, Filipino) had a rate lower than or the same as the natives (e.g., Chinese), Indochinese groups (Vietnamese, Laotian, and Cambodian) had a much higher rate. Thus, it is safe to conclude that, except for Indochinese groups, the majority of post-1965 Asian immigrants are less likely to participate in welfare assistance programs than natives.

Using the latest 2006–8 ACS data, I repeated the above analysis.

Table 5.4 The welfare participation rates of native and post-1965 Asian immigrant householders, 1999 and 2005–7

	1999		*2005–7*	
	% on welfare	*% base*	*% on welfare*	*% base*
All US natives	2.2	4,648,943	1.4	3,075,950
Post-1965 Asian immigrants	2.6	120,399	1.1	98,832
Post-1965 Asian immigrants excluding Indochinese	1.4	99,230	0.8	78,539
Immigration cohort				
1965–9	1.0	6,496	0.7	4,388
1970–4	1.3	11,405	0.6	7,548
1975–9	2.0	17,986	0.9	11,919
1975–9 excluding Indochinese	1.5	12,825	0.7	7,866
1980–4	3.5	23,053	1.3	15,653
1980–4 excluding Indochinese	1.8	16,235	0.9	10,234
1985–9	3.2	20,354	1.3	14,090
1985–9 excluding Indochinese	1.6	17,074	1.0	11,329
1990–4	3.6	20,640	1.6	14,159
1990–4 excluding Indochinese	1.6	16,597	1.0	10,599
1995–9	1.5	19,682	1.0	13,424
2000–4	1.3	783	0.8	12,238
Country of origin				
China	2.2	15,728	1.2	13,616
Hong Kong	0.6	3,385	0.4	2,802
Taiwan	0.6	6,137	0.6	4,778
Japan	0.4	5,328	0.6	3,510
Korea	1.9	14,029	1.0	10,942
India	0.4	17,730	0.3	16,982
Pakistan	1.0	3,378	0.7	2,438
Bangladesh	2.3	1,244	1.0	1,185
Philippines	1.5	20,397	0.7	17,496
Thailand	2.0	1,892	1.5	1,643
Vietnam	6.3	15,419	2.1	12,049
Laos	12.6	3,346	5.0	1,915
Cambodia	13.9	2,404	4.8	1,540

Table 5.4 (continued)

Note: Welfare participation in the PUMS and ACS only covers participation in public assistance income programs, including Supplemental Security Income (SSI), Aid to Families with Dependent Children, and General Assistance.

Source: Author's calculation based on the 2000 5 percent PUMS and the 2006–8 ACS.

The results show that, by 2005–7, post-1965 foreign-born Asians had a lower welfare participation rate than the natives, either including or excluding Indochinese (table 5.4). Each of the cohorts had a lower welfare participation rate, even including Indochinese (except for the 1990–4 cohort). Except for the Indochinese, most Asian groups had a welfare participation rate lower than, or similar to, that of the natives. Given their higher income, and therefore greater tax contributions, it is very unlikely that post-1965 Asian immigrants are a public charge.

Sociocultural impact

The sociocultural impact of Asian immigration is manifold. One aspect that has profoundly changed the daily life of Americans is Asian food. Food is part of culture: it reflects not just what we eat, but who we are and what we experience. As I recall, years ago one of my mentors at UCLA said, "Immigration makes Americans eat better." This observation certainly applies to new Asian immigration, as the number of Asian restaurants in the United States has mushroomed and the variety of cuisine styles has multiplied. Chinese food is an excellent case in point. Although it was introduced to America in the mid-nineteenth century, Chinese food did not pique the interest of mainstream America until after World War II and was confined largely to Cantonese cuisine (Lovegren 1995). However, according to the magazine *Chinese Restaurant News*, in 2007 the number of Chinese restaurants in the United States had reached almost 41,000, roughly three times the number of McDonald's franchise units, with $17 billion in annual sales, on a par with the gargantuan hamburger chain (Essman 2007; see also Liu and Lin 2009: 158). In addition to the so-called Chinese-American food that caters to American tastes, the varieties of cuisine (e.g., Cantonese, Shanghai, Beijing, Sichuan, Hunan) now more closely resemble those actually served in China and in Chinese communities around the world. Similarly, the number of Japanese restaurants soared to 9,000 in 2005 from about 4,500 a decade before (Faiola 2006). According to the statistics collected by the South Korean government, the number of Korean restaurants in America totaled about 1,400 as of May 2009 (*Korea Times* 2009). Incomplete counts show the number of Indian restaurants at 814 (Indians-abroad.com) and the number of Filipino restaurants at 481 (Filipino-americans.com). Most Asian restaurants are run by immigrants. Asian foods are not simply transplanted from the homeland, but include the creation of Americanized Asian dishes such as chop suey, egg roll, and Asian-inspired fast food salad, as well as the fusion style of pan-Asian dishes that blend Chinese, Indian, Thai, Vietnamese and other cuisines. The heavy reliance on grains, vegetables, and fruits rather than meat and dairy products in many Asian cuisines could help change American dietary habits and so deal with America's top health problems – heart disease, obesity, diabetes, and cancer, which are far less frequent in Asian countries.

Concomitant with the surge in post-1965 Asian immigration has been a growth in the popularity of traditional Oriental medicines, such as acupuncture, herbology, Qigong, and yoga. According to the National Institutes of Health, more than 10 million adults in the United States have used acupuncture at some time in the past or are using it currently. Acupuncture has become part of the American medical establishment, with a national organization, the American Academy of Medical Acupuncture (AAMA), and a publication, *Medical Acupuncture Journal*. The mission of the AAMA is to promote the integration of concepts from traditional and modern forms of acupuncture with Western medical training and thereby synthesize a more comprehensive approach to health care. Established in 1987, the AAMA claims a membership of over 1,800 physicians (of both Asian and non-Asian descent) and has eleven regional chapters, in California, Washington, Arizona, Texas, Pennsylvania, Ohio, New Jersey, Oregon, Illinois, Maryland, and Georgia. Although relatively few Asian immigrants can obtain an MD degree and therefore qualify for AAMA membership, many serve as non-physician acupuncturists, required by most states to pass an exam conducted by the National Certification Commission for Acupuncture and Oriental Medicine. Traditional Chinese herbology is also gaining a market as a result of an increasing number of Asian immigrants and non-Asians who use it. According to a study by the United States National Center for Complementary and Alternative Medicine, based on the 2002 National Health Interview Survey conducted by the Centers for Disease Control and Prevention's National Center for Health Statistics, 18.9 percent (or more than 38 million) of American adults used herbal therapy, or natural products other than vitamins and minerals, as a valid treatment option in 2001–2 (Barnes at el. 2004). Qigong, sometimes called "medical Tai Chi," is also gaining popularity, and there are more than 18.8 million practitioners. Introduced to America in the 1960s, yoga, a therapeutic mind–body exercise originating from India, boasts 20 million followers today. Barnes and her colleagues reported that 5.1 percent (or more than 10 million) of adult American adults practiced yoga in 2001–2.

New Asian immigration has also impacted science and technology. One indicator is the number of Nobel Prize laureates who are Asian immigrants. Among laureates since 1965 are Yoichiro Nambu from Japan (2008), Daniel Tsui from China (1998), Subramanyan Chandrasekhar from India (1983), Samuel C. C. Ting from China (1976),[9] and Leo Esaki from Japan (1973) in physics; Osamu Shimomura from Japan (2008) and Yuan Lee from Taiwan (1986) in chemistry; and Susumu Tonegawa from Japan (1987) and Har Gobind Khorana from India (1968) in physiology and medicine. In addition to the twelve Asian immigrant Nobel Prize winners (including three awarded before 1965), there are two laureates whose parents are Asian immigrants: Roger Tsien (chemistry, 2008) and Steven Chu (physics, 1997).

David Ho, who is an immigrant from Taiwan, was chosen as the person of the year by *Time* magazine in 1996 for his pioneering work in using protease inhibitors to treat HIV-infected patients.

With the influx of middle-class Asian immigrants, many children of Asian immigrants have emerged as recipients of prestigious awards and scholarships in math, science, and technology competitions. For example, half of the twelve USA Mathematical Olympiad winners in 2009 and a large proportion of US International Mathematical Olympiad (IMO) hall of famers were children of Asian immigrants. With the help of these children, team USA has been able to rank twenty-two times among the top three since the country began to participate in the competition in 1974, even though the average science and math scores of US students lagged behind their peers from many industrialized countries.[10] Many of the International Physics Olympiad, International Chemistry Olympiad, and International Biology Olympiad winners from the USA are children of Asian immigrants. Each year, many receive the prestigious Siemens Westinghouse Science and Technology scholarship awards. For instance, in the 2008–9 competition, two of the six individual scholarship winners were children of Asian immigrants, including the first-place $100,000 winner, Wen Chyan, and five of the six team winners consisted totally or partly of Asian students.

Post-1965 Asian immigration has made the United States more competitive in sport events, especially in some traditionally weaker disciplines, such as diving, ping-pong, and badminton. Among new Asian immigrants were a significant number of sport stars who become coaches or players for the United States. For example, "Jenny" Lang Ping, who helped the Chinese women's national volleyball team win the world championship crown in 1982, world cup titles in 1981 and 1985, and the Olympics gold medal in 1984, became the head coach of the US women's volleyball team in 2005 and led the team to the silver medal in the 2008 Olympic Games. Chow Liang, the coach for ten years of Shawn Johnson, the 2008 Olympic gymnastic gold medalist, came from China in 1991 and was a co-captain for the Chinese men's gymnastics national team by 1990. Chow was the head coach of the US women's gymnastics team in the 2008 Olympic Games. Many of the US Olympic ping-pong team members are Chinese immigrants. In the 2008 Olympic Games in Bejing, seven of the eight US ping-pong ball players were of Asian descent, including three born in China. One of the greatest badminton players in US history is Kevin Han, an immigrant from China, who was the only US player qualified for the 1996 and 2000 Olympics, and has won international regard for Americans in a sport dominated by Asians and Scandinavians. He is now the manager of sports partnerships on the US Olympic committee and helps coach American players. Howard Bach, who was born in Vietnam and came to the United States at the age of three, alongside his partner Tony Gunawan, a 2000 Olympic champion from Indonesia, won the men's doubles title at the 2005 world badminton championships, the first ever medal for the United States in an Olympic or world championship event.

In the public discourse, there is a claim that immigrants are more likely to engage in crime than the native born, but this argument has met with no evidence or counter-evidence in the academic literature (see, for example, Butcher and Piehl 1998; Hagan and Palloni 1998; Lee, Martinez, and Rosenfeld 2001; Martinez 2002, 2006). How has post-1965 Asian immigration impacted crime in the United States? While systematic statistics and studies are lacking, available data on incarceration rates can shed some light on this issue. Using the 5 percent PUMS from the 2000 census for adult males aged eighteen to thirty-nine, Rumbaut et al. (2006) reported the lowest incarceration rates in federal, state, or local prisons among foreign-born Asians, including Indians (0.11 percent), Chinese (0.18 percent), Koreans (0.26 percent), Filipinos (0.38 percent), Vietnamese (0.46 percent), with the exception of Laotians and Cambodians combined (0.92 percent). Excluding these last two, the rates were much lower than those of all US males (3.04 percent), all foreign-born males (0.86 percent), all US-born males (3.51 percent), US-born non-Hispanic white males (1.71 percent), US-born non-Hispanic black males (11.61 percent), and foreign-born and US-born males of Latino groups. Rumbaut and his colleagues also found that a longer US residence was associated with a higher incarceration rate among foreign-born Asian groups as well as foreign-born non-Asian groups and that US-born males of all groups, including Asian groups, registered a significantly higher incarceration rate than their respective foreign-born counterparts. These results appear to suggest that the process of "Americanization" increases incarceration rates. Additional research is needed to verify these findings.

Political impact

We now turn to the last question of this chapter: What is the impact of post-1965 Asian immigration on political partisanship and political orientation in America? Specifically, does it favor the DP more than the RP or vice versa, and does it favor liberals more than conservatives or vice versa?

However, direct evidence on these questions is sparse, since available studies seldom single out post-1965 Asian immigrants in any analysis of political partisanship and political orientation. What is available is some evidence on the orientation and partisanship of *Asian Americans*, both US born and foreign born combined, with mixed findings. For example, a couple of early studies showed that Asian Americans were more likely to identify with the RP than the DP (Cain and Kiewiet 1986; Cain, Kiewiet, and Uhlander 1991). On the other hand, Nakanishi (1991), using the survey data in Monterey Park, California, found that they were somewhat more Democratic than Republican. Confirming Nakanishi's results, the 1994 Field Institute poll in California reported 48 percent of Asian Americans as Democrats, 32 percent as Republicans, and 20 percent as Independents. A lopsided partisanship of Asian voters favoring the DP over the RP was also detected in the San Francisco Bay area in the 1994 (62 percent v. 22 percent) and 1996 surveys (62 percent v. 26 percent) by the Asian Law Caucus. A 1998 survey of Asian voters conducted by the Asian Pacific American Legal Center of Southern California also found a leaning toward the DP (42 percent) rather than the RP (34 percent). However, a *Los Angeles Times* poll in 1992–7 found a modest leaning toward the RP among Chinese (33 percent RP v. 30 percent DP) and Koreans (47 percent RP v. 44 percent DP), a strong leaning toward the RP among Vietnamese (61 percent RP v. 24 percent DP), but a slight leaning toward the DP among Filipinos (40 percent DP v. 38 percent RP). The 1994 and 1996 surveys of Asian voters in New York City conducted by the Asian American Legal Defense and Education Fund found a strong leaning toward the DP over the RP (43 percent v. 24 percent in 1994 and 54 percent v. 20 percent in 1996). Also note that, in many of these surveys, a significant percentage of the voters chose "other." A few available national surveys indicate that the partisanship of Asian Americans has been shifting. A national survey by *AsianWeek* (1996) detected an evenly splitting party affiliation among Asian Americans, with 28 percent Democrat, 27 percent Republican, and 41 percent neither. However, a few years later the 2000–1 Pilot National Asian American Political Survey (PNAAPS) of Chinese, Japanese, Korean, Filipino, Vietnamese, and South Asian Americans residing in Los Angeles, New York, Honolulu, San Francisco, and Chicago found a very strong inclination of these groups toward the DP (36 percent) over the RP (16 percent), with 13 percent Independents and 35 percent no-party identifiers (see Lien, Conway, and Wong 2004: table 4.2). Hence, the issue for Asian Americans is not just which party to affiliate with but whether to affiliate with a party at all. The PNAAPS also uncovered variation among these six groups. Chinese (32 percent DP v. 9 percent RP), Korean (43 percent DP v. 22 percent RP), Japanese (40 percent DP v. 12 percent RP), Filipino (40 percent DP v. 23 percent RP), and South Asian (44 percent DP v. 16 percent RP) Americans leaned toward the DP, while Vietnamese showed a slight tendency toward the RP (16 percent RP v. 12 percent DP). A large proportion of them were no-party identifiers. Note both that, since PNAAPS was conducted in the five metropolitan areas with a strong Democratic leaning, the results should not be generalized to the entire nation and that the respondents may or may not be voters.

Only a few studies include information on the partisanship of Asian immigrants. For example, a Chinese American Voter

Education Committee survey in San Francisco and Alameda County found that 41 percent of *foreign-born* Asian voters identified with the DP compared with 23 percent with the RP and 36 percent in the "other" category (Ong and Lee 2001: table 6.5). A *Los Angeles Times* survey reported that, in southern California, *foreign-born* Chinese, Korean, Filipino, and Vietnamese voters were more likely to affiliate with the RP than with the DP (ibid.). In both southern California and northern California, *foreign-born* Asians were generally more likely than US-born Asians to favor the RP. The PNAAPS revealed that 34 percent of Asian immigrants identified with the DP, 14 percent with the RP, 12 percent with Independent, and 20 percent with no party affiliation. This pattern was true for Chinese, Japanese, Koreans, Filipinos, and South Asians, but not for Vietnamese. Keep in mind that the PNAAPS included both citizens and non-citizens and involved voters and non-voters in the five metropolitan areas only. My own analysis of the American National Election Study (ANES)1948–2004 cumulative data shows that, among Asian *immigrants* (unweighted N = 127), 51.4 percent were Republicans compared with 26.7 percent Democrats, 18.4 percent Independents, and 3.5 percent apolitical. This nationally representative sample points to a strong leaning of Asian immigrants toward the RP.

The political orientation of Asian Americans has been changing as well. A 1996 Gallup Poll conducted by *AsianWeek* (1996) reported that half of Asian Americans self-identified as conservatives, compared with 38 percent liberal and 12 percent moderate. In contrast, the 2000–1 PNAAPS (Lien, Conway, and Wong 2004: table 3.1) found a stronger tendency among the six Asian groups toward liberals (36 percent) than conservatives (22 percent), with 32 percent middle of the road. This tendency was the same across the six groups, and middle of the road was the largest of all categories among Vietnamese (47 percent), Chinese (42 percent), and Japanese (37 percent). The PNAAPS does not provide separate information for Asian immigrants. A *Los Angeles Times* exit poll of the 1992 election showed that only 19 percent of the Asian *immigrant* voters self-proclaimed to be liberal, as opposed to 32 percent conservative and almost half (49 percent) middle of the road (Ong and Lee 2001: table 6.7). According to my own analysis of the ANES 1948–2004 cumulative data, among Asian *immigrants* (unweighted N = 124), 21.2 percent were liberal compared with 27.9 percent conservative, 23.5 percent middle of the road, and 27.5 percent responded "don't know" or "haven't thought much about it." Hence, the available evidence overall seems to suggest that Asian immigrants tend to be conservatives more than liberals.

Summary

Post-1965 Asian immigration has made a major contribution to the population growth of Asian Americans as a whole and of the six major Asian groups, but the effects have varied over time. Because of immigration, the Asian population has changed from being one born largely in the US to one born largely abroad, and the sex ratio now favors the female side. Asian immigration since 1965 has added over 9 million Asians to the US population, and its contribution to US population growth rose drastically up to the 1980s but decreased slightly thereafter.

Post-1965 Asian immigration has helped transform race and ethnic composition and relations substantially. The changing racial hierarchy has fueled a discourse on the prospect of Asian Americans "becoming white" in the American racial system in the foreseeable future. However, it is my belief that becoming white, joining non-blacks, or forming a non-white coalition may not be realistic scenarios. The most likely scenario is for Asian Americans to hold an intermediate position.

The evidence suggests that post-1965 Asian immigrants have improved the quality of the US labor force because they are more likely to be college-educated and professional and managerial workers with a higher average occupational standing. There is little evidence that post-1965 Asian immigration has adversely affected the employment opportunities or wages of the natives. However, there is evidence that new Asian immigrants have created jobs through investment and the operation of businesses.

Again, there is little evidence that new Asian immigrants have burdened US taxpayers. The available evidence indicates that, except for Cambodian, Laotian, and Vietnamese refugee groups, the majority of post-1965 Asian immigrants are less likely than natives to be welfare assistance program participants.

Asian immigration since 1965 has led to burgeoning Asian restaurants across the country and could change dietary habits in America. It has also popularized traditional Oriental medicines such as acupuncture, herbology, Qigong, and yoga. New Asian immigration has contributed to the growth of science and technology in America, and the influx of Asian athletic immigrants has strengthened American sport power, especially in traditionally weak events such as diving, ping pong, and badminton. New Asian immigrants contribute much less to crime in America than other groups. Foreign-born Asian men tend to have a much lower incarceration rate than their US-born counterparts as well as the total US male population, foreign-born and US-born men, and other groups.

The available evidence appears to suggest that, at the national level, Asian immigration favors the RP and conservatives more than the DP and liberals, as Asian immigrants are somewhat more likely to be Republicans and to identify with conservatives. But larger nationally representative samples are required to confirm such findings.

6

Adaptation of Asian Immigrants and their Children

Chapters 4 and 5 have examined the causes and effects of post-1965 Asian immigration. The central question of the present chapter is: How do post-1965 Asian immigrants and their children adapt to American life? As mentioned in chapter 1, there is no paucity of research on this issue. What is inadequate is research that simultaneously investigates all important dimensions of adaptation for all major groups of *post-1965 Asian immigrants* and their children, rather than Asian Americans, using the latest nationally representative quantitative data and guided by theories of adaptation. Existent studies often lump all Asians together regardless of their place of birth, seldom distinguish between post-1965 immigrants and all immigrants, or use non-national or non-representative samples, especially for identificational and religious adaptation. In addition, many studies are not theory based, do not make cross-group comparisons, and do not consider gender. To remedy these limitations in the literature, this chapter analyzes the cultural, socioeconomic, structural, marital, identificational, and political adaptation of post-1965 Asian immigrants and their progeny.

Theories of adaptation

Before examining empirical evidence, it will be beneficial to review briefly some major theories of adaptation, as they provide guidance for understanding the adaptation experience of immigrants and their children. The relevant theories reviewed here are classic assimilation theory, melting-pot theory, cultural pluralism theory, segmented assimilation theory, and revisionist assimilation theory.

Classic assimilation theory can be traced back to the Chicago School of sociology in the 1930s and was the dominant theory of adaptation until the 1960s. The basic idea of this theory is that, generation by generation, all new immigrant groups will eventually lose their cultural traditions and social institutions and completely assimilate into the dominant Anglo culture and institutions. Because of its emphasis on assimilation into the Anglo core, this theory is also dubbed the Anglo-conformity perspective (see Greeley 1974). To address the process and outcome of assimilation, Robert Park ([1937] 1950) formulated the earliest version of assimilation theory, known as the *race relations cycle*, which has four stages: (1) contact, (2) competition, (3) accommodation, and (4) assimilation. Park envisioned this cycle as universally applicable and the sequence as "apparently progressive and irreversible." This vision later brought a flood of criticism as research uncovered contradictory evidence. A couple of decades later, Milton Gordon (1964) famously depicted his seven stages or types of assimilation:

1 cultural assimilation (acculturation), or assimilation into the dominant group's culture (e.g., language, religion, customs, traditions);
2 structural assimilation, or assimilation into the host's social groups (e.g., friends, peers, and neighborhoods) and social institutions and organizations;[1]
3 marital assimilation (amalgamation), or large-scale intermarriage;
4 identificational assimilation, or development of a sense of peoplehood based solely on the host society;
5 attitude receptional assimilation, or absence of prejudice;
6 behavioral receptional assimilation, or absence of discrimination; and
7 civic assimilation, or absence of value and power conflict.

Notwithstanding many critiques on the order of the stages, the overlapping of some stages, and the exclusion of secondary-level structural assimilation, Gordon's framework, especially the first four stages/types, laid the groundwork for many studies of immigrant adaptation in the following decades.

A major problem with classical assimilation theory lies in the fact that it is virtually impossible to find evidence of total assimilation of an immigrant group into Anglo culture and institutions, even after many generations, although partial assimilation is undeniable for any group. Moreover, a perceived superiority of Anglo culture and institutions over that of others is embodied in the idea of Anglo-conformity (Yang 2000a). As a result, the idea that assimilation is inevitable or desirable had lost legitimacy by the 1960s (see Yinger 1961).

A competing theory is *melting-pot theory*, which emerged in the early twentieth century. Unlike assimilation theory, melting-pot theory envisions adaptation as a process that melts together the host group and immigrant groups culturally and biologically in the America cauldron and creates a new group called "American" and a new culture called "American culture." The outcome of adaptation is the disappearance of both the host group and its culture and the immigrant group and its culture and the making of a brand new group and culture. The melting pot is certainly very appealing, as it is free from the ethnocentric idea of Anglo conformity and represents equal group relations. Furthermore, it symbolizes dynamic and progressive changes in society. However, most researchers today consider the melting pot a myth rather than a reality in American society because there is a lack of supporting evidence for the single melting pot model in terms of biological and cultural fusing (Yang 2000a).

As an alternative, *cultural pluralism theory* rose to prominence in the mid-twentieth century as a more accurate descriptor of American reality. While assimilation theory and melting-pot theory stress the homogenization process of group interaction, cultural pluralism theory underlines the differentiation process (Greeley 1974). According to this theory, immigrant adaptation to the host society will engender neither total assimilation nor a melting pot, but partial assimilation to the dominant culture and institutions and partial retention of ethnic cultures and institutions. Its emphasis is on the coexistence of both the dominant culture and the ethnic culture – thus "cultural pluralism." Other terms such as "salad bowl," "multiculturalism," "mosaic," and "kaleidoscope" depict the same process and outcome. In America, cultural pluralism was a reality before it became a theory (Gordon 1964).

In the last two decades, grave challenges to classic assimilation theory and new research have led to the reformulation of assimilation theory in different fashions. Two influential versions are segmented assimilation theory and revisionist assimilation theory. First formulated by Alejandro Portes and Min Zhou (1993), *segmented assimilation theory* seeks to challenge classic assimilation theory and to address the processes and outcomes of second-generation adaptation to the host society. Challenging the arguments of classic assimilation theory that assimilation is a straight-line process and its outcome is uniform upward mobility for all new groups, it contends that the process of second-generation adaptation does not proceed in a straight line and the outcomes are diverse and segmented. Since American society consists of segregated and unequal segments, the outcomes of adaptation depend on the segment of society into which the individual group assimilates. According to Portes and Zhou, there are three possible outcomes of mobility: (1) upward mobility into normative, middle-class America; (2) downward mobility into the underclass; and (3) economic upward mobility into middle-class America, with lagged acculturation and deliberate preservation of the immigrant community's cultures and institutions. Zhou (1997) and Portes and Rumbaut (2001) later discussed further the factors that determine which segment of American society will be the one into which a particular immigrant group assimilates.

Segmented assimilation theory appears to offer a viable framework for capturing the diverse patterns of intergenerational mobility in contemporary America. As a result, it is gaining growing popularity in the fields of immigration and ethnic/racial studies. One major limitation is that, with a focus on the second generation, it addresses the diverse outcomes only within one generation (horizontal outcomes) across different groups and does not attempt to explain vertical outcomes (especially non-linear outcomes) across generations (*intergenerational* mobility). Another limitation is that, even just for the second generation, there are more than three possible outcomes. Economic downward mobility but fast acculturation is one example.

Unlike segmented assimilation theory, what I call *revisionist assimilation theory* addresses assimilation in general rather than just that of the second generation. In *Remaking the American Mainstream*, Richard Alba and Victor Nee (2003) offer a systematically reformulated assimilation theory tit-for-tat against the challenges to classic assimilation theory. Alba and Nee (2003: 38) redefined assimilation "as the attenuation of distinctions based on ethnic origin." That is, new groups gradually lose their ethnic distinction and become more and more similar to the dominant group. Thus, assimilation is emphasized as a process and a matter of degree rather than the final outcome. Alba and Nee have modified the major arguments of classic assimilation theory being criticized as follows. First, assimilation is not a one-way process but a two-way street: immigrants become assimilated into the mainstream culture and they also profoundly change mainstream society and culture in becoming Americans. Second, assimilation may not necessarily be a straight-line process, but it could be a "bumpy-line" process. Third, assimilation is not a universal outcome but an important one. It is not inevitable or irreversible, but remains a central social process in the adaptation of immigrants and their descendants, even in contemporary America. Finally, assimilation may be an unintended outcome of immigrants' pursuit of other goals. It is a contingent outcome deriving from the cumulative effect of individual choices and collective action in close-knit groups, occurring at different rates both within and across ethnic groups.

Through these "operations," Alba and Nee have produced an almost total makeover of classic assimilation theory capable of fending off the critics. Nonetheless, such a makeover that departs totally from the original meaning of assimilation also calls into question whether assimilation best characterizes the experience of immigrants and their children. Perhaps "integration" is a more apposite term.

Which of these theories better captures the adaptation experience of new Asian immigrants and their children? Let us look at empirical data.

Cultural adaptation

I will first examine the extent to which post-1965 Asian immigrants and their offspring have become assimilated into American culture and maintained their ethnic cultures. Cultural assimilation is the first dimension identified by Gordon (1964). Cultural assimilation or retention can be measured differently, but the most common and often available indicators are English-language acquisition, an ability to speak one's native language, and religious affiliation or conversion. Measurements of English-language competence and ability to speak a native language can be easily found from census and survey data. Table 6.1 shows the language assimilation of native-born and post-1965 foreign-born Asians aged eighteen or older. A high level of partial language assimilation appeared to be the dominant pattern of new Asian immigrants' language adaptation. As a whole, two-thirds (66.6 percent) of post-1965 Asian immigrants had a high degree of partial language assimilation. If a low degree of partial assimilation is included, the rate of partial language assimilation rose to 83.4 percent. Total language assimilation (10.8 percent) and no language assimilation (5.8 percent) constituted the experience of only a minority. Also note that post-1965 Asian immigrants had a higher degree of language assimilation than Hispanic immigrants (19.8 percent no assimilation, 76.3 percent partial assimilation, and 3.9 percent total assimilation). All separate Asian immigrant groups showed a high degree of partial (both high and low) language assimilation (in the 80 percent range), although Vietnamese, Koreans, Chinese, and Japanese tended to have higher proportions of low partial language assimilation, since English is not an official language in their home countries.

Table 6.1 Percentage distribution in English-language assimilation of US-born and post-1965 foreign-born Asians and Hispanics aged eighteen or older by ethnicity and gender, 2006–8

Group	Language assimilation (%)							
	No		Low partial		High partial		Total	
	F	US	F	US	F	US	F	US
Asians total	5.8	0.2	16.8	1.6	66.6	33.1	10.8	65.1
Men	4.4	0.2	15.1	1.6	69.9	32.3	10.6	65.9
Women	7.0	0.3	18.3	1.6	63.6	33.9	11.1	64.2
Chinese total	12.4	0.3	21.9	2.0	59.2	43.9	6.5	53.8
Men	11.1	0.2	21.0	2.0	61.6	43.5	6.3	54.3
Women	13.5	0.4	22.8	1.9	57.0	44.4	6.7	53.3
Japanese total	2.4	0.1	17.7	1.4	64.5	13.6	15.3	85.0
Men	1.9	0.1	18.2	1.1	66.6	12.9	13.3	85.9
Women	2.8	0.1	17.4	1.6	63.3	14.3	16.5	84.0
Korean total	5.3	0.2	26.1	2.5	55.2	43.1	13.4	54.2
Men	3.4	0.1	25.0	2.4	59.6	41.7	11.9	55.8
Women	6.7	0.4	26.9	2.5	51.9	44.5	14.5	52.6
Indian total	2.5	0.2	7.0	1.3	76.5	6.0	14.1	52.5
Men	1.0	0.1	4.8	1.4	79.5	43.4	14.6	55.0
Women	4.3	0.3	9.4	1.2	72.9	48.8	13.4	49.7
Filipino total	0.6	0.1	6.5	1.0	78.9	18.1	14.0	80.8
Men	0.5	0.0	6.2	0.9	79.6	17.0	13.7	82.1
Women	0.6	0.1	6.7	1.2	78.5	19.3	14.2	79.4
Vietnamese total	8.4	0.6	29.7	2.5	56.2	47.9	5.7	49.1
Men	5.6	0.5	26.5	2.6	62.4	47.8	5.5	49.1
Women	11.0	0.6	32.7	2.3	50.3	48.0	5.9	49.0
Hispanics total	19.8	0.7	30.0	2.3	46.3	56.2	3.9	40.7
Men	17.3	0.6	30.5	2.4	48.3	55.6	3.9	41.4
Women	22.7	0.8	29.4	2.3	44.0	56.8	4.0	40.1

Notes: No language assimilation means that the respondent cannot speak English; low partial assimilation means that the respondent speaks English, but not well; high partial assimilation means that the respondent speaks English well or very well; total assimilation means that the respondent speaks only English.
F denotes the foreign-born admitted since 1965, US those born in the United States.

Source: Author's calculation based on the 2006–8 ACS data for single race. The data were weighted so that the results can be generalized to the population. The unweighted sample size is 228,073 for foreign-born and 59,428 for US-born Asians. All the subsamples are sizable.

In sharp contrast, total language assimilation was the dominant pattern among US-born Asians. Close to two-thirds of all native-born Asians could speak English only. Group variations cannot be ignored, however. US-born Japanese registered the highest total language assimilation rate (85 percent) because of a higher proportion of third or later generation. The very high rate of total language assimilation of native-born Filipinos was largely a result of their greater degree of Westernization and Americanization. Only modestly or slightly more than half of US-born Chinese, Koreans, and Indians (even with English as an official language in their country of origin) experienced total language assimilation. Conscious efforts by the immigrant parents and ethnic communities of these groups to keep their native language and cultures alive certainly had bearings on this pattern (Bhattacharyya 2005; Lai 2004: part III; Zhou 2009a; Zhou and Kim 2006). US-born Vietnamese were the only group whose dominant language adaptation pattern was partial assimilation. Cultural maintenance endeavors and the younger age structure of this group may explain this pattern.

There were some small gender differences in language adaptation patterns. For example, foreign-born Asian men were more likely to exhibit a high partial language assimilation pattern than their female counterparts, and US-born Asian men as a whole, and among more separate groups, were slightly more likely to experience total language assimilation than US-born Asian women.

Whether one can speak one's native language is another indicator of language adaptation. According to the 2006–8 ACS data, roughly 88 percent of post-1965 Asian immigrants spoke their native languages at home, but only 32 percent of native-born Asians did so (table 6.2). This pattern of high native-language retention rates among immigrants but low retention rates among the native born existed across all Asian subgroups. Nonetheless, notice that native-language retention rates were very or quite high among US-born Vietnamese, Chinese, Koreans, and Indians but very low among native-born Filipinos and Japanese. Compared with Hispanics, both foreign-born and native-born Asians tended to show a lower level of native-language retention.

As is well known, the dominant religions in Asian sending

Table 6.2 Percentage distribution in native-language maintenance of US-born and post-1965 foreign-born Asians and Hispanics aged eighteen or older by ethnicity and gender, 2006–8

Group	Native language spoken at home (%)	
	Foreign-born	*US-born*
Asians total	87.5	32.2
Men	87.7	31.5
Women	87.3	33.0
Chinese total	86.5	42.0
Men	86.7	41.5
Women	86.4	42.6
Japanese total	76.1	13.2
Men	77.4	12.1
Women	75.4	14.2
Korean total	82.5	40.5
Men	84.0	39.4
Women	81.4	41.7
Indian total	62.3	35.9
Men	61.9	33.8
Women	62.8	38.2
Filipino total	83.8	15.6
Men	84.1	14.9
Women	83.7	16.4
Vietnamese total	88.3	43.5
Men	88.7	43.7
Women	87.9	43.4
Hispanics total	95.6	58.9
Men	95.7	58.2
Women	95.5	59.6

Source: Author's calculation based on the 2006–8 ACS data for single race. The data were weighted so that the results can be generalized to the population. The unweighted sample size is 228,073 for foreign-born and 59,428 for US-born Asians. All the subsamples are sizable.

countries (except for the Philippines) are Buddhism, Hinduism, and Islam. However, conversion to Christianity, the dominant religion in the United States, has become very common among new Asian immigrants and even more prevalent among US-born

Asians. Existing qualitative studies (e.g., Chen 2008; Jeung 2005; Min and Kim 2002; F. Yang 1999) have provided some evidence on this. However, despite some local surveys (e.g., Hurh and Kim 1990; Min and Kim 2005), quantitative data based on nationally representative samples are almost non-existent. The closest approximation of a nationally representative sample is the PNAAPS, but this survey was confined to the six groups of Asian Americans residing in Los Angeles, New York, Honolulu, San Francisco, and Chicago. The analysis of the PNAAPS by Lien and Carnes (2004) found that Christianity (46 percent, including Protestantism and Catholicism) was the dominant preference of Asian Americans; Buddhism, Hinduism, and Islam also attracted a significant segment (23 percent); and almost one-fifth of Asian Americans had no religious identification. Their analysis by ethnicity reveals that non-religious believers dominated the Chinese community; Filipinos were most religious among Asians and largely Catholic; Hinduism followed by Islam dominated among South Asian Americans; Buddhism overshadowed other religions in the Vietnamese community; Koreans were largely Christian, especially Protestant; and, among Japanese Americans, Christianity occupied a leading position, though there was a relatively large proportion of Buddhists and also non-believers. However, short of being a nationally representative sample, the PNAAPS lumps all Asians together without distinguishing the foreign born from the native born, so we do not know to what extent these findings apply to Asian immigrants and their offspring.

Using the cumulative data from the 1972–2008 General Social Surveys, a nationally representative sample of US adult population with a large sample size of Asians, allows us to address the major limitations in previous studies. As shown in table 6.3, collectively more than half of the post-1965 Asian immigrants had converted to Christianity, only around 30 percent had retained their original religions, and 18 percent had not identified with any religion. The US-born Asians even evinced a somewhat higher degree of Christianization, especially Protestantization, and a lower degree of ethnic religion retention. Compared

Table 6.3 Percentage distribution in religious affiliation of US-born and post-1965 foreign-born Asians and Hispanics aged eighteen or older by ethnicity, 1972–2008

Group	Protestant	Catholic	Buddhist	Hindu	Muslim	Other	None	DK/NA	N (weighted)
Asians F	19.3	31.7	5.3	6.3	4.5	14.8	18.1	0	674
US	30.3	24.0	8.0	0.4	0.6	11.6	24.7	0.5	236
Chinese F	24.6	11.5	8.8	0	0	9.5	45.6	0	160
US	29.1	14.6	7.0	0	0	8.0	41.2	0	63
Japanese F	17.1	6.2	4.7	0	0	30.0	41.9	0	42
US	25.5	14.3	17.7	0	0	19.4	23.1	0	61
Korean F	58.3	18.0	7.7	0	0	6.0	9.9	0	22
US[a]	100.0	0	0	0	0	0	0	0	2
Indian F	13.4	7.8	0.3	27.2	7.5	33.4	10.4	0	155
US	55.9	10.7	0	2.2	1.1	7.6	22.5	0	39
Filipino F	14.1	82.6	0	0	0.5	1.6	1.2	0	196
US	24.1	57.4	0	0	0	4.2	12.1	0	51
Vietnamese F	0	21.6	72.2	0	0	0	3.5	2.1	16
US[a]	0	36.6	48.8	0	0	14.6	0	2.7	6
Hispanics F	16.6	72.7	0	0	0	2.2	8.5	0	1,194
US	23.8	61.7	0.1	0	0	3.9	9.9	0.5	1,500

Notes: F denotes the foreign-born admitted since 1965, US those born in the United States. DK/NA = don't know/no answer.

a The N is too small, so the result should be taken as suggestive.

Source: Author's calculation based on the 1972–2008 cumulative file of the General Social Survey. Unless otherwise specified, the calculation for ethnic groups was based on the ETHNIC variable. For Koreans and Vietnamese, the calculation was based on the RACECEN1 variable, since the ETHNIC variable lumps these two groups in "other Asians." The data were weighted by the variable WTSSALL, so that the results can be generalized to the population.

with foreign-born or native-born Hispanics, Asians were more likely to be Protestantized. Korean immigrants had been largely Protestantized.[2] A great majority of foreign-born Filipinos retained their traditional Catholicism. A significant percentage (though way shy of a majority) of foreign-born Chinese, Japanese, Indians, and Vietnamese had become Christians, while a significant proportion of these four groups also kept their ethnic religions. In particular, a large majority of Vietnamese immigrants had remained Buddhists. For all separate Asian groups apart from Vietnamese, the US born were more likely to be converted to Protestantism. Non-believers made up more than 40 percent of the foreign-and native-born Chinese and the foreign-born Japanese. These data point to a picture of partial religious assimilation and partial religious retention, with large variation across groups.

Socioeconomic adaptation

Socioeconomic assimilation was not mentioned by Gordon (1964) but it is an important aspect of adaptation. What are the patterns of socioeconomic mobility of post-1965 Asian immigrants and their offspring? How do they fare socioeconomically compared with other major racial and ethnic groups? There are many measurements of socioeconomic attainment. This section focuses on a few of the most common indicators: educational attainment, occupational status, personal income, entrepreneurship, and poverty. Education is one of the most important measures of socioeconomic status and a great status equalizer. Until around 1970, a typical American had a high-school diploma, but today a typical American has attended college and had slightly more than thirteen years of schooling. For Asians in America, completing college is almost taken for granted, not to mention high-school completion. Hence, in the case of Asians it is more important to examine attainment in higher education than in high school. Where do post-1965 Asian immigrants and their children stand comparatively in their attainment of higher education? Table 6.4 presents the results based on the 2006–8 ACS data for single race.[3]

Table 6.4 Percentage distribution in higher education attainment of US-born and post-1965 foreign-born Asians and others aged twenty-five to sixty-four by ethnicity and gender, 2006–8

Group	Some college		College completion		Advanced degree	
	F	US	F	US	F	US
Asians total	18.7	27.0	30.7	35.5	21.2	20.2
Men	18.3	27.5	29.1	34.4	25.7	19.1
Women	19.0	26.4	32.1	36.7	17.2	21.4
Chinese total	13.7	17.9	24.1	44.4	28.7	28.6
Men	11.7	18.5	21.4	43.4	34.1	28.0
Women	15.5	17.1	26.5	45.5	24.0	29.3
Japanese total	25.2	31.1	39.0	36.0	16.7	17.4
Men	17.1	31.3	43.9	34.8	22.1	16.5
Women	30.2	30.8	35.9	37.3	13.3	18.4
Korean total	19.9	20.1	36.2	42.2	18.1	23.4
Men	20.1	19.0	36.5	43.7	24.9	20.7
Women	19.8	21.3	35.9	40.6	13.0	26.4
Indian total	10.6	12.8	33.2	36.6	37.8	39.7
Men	9.5	13.7	32.1	37.1	42.9	38.3
Women	11.8	11.9	34.5	36.0	31.8	41.3
Filipino total	28.4	37.5	44.4	29.3	7.9	9.9
Men	32.9	38.4	39.8	27.7	7.4	8.8
Women	25.4	36.5	47.5	31.1	8.2	11.0
Vietnamese total	23.2	27.2	19.1	29.4	7.3	17.0
Men	25.4	29.2	20.9	26.9	8.5	16.1
Women	21.1	25.1	17.4	32.0	6.2	18.0
White NH total		31.3		21.1		11.5
Men		29.6		20.8		11.3
Women		32.9		21.3		11.6
Black NH total		32.4		11.7		5.5
Men		29.2		10.5		4.2
Women		35.2		12.8		6.6
Indian NH total		33.9		9.1		4.5
Men		31.0		8.3		4.0
Women		36.6		9.9		4.9
Hispanics total	14.7	32.8	7.3	11.9	3.2	5.1
Men	13.3	31.0	6.6	11.2	3.0	4.6
Women	16.3	34.7	8.2	12.6	3.4	5.6

Table 6.4 (continued)

Notes: Some college includes college without a degree and associate degrees; advanced degrees include professional degrees, master's degrees, and doctoral degrees.
F denotes the foreign-born admitted since 1965, US those born in the United States. NH denotes non-Hispanic.

Source: Author's calculation based on the 2006–8 ACS data for single race. The data were weighted so that the results can be generalized to the population. The unweighted sample size is 184,777 for foreign-born and 34,424 for US-born Asians. All the subsamples are sizable.

A much higher percentage of all post-1965 Asian immigrants completed four-year college or had a professional or graduate degree than US-born non-Hispanic whites and other racial or ethnic groups. Summing up the percentages of higher education categories, nearly 71 percent of post-1965 Asian immigrants had some college or higher education, way ahead of any other racial or ethnic groups. US-born Asians did even better. The 2006–8 ACS data show rates somewhat higher for college completion, advanced degree possession, and total college education for both foreign- and US-born Asians than the 5 percent PUMS data (not shown). Both sets of data lump all US born together, regardless of generation. Using the 2003–6 March CPS data, which include the birthplace, mother's birthplace, and father's birthplace of respondents, I was able to distinguish three generations for all Asians: first generation (immigrants born abroad), second generation (born in the United States with at least one foreign-born parent), and third generation (born in the United States with US-born parents).[4] The analysis of the CPS data reveals that second-generation Asians had the highest college completion rate (39.5 percent), followed by third-generation Asians (34.7 percent) and first-generation Asians (32.3 percent). The second generation also had the highest advanced degree possession rate (21.2 percent), followed by the first generation (20.2 percent) and the third generation (16.9 percent). The overall rate of having some college or more was 83.8 percent for the second generation, 78.1 percent for the third generation, and 68.8 percent for the first generation. Thus, there appeared to be a non-linear pattern of educational mobility over generations. These findings confirm what I found earlier using the 1994–9 CPS data (Yang 2004) and coincide with segmented assimilation theory.

One should also understand the variation among Asian groups in higher education attainment. Among post-1965 foreign-born Asians, Filipinos led in college completion rate (44.4 percent), and all groups but Vietnamese (19.1 percent) had a rate higher than native-born non-Hispanic whites (21.1 percent). Among US-born Asians, the Chinese stood out, with a 44.4 percent college completion rate, and all groups were significantly ahead of native-born non-Hispanic whites.[5] It is also interesting to observe the diverse mobility patterns in college completion from the immigrant generation to the US-born generation. While the rates of US-born Chinese, Koreans, Vietnamese, and Indians improved, those of Filipinos and Japanese worsened. In terms of advanced degree attainment, all Indians, Chinese, Japanese, and Koreans, as well as US-born Vietnamese, had a higher rate than native-born non-Hispanic whites, but both foreign- and native-born Filipinos and foreign-born Vietnamese showed a lower rate than native-born non-Hispanic whites while still being higher than those of other racial or ethnic groups. The mobility patterns in advanced degree attainment were also diverse, with both upward movement (Koreans, Vietnamese, Filipinos, and Indians) and virtually no movement (Japanese and Chinese). Once again, these patterns are consistent with segmented assimilation theory.

It is also important to understand gender differences in higher education attainment among Asian immigrants and their children. Collectively, both foreign- and US-born Asian women fared somewhat better than their male counterparts in college completion rates. This pattern is replicated for the Chinese and Filipinos, but reversed for Koreans and mixed for other groups, depending on their place of birth. In terms of advanced degree possession rate, foreign-born Asian men did better than their female counterparts, but this reversed among US-born Asians. This pattern held for all Asian groups apart from foreign-born Filipinos. This reflects male domination in Asian societies. The very small gender gaps in college completion and advanced degree attainment rates and the higher rates for women across US-born Asian groups suggest the relatively higher status of Asian women relative to men in American society. Again, the diverse intergeneration educational mobility patterns can be observed across groups within each gender.

High professionalization appears to be a hallmark of both post-1965 Asian immigrants and native-born Asians. Table 6.5 shows that, in 2006–8, as a whole both US-born and post-1965 foreign-born Asians were 6 percent or 5 percent more likely than native-born non-Hispanic whites, and even more likely than other racial or ethnic groups, to be professional workers. US-born Asians fared slightly better than their foreign-born counterparts. A higher rate of professional workers is expected, given Asians' greater educational attainment. However, there were variations across Asian groups. While foreign-born Vietnamese lagged behind native-born non-Hispanic whites, all other foreign-born groups, particularly Indians and Japanese, had a higher rate of professional workers. Among the US born, all six Asian groups, especially Chinese, Asian Indians, Koreans, and Japanese, outshone native-born non-Hispanic whites in professional rate. The intergenerational mobility patterns varied. While US-born Chinese, Vietnamese, Koreans, and Indians displayed significant or slight upward mobility compared with their foreign-born counterparts, US-born Filipinos and Japanese showed downward mobility. Among the foreign-born Asian groups, Chinese, Vietnamese, and Korean men fared better than their respective female counterparts in professional rate, but the gender advantage was reversed among Filipinos, Indians, and Japanese. Among the US-born Asian groups, except for the Chinese, women were more likely to be professionals than men, indicating their advantage relative to men in the United States.

The literature reveals that Asian immigrants have disadvantages in obtaining executive, administrative, and managerial positions because of their lack of English communication skills and a stereotype of Asians as being not suitable as managers (Min 1995, 2006a). Table 6.5 indicates that post-1965 Asian immigrants as

Table 6.5 The occupational attainment and average personal income of US-born and post-1965 foreign-born Asians and others aged sixteen to sixty-four by ethnicity and gender, 2006–8

Group	Professional (%)		Managerial (%)		Personal income ($)	
	F	US	F	US	F	US
Asians total	22.4	23.6	14.4	14.9	47,574	43,122
Men	22.5	22.0	15.2	15.1	57,474	49,963
Women	22.4	25.4	13.7	14.7	37,116	35,743
Chinese total	24.9	30.0	16.8	18.4	48,172	52,037
Men	26.9	29.5	15.9	17.9	57,005	59,729
Women	22.8	30.6	17.6	19.0	39,154	43,591
Japanese total	25.8	25.0	21.2	18.2	52,275	56,780
Men	25.1	21.9	29.4	19.1	75,898	66,521
Women	26.5	28.5	14.4	17.3	32,452	45,892
Korean total	22.0	25.9	16.4	14.8	44,986	42,493
Men	23.0	23.7	19.2	16.1	57,742	49,656
Women	21.2	28.4	13.9	13.5	33,430	34,865
Indian total	28.5	29.9	17.6	15.9	61,655	43,503
Men	27.8	27.0	19.4	17.7	74,203	52,352
Women	29.6	33.2	15.0	13.8	42,139	33,481
Filipino total	21.9	18.8	11.6	12.3	43,073	36,325
Men	17.0	17.7	11.0	11.6	45,556	40,645
Women	25.5	19.9	12.1	13.1	41,235	31,591
Vietnamese total	13.3	19.1	8.6	11.3	37,976	32,439
Men	15.1	17.2	7.9	11.0	44,771	38,074
Women	11.4	21.0	9.3	11.6	30,621	26,468
White NH total		17.6		13.6		44,094
Men		13.5		14.7		55,234
Women		21.9		12.3		32,292
Black NH total		11.6		8.2		28,471
Men		8.2		7.1		30,665
Women		14.5		9.1		26,559
Indian NH total		10.9		8.1		27,337
Men		7.7		7.5		31,851
Women		14.0		8.7		22,963
Hispanics total	5.1	11.1	4.8	8.9	25,623	29,694
Men	3.5	8.2	4.6	8.5	29,464	34,482
Women	7.7	14.1	5.2	9.3	19,481	24,671

Table 6.5 (continued)

Notes: Managerial workers include executive, administrative, managerial, and management-related occupations.
F denotes the foreign-born admitted since 1965, US those born in the United States. NH denotes non-Hispanic.

Source: Author's calculation based on the 2006–8 ACS data for single race. The data were weighted so that the results can be generalized to the population. The analysis is restricted to respondents active in the labor force. The unweighted sample size is 173,250 for occupation and 173,028 for income for foreign-born and 46,891 for occupation and 46,860 for income for US-born Asians. All the subsamples are sizable.

a whole edged out native-born non-Hispanic whites in the rate of managerial workers and did much better than other racial or ethnic groups. The particularly high rate of Japanese immigrants was probably due to the fact that Japanese companies routinely send their upper-level white-collar employees to their overseas branch offices and subsidiaries to acts as supervisors. Many of these managerial workers had no intention of settling permanently, despite their green card, and were very likely to return to Japan after their service (Fang 1996). Filipino and Vietnamese immigrants were less likely to work in managerial jobs than native-born non-Hispanic whites, but Chinese, Indian and Korean immigrants were slightly more likely to do so. US-born Asians as a whole also had a slight edge on native-born non-Hispanic whites in managerial rate. Native-born Chinese, Japanese, Indians, and Koreans had an advantage, but native-born Filipinos and Vietnamese had a disadvantage compared with native-born non-Hispanic whites. Collectively, native-born Asians did slightly better than foreign-born Asians; this pattern held true for native-born Chinese, Vietnamese, and Filipinos but not for native-born Japanese, Koreans, and Indians. These results again point to diverse intergenerational mobility patterns. The advantage of males over females was true only for foreign- and US-born Asians as a whole, Japanese, Koreans, and Indians.

Entrepreneurship, often measured by self-employment, is an

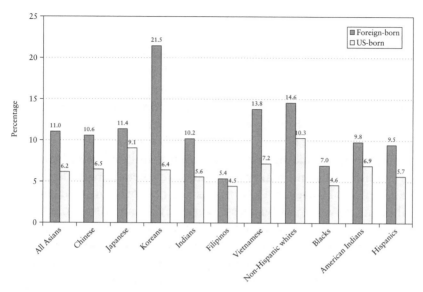

Figure 6.1 Self-employment rates of native-born and post-1965 foreign-born Asians aged sixteen to sixty-four by ethnicity, 2006–8

avenue of economic adaptation and upward social mobility (Portes and Rumbaut 2006; Zhou and Cho 2010). Zhou and Cho (2010) go further, to argue that ethnic entrepreneurship has the non-economic effects of building ethnic community, thereby creating a unique social environment conducive to the upward mobility of its members. To what extent do post-1965 Asian immigrants use entrepreneurship for economic survival and mobility? To what extent do US-born Asians follow the footsteps of their immigrant forebears in entrepreneurship? Figure 6.1 provides answers to these questions by presenting the self-employment rates of Asians in comparison with other racial or ethnic groups by generation and ethnicity, based on the 2006–8 ACS for those active in the labor force.[6] It is evident that post-1965 foreign-born Asians, jointly or separately by ethnicity, were more likely to be entrepreneurs than their respective US-born counterparts, as also observed in all other racial or ethnic groups. Asian immigrant groups, however, were not equally likely to run their own businesses. While the majority of foreign-born Asian groups showed approximately the same rate (around 10 percent) as native-born non-Hispanic whites, Filipinos had a low inclination to engage in businesses and the rate for Koreans was about 22 percent. These results, which are national in scale and more accurate because of proper restrictions and weighting, are largely consistent with previous findings (see, for example, Cheng and Yang 1996; Light and Bonacich 1988; Min 1988, 1996, 2006b). The greater propensity of Asian immigrants toward entrepreneurship, mostly small businesses, is due to their desire for economic survival and mobility and their disadvantages in English skills and mainstream labor market characteristics and experiences. However, US-born Asians do not want to engage in labor-intensive small-business work involving long hours, nor do they need to be involved in such work, because their educational credentials, occupational skills, and English proficiency enable them to land much better jobs in the mainstream economy. This explains why native-born Asians had a lower rate of self-employment. In particular, the self-employment rate of US-born Koreans (6.4 percent) is in stark contrast to that of foreign-born Koreans (21.5 percent). Note that, compared with the 5 percent PUMS data from the 2000 census (not shown), almost all Asian groups, as well as non-Asian groups, regardless of birthplace, saw a slight rise in the rate of self-employment in 2006–8. Vietnamese increased their entrepreneurship rate significantly in the same period, from 9.8 percent for the foreign born and 3.5 percent for the native born to 13.8 percent and 7.2 percent, respectively.

Income is certainly a very important indicator of economic adaptation. For this analysis, personal income is a better indicator than family income because the latter tends to inflate Asians' income level owing to the greater average size of Asian families. The 2006–8 ACS provides the latest available data on personal income in the period 2005–7. As shown in table 6.5, as a group, post-1965 foreign-born Asians ($47,574) fared somewhat better than native-born non-Hispanic whites and much better than other racial or ethnic groups in average personal income. Nevertheless, group variation existed. Compared with native-born non-Hispanic whites, on average post-1965 foreign-born Indians, Japanese, Chinese, and Koreans earned more, but foreign-born Filipinos,

Koreans, and Vietnamese earned less. The patterns for US-born Asians differed to some extent. Collectively, at $43,122, they trailed slightly behind native-born non-Hispanic whites. US-born Japanese and Chinese pulled ahead of native-born non-Hispanic whites in personal income, but native-born Filipinos, Koreans, Asian Indians, and Vietnamese fell behind, probably because these groups were on average younger and needed some time to boost their income profiles.[7] Also note that, with the exception of Chinese and Japanese, post-1965 Asian immigrants collectively and in each of separate ethnic groups had a significantly higher income than their US-born counterparts, indicating downward income mobility. Again, this may be due to the younger age structure of most US-born Asian groups. Jointly or separately, for both foreign-born and native-born groups, all Asian men fared much better than Asian women. This was also true for all other racial or ethnic groups. Interestingly, while US-born Asian men earned a lower income than native-born non-Hispanic white men, both foreign- and US-born Asian women outperformed native-born non-Hispanic white women.

Poverty is based on income but takes into account family size and geographic location (Alaska and Hawaii are different from the forty-eight continental states). Figure 6.2, based on the latest 2006–8 ACS, shows the poverty rates of Asian household heads compared with those of other racial and ethnic groups.[8] As a whole, post-1965 Asian immigrants had a higher poverty rate (2.3 percent) than non-Hispanic whites, both native born (1.0 percent) and foreign born (2.0 percent). The rate of foreign-born Koreans (5.5 percent) was the highest. The high rate of foreign-born Japanese is especially puzzling given their greater educational attainment, occupational status, and personal income. US-born Asians did slightly better than their foreign-born counterparts as a whole and among Japanese, Chinese, and Koreans; but US-born Indians, Filipinos, and Vietnamese were much more likely to live in poverty than their respective foreign-born counterparts. These results paint a diverse picture of the economic adaptation of Asian immigrants and their offspring more or less consistent with segmented assimilation theory.

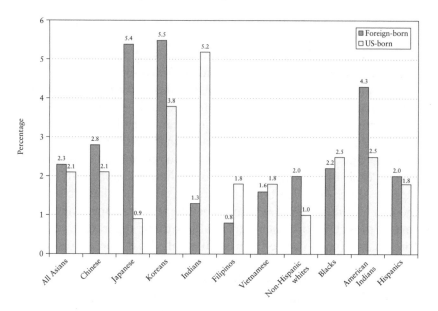

Figure 6.2 Poverty rates of native-born and post-1965 foreign-born Asians householders by ethnicity, 2006–8

It is intriguing to note that children of new Asian immigrants perceive socioeconomic success differently because of the effects of the "model minority" stereotype and the double standard imposed by society. Zhou et al. (2008) reported that many children of Asian immigrants felt unsuccessful or even embarrassed by their "failure," despite having a college education and a very decent income, because they compared their achievements with those of other higher achieving Asians (often their siblings and friends) and felt they had not lived up to the expectations of graduating from an elite college and/or securing a better-paid professional job.

Structural adaptation

Structural assimilation suggested by Gordon (1964) is an important dimension of adaptation. However, measurements and empirical data on structural adaptation are often lacking. Residential

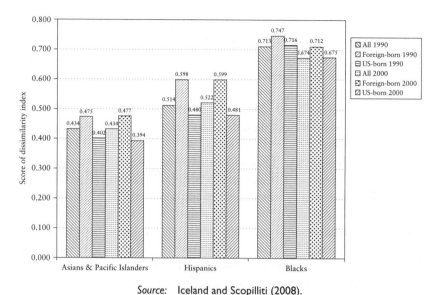

Source: Iceland and Scopilliti (2008).

Figure 6.3 Dissimilarity from US-born, non-Hispanic whites by race/ethnicity and place of birth, 1990–2000

segregation or integration is one aspect of structural adaptation with available data. One indicator of residential segregation or integration is the dissimilarity index, which measures the extent to which a group is evenly distributed across neighborhoods or tracts. A score of .60 or above indicates extreme segregation between two groups.[9] Nevertheless, existing data normally do not distinguish the foreign born from the US born. Two exceptions are studies by Iceland and Scopilliti (2008) and Iceland (2009). Figure 6.3 was constructed using the result of Iceland and Scopilliti's (2008) analysis, based on the 1990 and 2000 census data for US metropolitan areas, with at least 1,000 members of the group in question in 1990 and 2000.[10] Several observations can be made. First, in both 1990 and 2000, Asian and Pacific Islander immigrants had a higher level of residential segregation from native-born non-Hispanic whites than their US-born counterparts. This may be taken as evidence of residential assimilation, as the social distance between the groups had decreased over generations. Second, the degree of residential segregation between Asian and Pacific Islander immigrants and their progeny and native-born non-Hispanic whites remained quite significant, as the dissimilarity index scores stood between .394 and .477. This is evidence of ethnic resilience rather than total residential assimilation, which would require a dissimilarity index score of 0 or close to 0. Third, both foreign- and US-born Asian and Pacific Islanders displayed a significantly lower level of residential segregation than their respective counterparts of Hispanics and especially blacks. This indicates that Asians have a significantly higher degree of residential assimilation than Hispanics and blacks. In other words, these results suggest that Asian immigrants and their children were more likely than Hispanics and blacks to share residential neighborhoods with native-born non-Hispanic whites. Iceland and Scopilliti (2008) also found that, for Asian and Pacific Islander immigrants (as well as Hispanics), a longer US residency was associated with a lower degree of residential segregation from native-born non-Hispanic whites, but the opposite was true for blacks. These results for Asian immigrants and their offspring are consistent with the prediction of the cultural pluralism perspective. If Hispanics and blacks are considered, the evidence coincides with the prediction of segmented assimilation theory.

Iceland (2009) further analyzed intergroup variation in segregation for Asian immigrants using the 2000 census data. Table 6.6, based on his analysis, shows that, in terms of both dissimilarity index and isolation index, Japanese immigrants were most likely to live in the same neighborhoods with native-born non-Hispanic whites, but Cambodian immigrants were least likely to do so. Korean, Filipino, and Indian immigrants also exhibited a relatively lower degree of residential segregation than immigrants of other Asian groups in terms of the dissimilarity index. The other groups passed the cutoff point of .60 on the dissimilarity index, indicating an extreme level of segregation, especially among Cambodians, Laotians, Pakistanis, and Thais. The isolation index can be interpreted as the percentage of the same group in a neighborhood or tract in which an average group member lives. A score of .70 or higher is considered extreme segregation. The scores of the isolation index are all well below the cutoff point of .70, suggesting

Table 6.6 Residential segregation indexes for Asian immigrants by country of origin, 2000

Country of origin	# of metropolitan areas	Dissimilarity index	Isolation index
Asia & Pacific Islands	266	.474	.276
China	35	.606	.266
Japan	12	.533	.067
Korea	28	.583	.158
India	33	.576	.108
Philippines	34	.572	.234
Vietnam	28	.663	.232
Laos	1	.763	.169
Cambodia	1	.863	.330
Pakistan	5	.721	.106
Thailand	3	.700	.079

Notes: Only metropolitan areas with 1,000 or more members of the group and countries of origin with 100,000 immigrants or more were included in the analysis. A higher value on either index indicates a higher degree of segregation. The reference group is US-born, non-Hispanic whites.

Source: Adapted from Iceland (2009), table B.3.

a very low level of segregation. For example, the score of .067 indicates that an average Japanese immigrant lived in a neighborhood that consisted of 6.7 percent of Japanese in 2000, whereas the score of .330 manifests that an average Cambodian immigrant lived in a neighborhood with 33 percent of Cambodians. The evidence presented here appears to lend support to the prediction of revisionist assimilation theory about varying rates of assimilation across groups. Iceland's (2009) analysis also reveals that, among these immigrant groups, a longer period of US residence was generally associated with a lower degree of residential segregation, but segregation remained very significant for all groups. This evidence matches the prediction of cultural pluralism theory.

Structural adaptation may include changes in intergenerational relations within and beyond immigrant families. Many studies (e.g., Espiritu 2009; Kibria 2009; Louie 2004; Zhou 2009b; Zhou and Bankston 1998) have demonstrated tensions between Asian immigrant parents and their US-born or US-raised (second or 1.5 generation) children over educational expectations, career choices, dating, marriage choices, and parental discipline. For example, Asian immigrant parents normally expect more diligence and nothing less than an A from their children, but the children are accustomed to the American norm of doing good work (B, or even C) as long as one has tried. Parents often want their children to pursue "safe," high-paid, and high prestige careers such as law, medicine, engineering, math, and hard sciences, while some children wish to pursue their preferred occupations in art, music, humanities, social sciences, and so on. Parents seldom permit their daughters to date, to stay out late, to sleep over at a friend's house, or take out-of-town trips, whereas daughters gripe about constant surveillance. Parents often expect their children to choose a spouse from their own ethnic group and in some cases to follow the tradition of arranged marriage, but their children resist such pressures and fight for the freedom to marry the person of their choice. Parents expect their children to be respectful and compliant, while their children are used to the American way of independence and assertiveness. However, strain and conflict are not the only characteristics of intergenerational relations; there are also bonds that bind Asian immigrants and their children and accommodations and compromises between them. Although these family tensions may have undesirable consequences, the act of balancing Asian and American cultures can produce positive outcomes (Zhou and Bankston 1998).

Moreover, Asian intergenerational relations are also shaped by factors beyond immigrant families, such as ethnic institutions. For instance, Zhou (2009b) found that Chinese language schools provide a place for children of Chinese immigrants to share their common problems with their parents, to vent their feelings, and to work out coping strategies; the schools also help reinforce parental values about the importance of education, the norm of respecting parents, and an ethnic pride of being Chinese. Children of Asian immigrants who work in family businesses also experience role reversal because they have to translate for their parents and deal on a daily basis with customers, as well as dealers, business partners, and lawyers, as documented in a recent study of the children of Korean and Chinese immigrant entrepreneurs (Park 2005). The arrangement of cross-border transnational families, such as the "parachute kids" – children studying in the host country while their parents remain in the home country – discussed by Zhou (1998), also influences intergenerational relations.

Another aspect related to structural adaptation is the delinquency of the children of Asian immigrants. Unfortunately, only a handful of studies in this area exist. Zhou and Bankston's (1998) study of Vietnamese high-school students in New Orleans detected a bifurcated pattern of "valedictorians" or "achievers" and "delinquents" or "gangsters." Their follow-up study about a decade later found the continuation of this pattern and a shrinking segment of "valedictorians" together with a growing segment of "delinquents" (Zhou and Bankston 2006). Interestingly, being "too Americanized" into the "wrong" part of America was found to be associated with a higher rate of delinquency, while maintaining some Vietnamese cultural traditions was correlated with a lower rate. Using the 5 percent PUMS data from the 2000 census, Rumbaut et al. (2006) found that, while foreign-born Asians tended to have the lowest rates of incarceration in federal, state, or local prisons compared with other groups, their US-born counterparts (mostly second generation) registered significantly higher rates across the board. In particular, the incarceration rate jumped to 5.6 percent for US-born Vietnamese compared with 0.46 percent for foreign-born Vietnamese and to 7.26 percent for US-born Laotians and Cambodians as opposed to 0.92 percent for their foreign-born counterparts. There were large differences among US-born Asian groups, ranging from 0.65 percent for the Chinese to 7.26 percent for Laotians and Cambodians. These findings coincide with segmented assimilation theory.

Intermarriage

Intermarriage intersects with cultural adaptation because it can influence the preservation of ethnic language and other cultural traditions. According to Gordon (1964), it is part of assimilation called marital assimilation or amalgamation, which blurs the boundaries of minority groups and the dominant group. While the meaning of intermarriage is subject to debate, at minimum it can be viewed as an indicator of diminished social distance between the groups involved (Lee and Fernandez 1998). Intermarriage can be inter-racial (e.g., Chinese–white) or inter-ethnic (e.g., Chinese–Korean). What are the patterns of intermarriage among Asian immigrants and their offspring? How have the patterns of intermarriage changed over time? These are the questions to be addressed in this section.

The past three decades have produced a significant body of literature on the intermarriage of Asians in the United States. While some studies focus on one particular group (e.g., Min 1993; Sung 1990; Wong 1989), more analyze Asians as a whole or several Asian groups together (e.g., Hwang, Saenz, and Aguirre 1997; Kitano et al. 1984; Lee and Boyd 2008; Lee and Fernandez 1998; Lee and Yamanaka 1990; Okamoto 2007; Qian, Blair, and Ruf 2001; Shinagawa and Pang 1996). Although a few studies are confined to the local or state level (e.g., Hwang, Saenz, and Aguirre 1994; Kitano et al. 1984; Liang and Ito 1999), many are conducted at the national level using the census data (e.g., Hwang, Saenz, and Aguirre 1997; Lee and Boyd 2008; Lee and Fernandez 1998; Lee and Yamanaka 1990; Okamoto 2007; Qian, Blair, and Ruf 2001). Some studies lump all Asians together without considering birthplace because of their emphasis on Asian Americans. For the purpose of this study, it is important to distinguish between immigrants and the US born in intermarriage patterns. The US decennial censuses and the ACSs (the annual continuation of the census long form since 2001) provide the best source of data because they contain sufficiently large national representative samples of married Asian immigrants and their offspring.

To answer the research questions of this section, I pulled the relevant information on intermarriage rates from studies conducted by Sharon Lee and her collaborators (Lee and Boyd 2008; Lee and Fernandez 1998) using the nationally representative samples from the 5 percent PUMS data of the 1980, 1990, and 2000 censuses (see table 6.7). Several clear patterns emerge when

Table 6.7 Intermarriage rates of foreign- and US-born Asians by ethnicity and gender, 1980–2000

Group	1980 (%) F	1980 (%) US	1990 (%) F	1990 (%) US	2000 (%) F	2000 (%) US
Asians total	22.3	34.7	17.4	40.1	15.0[a]	47.7[a]
Men	10.5	33.1	9.1	37.7	8.7	43.1
Women	30.1	35.9	24.3	42.5	21.3	52.3
Chinese total	10.3	37.2	9.1	46.4	9.8	47.5
Men	8.2	37.6	6.7	44.5	6.6	42.3
Women	11.9	36.8	11.3	48.2	12.8	52.5
Japanese total	50.9	24.0	42.3	31.2	44.2	39.0
Men	16.2	23.0	17.3	28.2	20.7	35.8
Women	62.1	24.8	54.3	34.2	55.6	42.3
Korean total	30.3	68.0	20.9	71.7	18.9	62.1
Men	4.2	69.4	3.5	69.7	5.1	52.6
Women	43.8	66.9	33.0	73.3	29.1	69.4
Indian total	9.8	NA	8.9	38.0	8.3	40.7
Men	14.1	NA	12.4	45.1	9.5	40.6
Women	5.2	NA	5.2	32.2	7.0	40.8
Filipino total	24.0	58.5	24.8	64.8	24.4	63.4
Men	12.9	60.4	11.9	64.0	11.3	58.2
Women	31.4	56.9	34.4	65.5	34.1	68.0
Vietnamese total	30.3	NA	13.0	23.7	NA	NA
Men	4.2	NA	7.2	18.1	NA	NA
Women	43.8	NA	18.2	27.4	NA	NA

Notes: Intermarriage includes both inter-racial marriage (e.g., Chinese and whites) and inter-ethnic marriage (e.g., Chinese and Japanese).
F denotes foreign-born Asians, US those born in the United States.
[a] Estimate calculated by the author using the relevant numbers and percentages in Lee and Boyd (2008), table 1.
NA = not available.

Sources: Adapted from Lee and Fernandez (1998), table 4, which was based on the 5 percent PUMS data from the 1980 and 1990 censuses for Asians aged eighteen to sixty-four, and Lee and Boyd (2008), table 3, which was based on the 5 percent PUMS data from the 2000 census for single-race Asians.

examining foreign- or US-born Asians as a whole. First, US-born Asians were much more likely to be exogamous than foreign-born Asians. For instance, in 2000 they were more than three times as likely as foreign-born Asians to out-marry. One possible reason is that foreign-born Asians may be already married or engaged at the time of their arrival (Hwang and Saenz 1990). Another reason is that traditional cultural norms against exogamy may prevent or hinder foreign-born Asians from marrying out (Lee and Fernandez 1998). Moreover, being born in the United States reduces the social distance between Asians and other groups and increases their chance of outmarriage. Second, Asian women were more likely to out-marry than Asian men, but the gender gaps for the US born were narrower than those for the foreign born. The US military presence in Japan, Korea, and the Philippines may largely explain the higher intermarriage rate among foreign-born Asian women than foreign-born Asian men. Portraits of Asian women as feminine, submissive, and exotic may have enhanced their appeal to non-Asian men, while stereotypes of Asian men as dominant, authoritarian, and asexual may have decreased their attractiveness (Espiritu 2008). Third, the intermarriage rate of foreign-born Asians declined steadily from 1980 to 2000. This downward pattern was true for both male and female Asian immigrants. Although the causes await further research, continuing Asian immigration and the growing size of each Asian group may have increased the likelihood of endogamy and reduced the need for exogamy. Finally, in marked contrast, the intermarriage rate of US-born Asians increased between 1980 and 2000, a pattern that applied to both men and women. This rise may be an outcome of demographic changes and growing Asian panethnic identification (Espiritu 1992; Shinagawa and Pang 1996). Overall, all the patterns largely confirm the results found in the literature.

Diverse patterns can be observed from the data for foreign-born Asian groups. The Japanese were the most exogamous at all times, Indians were the least exogamous, while Filipinos, Koreans, Vietnamese, and Chinese fell somewhere in between. The inter-marriage rates of Filipinos, Indians, and Chinese had remained relatively stable over time, but the rates of Koreans and Vietnamese had slid significantly and that of Japanese had fluctuated. For all foreign-born Asian groups apart from Indians, women were more likely to out-marry than men. This was especially evident among the Japanese, Filipinos, Koreans, and Vietnamese, a phenomenon perhaps tied to the past and present US military involvements in their countries (Lee and Fernandez 1998). Nevertheless, for Indians a reversed gender pattern was present at all times (albeit weaker in 2000): Indian men were more likely to out-marry than Indian women because tighter control is imposed on daughters than on sons (Lee and Fernandez 1998; Lee and Yamanaka 1990).

Heterogeneity also exists among US-born Asian groups. Koreans and Filipinos were most exogamous, followed by Chinese, Indians, and Japanese, and Vietnamese fell at the other end of the spectrum.[11] There appeared a growing trend in exogamy among Chinese, Japanese, and Indians, but a fluctuating pattern among Koreans and Filipinos. Gender differences across groups seem to be shifting over time. In 1980, the gender gaps appeared to be quite small, though men were somewhat more likely to out-marry than women among Filipinos, Koreans, and Chinese. However, in 1990 and 2000 the gaps were growing bigger, with women more likely to out-marry than men for all Asian groups. With the exception of Japanese women and all Japanese, all US-born Asian groups, usually by a large margin, were more likely to out-marry than their foreign-born counterparts. Lee and Boyd (2008)˙ also found that the 1.5 generation (i.e., those who were born abroad and immigrated before the age of thirteen) was much more likely to out-marry than immigrants who came to the United States at thirteen years old or older, but less likely to do so than the native born.

One limitation of these existing studies is that, since intermarriage includes both interracial and interethnic marriages, we do not know *for Asian immigrants or US-born Asians* whether interracial marriage or inter-ethnic marriage dominates and how the dominant type of intermarriage has changed over time. What we do know from the literature is that, for Asians as a whole, interracial marriages, especially with whites, constituted the majority of intermarriages, but the rate of inter-ethnic marriages had increased significantly, from 10.7 percent in 1980 to 21.2 percent in 1990 (Lee and Fernandez 1998). Nonetheless, according to my calculation, based on the data from Lee and Boyd (2008: table 1), this rate had slightly decreased, to 18.1 percent in 2000. A later study using the 2001–6 ACSs, however, found that, among Asians born in the United States after 1965, inter-racial marriages were much more frequent than inter-ethnic marriages and that this observation was valid for both men and women and for all the six largest Asian groups (Min and Kim 2009).

Identity construction and reconstruction

Identity change is another dimension of adaptation, which Gordon (1964) referred to as "identificational assimilation." This section examines how post-1965 Asian immigrants and their children construct and reconstruct their identities and the factors that contribute to their identity formation and change. A review of the existing literature reveals that there is little systematic research on the identity of Asian *immigrants*, an area that merits attention in the future, but there are numerous studies of the identity of Asian immigrants' offspring, mostly on the second generation but a few on third or later generations (e.g., Kibria 2002; Min 2002; Min and Kim 1999; Tuan 1999). With a couple of exceptions, most of these studies take a qualitative approach with in-depth interviews as data. While they are rich, informed, and intriguing, data in these studies cannot be generalized.

One can expect that Asian immigrants (i.e., the first generation), like immigrants in other groups, tend to maintain their ethnic identities, but they also undergo identificational change after migration to the host country. Only sparse information on the identity of Asian immigrants exists in scattered places. For example, Lien, Conway, and Wong (2003: table 2) showed that, in their sample from the PNAAPS, out of 913 Asian immigrants 37 percent identified themselves as "ethnic Asian" (e.g., Chinese, Filipino, Indian), 5 percent chose "Asian," 34 percent selected "ethnic American" (e.g., Chinese American, Filipino

American, Asian Indian American), 15 percent identified with "Asian American," and only 5 percent opted for "American."[12] In other words, more new Asian immigrants chose to retain their ethnic or national identities and a very high percentage experienced partial identificational assimilation by adding the suffix "American"; in the racialized US context, one-fifth of them reconstructed their identity as "Asian American" or "Asian"; and only 5 percent experienced a total identificational assimilation. Lien, Conway, and Wong also found that, with a longer length of US residence, identification as "ethnic Asian" declined, but identification as "ethnic American" or "Asian American" rose. Acquiring US citizenship increased the likelihood of "American," "Asian American," and "ethnic American" identities while decreasing the identities of "ethnic Asian" and "Asian." Marrying a non-Asian substantially increased the chance of "American" identification, while marrying an Asian largely increased the "ethnic Asian" identification. All of the evidence appears to coincide with conventional wisdom and the cultural pluralism perspective.

Many qualitative studies of second-generation identities found that most children of Asian immigrants tend to select ethnic American as their primary identity, but they also increasingly embrace the panethnic identity "Asian American" at a moderate level (e.g., Kibria 2002; Min and Hong 2002; Min and Kim 1999). *Asian American panethnicity* can be defined as the development of solidarity and a common identity among all Asian subgroups.[13] Albeit not generalizable, these observations are confirmed by the PNAAPS. Lien, Conway, and Wong (2003: table 2) reported that, among the second-generation respondents in the PNAAPS (N = 172), "ethnic American" was the top choice of self identity (41 percent), followed by "American" (28 percent) and "Asian American" (17 percent), and only a small proportion identified themselves as "ethnic Asian" (8 percent) or "Asian" (2 percent). Among the third generation (N = 122), the "American" identity (43 percent) topped all other choices, "ethnic American" (25 percent) was relegated to second place, "Asian American" rose slightly, to 19 percent, and "ethnic Asian" and "Asian" further shrank to 3 percent apiece. Conflated with the evidence for the first generation presented in the preceding paragraph, it is evident that, the later the generation, the more Americanized and less ethnicized in identity the respondents became; nonetheless, identificational assimilation was never total, and ethnic Asian and especially ethnic American identities remained very much alive. The evidence again negates classic assimilation theory and lends support to the cultural pluralism perspective.

A more challenging question is: How do we explain the identity construction and reconstruction of Asian immigrants and their children? A number of theoretical perspectives on ethnicity can help shed light on this question. *Primordialism* views ethnicity as an *ascribed* or inherited identity and an extension of kinship, and ethnic boundaries as immutable. This perspective stresses the role of primordial factors such as lineage and cultural ties in determining ethnicity. To primordialists, it is the primordial bonds that give rise to and sustain ethnicity (Geertz 1973; Isaacs 1975; van den Berghe 1981). Unlike primordialism, *instrumentalism* sees ethnicity as an instrument or a strategic tool for gaining resources (Glazer and Moynihan 1975; Greenberg 1980). According to this theoretical framework, people become and remain ethnic when their ethnicity yields significant returns. In other words, ethnicity exists and persists because it is useful. The functional advantages range from "the moral and material support provided by ethnic networks to political gains made through ethnic bloc voting" (Portes and Bach 1985: 24). To instrumentalists, ethnicity is something manipulable, variable, situationally expressed, and subjectively defined.[14] *Social constructionism* conceptualizes ethnicity as a socially *constructed* identity and treats ethnic boundaries as flexible or changeable. Thus, ethnic affiliation or identification is determined or constructed by society, and ethnicity is a reaction to the changing social environment. There are different versions of constructionism. The *emergent ethnicity* perspective, an early form of constructionism developed by Yancey, Erikson, and Juliani (1976), downplays the effect of cultural heritage and views ethnicity as an "emergent phenomenon" created by structural conditions. Sarna (1978) argued that ethnicity is created by ascription or the assignment of individuals to particular ethnic groups by outsiders such as governments, churches, schools, presses, natives, and other immigrants, and by adversity such as prejudice, discrimination, hostility, and hardship. Advancing a more explicit version of social constructionism, Nagel (1994, 1996) contended that ethnicity is socially constructed and reconstructed by internal forces (i.e., actions taken by ethnic groups themselves, such as negotiation, redefinition, and reconstruction of ethnic boundaries) and external forces (i.e., social, economic, and political processes and outsiders), and that it is a dynamic, constantly changing property of individual identity and group organization. The theory of racial formation developed by Omi and Winant (1986) is also in line with social constructionism if we treat race as a special case of ethnicity and focus on the construction of racial or panethnic identity. Omi and Winant contended that, as a constantly changing phenomenon, race is constructed or shaped by both social structure and cultural representation, by both macro-level social process and micro-level individual experience, and by the historical process. In particular, they argued that, today, race is a primarily political phenomenon shaped by the political process.

In the case of new Asian immigrants and their offspring, a number of factors suggested by the foregoing theoretical perspectives are at play, but the importance of these factors varies across generations and groups. One factor is the bonds suggested by the primordialist perspective. To be sure, familial, cultural, and emotional ties to the homeland play a very important role in sustaining the ethnic identities of Asian immigrants (Min 2002). However, the importance of such ties fades over generations as the attachment to the host country weakens. This explains the declining ethnic Asian identification and increasing American and ethnic American identification. Nevertheless, the effect of such bonds on the second-generation identity varies across groups because of differences in parental emphasis on the retention of ethnic culture. For instance, while second-generation Koreans and Chinese have stronger ethnic attachment as a result of parental efforts in maintaining ethnic culture, Filipino parents considered the retention of ethnic culture less important or even a hindrance to the mobility of their children (Espiritu 1994).

Structural conditions suggested by social constructionism exert an important impact on the identities of Asian immigrants and their offspring. The government's racial lumping of smaller Asian groups into the broader racial or panethnic category "Asian" certainly contributed to the rise of an "Asian American" identity among immigrants, and especially their US-born children (Espiritu 1992). The emergence of Asian American studies programs and the offering of the Asian American curriculum have facilitated the acceptance of this identity, especially among US-born Asians. Asians' experiences with prejudice and discrimination also contributed to their ethnic American identities. Since white immigrants can easily blend into white society, ethnicity for them becomes an option (Waters 1990). However, for Asian immigrants and their US-born progeny, even the third or later generation, ethnicity is not an option but an everyday reality. Their "perpetual foreigner" experience reminds them that they are not perceived as full Americans (Tuan 1999). This is exemplified by MSNBC's headline on the Internet "American beats out Kwan," after Tera Lipinski edged past Michelle Kwan for the gold medal in the ladies' figure skating competition in the 1998 Olympic Games in Nagano, Japan.[15] The secondary headline "American outshines Kwan, Slutskaya in skating surprise," following the main headline "Hughes [Sarah Hughes] good as gold" in the sports section of *Seattle Times* on February 23, 2002, during the Olympics in Salt Lake City, further demonstrates that this "perpetual foreigner" perception is deeply embedded.

Finally, self-interest of Asian immigrants and their offspring suggested by instrumentalism also had a direct effect on the formation and acceptance of the Asian American identity. "Asian American" is a political construct that can help Asians coalesce in the promotion of their economic, political, and social interests. The inability of the American public to distinguish among different Asian ethnic groups and the anti-Asian violence associated with mistaken identities, such as the case of Vincent Chin, also help fortify the pan-Asian identity (Espiritu 1992). The Asian

American movement and the reclassification movement of Indians in the 1970s represented the internal actions taken by Asians to define and redefine themselves.

Political incorporation and participation

Not only do Asian immigrants and their offspring go through cultural, structural, socioeconomic, marital, and identificational adaptation, they also undergo political integration. Note that none of the theories reviewed earlier in this chapter touches upon political adaptation – probably because of disciplinary boundaries – but political adaptation is an important part of the immigrant experience. Compared with research on other types of adaptation, the literature on the political incorporation and participation of Asian immigrants and their children is relatively thin. Our main questions in this section are: How well do post-1965 Asian immigrants integrate into American society politically, and to what extent do new Asian immigrants and their children participate in the American political system?

One important and often used indicator of immigrant political incorporation is naturalization or acquisition of citizenship. Since naturalization symbolizes the acquisition of full political and social membership in a new country and a shift in national identity and allegiance, it gauges immigrants' degree of integration into the host society (Yang 1994). Notwithstanding the importance of this subject, surprisingly only limited studies of post-1965 Asian immigrants exist (Liang 1994; Yang 2002). My earlier study, using the 5 percent PUMS data from the 1990 census (Yang 2002), found a very high average naturalization rate of post-1965 Asian immigrants and a bifurcated pattern in citizenship acquisition among the six Asian immigrant groups. I have updated the analysis using the 5 percent PUMS data from the 2000 census and the 2006–8 ACS. The results basically corroborate my previous findings. I show here only the findings from the latest ACS. The last column of table 6.8 shows that about 73 percent of all post-1965 Asian immigrants who arrived in 1965–99 (i.e., those who

Table 6.8 Naturalization rates of post-1965 Asian and non-Asian immigrants aged eighteen or older by immigration cohort and ethnicity, 2006–8

Group	Immigration cohort							
	1965–9	1970–4	1975–9	1980–4	1985–9	1990–4	1995–9	1965–9 total
Asians %	92.0	91.2	89.7	83.6	77.6	66.8	42.4	72.7
N	7,032	12,893	20,545	26,528	24,456	23,469	14,145	129,068
Chinese %	95.5	95.7	94.0	90.4	85.1	64.9	40.3	74.9
N	2,205	2,851	4,692	6,780	7,273	5,724	3,439	32,964
Japanese %	70.0	63.3	54.5	44.5	33.0	23.5	11.0	37.8
N	353	408	311	238	226	198	105	1,839
Korean %	91.6	92.8	88.4	80.0	73.4	53.7	28.5	70.0
N	618	2,092	2,855	2,879	2,734	1,423	770	13,371
Indian %	92.9	92.8	91.3	85.7	78.9	68.4	38.7	67.8
N	1,048	2,254	2,830	3,761	4,205	4,258	3,663	22,019
Filipino %	94.6	92.2	90.9	85.8	79.3	70.8	52.4	78.2
N	2,215	3,645	3,751	4,760	5,196	4,720	2,752	27,039
Vietnamese %	90.9	91.6	93.4	88.6	84.1	77.7	63.6	82.1
N	193	599	3,919	4,114	2,306	4,959	1,936	18,026
White NH %	77.0	75.8	77.4	71.0	66.8	64.0	42.8	64.5
N	11,274	9,120	10,795	9,526	11,156	14,723	10,656	77,250
Black NH %	85.1	80.8	78.7	71.3	65.8	54.5	42.6	62.8
N	2,525	3,433	3,589	5,347	5,335	4,338	4,113	28,680

Table 6.8 (continued)

Group	Immigration cohort							
	1965–9	1970–4	1975–9	1980–4	1985–9	1990–4	1995–9	1965–9 total
Indian NH %	78.2	66.2	86.9	69.2	80.4	43.3	44.9	62.7
N	27	35	41	42	56	49	33	283
Hispanics %	75.6	64.7	56.4	50.5	35.3	22.7	13.5	35.8
N	12,081	15,421	15,654	20,553	19,627	12,686	8,831	104,853

Note: NH denotes non-Hispanic.

Source: Author's calculation based on the 2006–8 ACS data for single race. The data were weighted so that the results can be generalized to the population, but the N's shown are unweighted.

met the normal five-year residence requirement) had become US citizens by 2006–8, the highest naturalization rate among all post-1965 immigrant groups. If based solely on naturalization, new Asian immigrants appear to be most assimilable. The bifurcated pattern in naturalization remained in 2006–8. Vietnamese (82.1 percent) had the highest propensity to naturalize, but Japanese had a very low rate (37.8 percent), which was only slightly higher than the average rate of Hispanic immigrants. The lack of desire for Japanese immigrants to naturalize can be explained largely by the very high living standards in Japan and the fact that many Japanese green-card holders were sent by Japanese corporations to work for a period in their US branches or subsidiaries and would eventually return to Japan. Table 6.8 also shows that, with a few minor deviations (for example, Vietnamese, non-Hispanic American Indians, and non-Hispanic whites), the longer the US residence (or the earlier the immigration cohort), the higher the naturalization rate among Asian and non-Asian immigrant groups.

Albeit primary sources of data used to calculate the naturalization rate, US census or ACS data measure only the proportion of the foreign-born population that is naturalized at one particular point in time, but not how frequently immigrants have naturalized (Cornwell 2006). Moreover, the numerator – the number of naturalized population – does not include immigrants who have died or emigrated, and the denominator – the total foreign-born population – may include those who are ineligible for naturalization (e.g., foreign students, temporary workers, undocumented immigrants). These problems with the numerator and the denominator tend to underestimate naturalization rates. The longitudinal data from the DHS are more accurate than the census data because only eligible immigrants are included in the calculation of naturalization rates, although subsequent emigration or mortality of immigrants is still not taken into account. Figure 6.4, based on the DHS data on the naturalization rates for a cohort of immigrants admitted in fiscal year 1977 and traced through fiscal year 1995, indicates that Chinese (including those from Taiwan, Hong Kong, and mainland China), Vietnamese, Filipinos, Koreans, and Indians had a much higher naturalization rate than the overall average of all immigrant

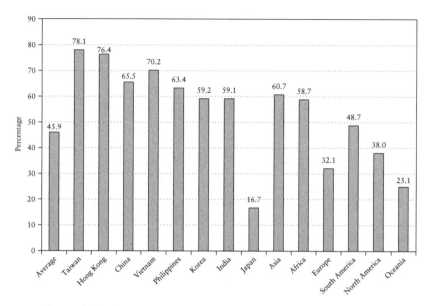

Figure 6.4 Naturalization rates for a cohort of Asian and non-Asian immigrants admitted in 1977 and traced through 1995

groups (46 percent). Asians had the highest rate (61 percent) of all immigrants. In sharp contrast, only about 17 percent of Japanese immigrants became US citizens, a rate that was much lower than the averages of immigrants from Africa, Europe, South America, North America, and Oceania. Despite some differences in rates and the time period, in comparison with table 6.8, the DHS data confirm the highest naturalization rate of post-1965 Asian immigrants and the bifurcated pattern among Asian immigrant groups.

Naturalization is not tantamount to political participation, but is the first step toward this. What are the patterns of political participation among Asian immigrants and their children? Table 6.9 offers some answers. Among immigrants who had become naturalized citizens, apart from 2006, when they basically tied with Hispanic immigrants, Asians had the lowest voter registration rate. However, over time their rate has been climbing overall. Asian naturalized citizens also recorded the lowest voting rates, with oscillation over time. US-born Asians did not do much better

Table 6.9 Reported voting and registration among Asian and non-Asian native-born and naturalized citizens by race/ethnicity, 1998–2006

Group	1998		2000		2002		2004		2006	
	Registered	Voted	Registered	Voted	Registered	Voted	Registered	Voted	Registered	Voted
Naturalized citizens										
All races	54.8	38.0	58.1	50.6	54.4	36.2	61.2	53.7	54.3	36.6
White NH	63.9	46.6	63.4	55.9	62.5	45.0	68.2	61.8	61.1	43.5
Black	53.9	36.5	60.3	56.8	57.9	40.2	61.8	54.4	52.3	35.1
Hispanic	53.6	37.4	57.7	49.6	51.9	33.4	60.0	52.1	51.2	34.3
Asian	44.8	28.1	51.7	43.4	48.8	30.5	54.6	46.4	51.5	33.5
Native-born citizens										
All races	67.8	45.7	70.2	60.0	67.3	46.8	72.9	64.5	68.6	48.6
White NH	69.4	47.4	71.8	62.0	69.6	49.2	75.3	67.3	71.5	51.8
Black	64.1	42.0	67.7	56.8	62.7	42.4	69.1	60.4	61.5	41.4
Hispanic	55.7	31.4	57.2	43.6	52.7	29.5	57.1	45.5	54.6	31.6
Asian	55.3	38.5	53.5	43.2	49.9	32.3	47.1	40.5	45.0	30.7
All citizens										
All races	67.1	45.3	69.5	59.5	66.5	46.1	72.1	63.8	67.6	47.8
White NH	69.3	47.4	71.6	61.8	69.4	49.1	75.1	67.2	71.2	51.6
Black	63.7	41.8	67.5	56.8	62.4	42.3	68.7	60.0	60.9	41.0
Hispanic	55.2	32.8	57.3	45.1	52.5	30.4	57.9	47.2	53.7	32.3
Asian	49.1	32.3	52.4	43.3	49.2	31.2	51.8	44.2	49.1	32.4

Notes: Asians included Pacific Islanders before 2004.
Race refers to single race after 2002.
NH denotes non-Hispanic.

Sources: US Bureau of the Census, Current Population Surveys, November, 1998–2006.

than naturalized Asian immigrants. They recorded the lowest voter registration rate at all times and the lowest voting rates in 2000, 2004, and 2006. While they registered to vote at a higher rate than their foreign-born counterparts up to 2002, the foreign born outshone them after that year; US-born Asians voted at a higher rate than foreign-born Asians only in 1998 and 2002. These statistics seem to paint a picture of Asian immigrants and their offspring as politically indolent in spite of their high socioeconomic status.

Perhaps aggregating all Asian groups conceals the real state of affairs. Unfortunately, the Census Bureau provides no information on political participation by Asian ethnic groups. Although there exists some information on group variation in political participation (see Lien 2004; Lien, Conway, and Wong 2004), no distinction has been made between immigrants and US-born Asians. The only exception is Lien's latest study (2008). The study reveals that, in 2004 among foreign-born naturalized citizens, Indians were most likely to register (60 percent), followed by Filipinos (57 percent), Koreans (54 percent), Vietnamese (54 percent), and Chinese (51 percent), while Japanese were least likely to do so; once registered, all Asian ethnic groups showed at a very high voting rate, from 81 percent for Filipinos to 95 percent for Japanese. Among US-born Asian citizens, Chinese showed the highest registration rate (66 percent) followed by Japanese (61 percent), Filipinos and Koreans (41 percent), and Indians (34 percent), with Vietnamese recording the lowest rate (19 percent). The actual voting turn-out rates were very high, mostly in the 80 percent range (except for Filipinos, at 75 percent). Although US-born Chinese and Japanese registered to vote at a much higher rate than their respective foreign-born counterparts, foreign-born Indians, Filipinos, Koreans, and Vietnamese surpassed their respective US-born counterparts; foreign-born Japanese, Korean, Filipino, and Vietnamese registered voters were more likely to vote than their respective US-born counterparts, but the reversal was observed for Indians.

It should be mentioned that electing Asians into positions of power can boost Asian political participation and incorporation, as evidenced by the Chinese ethnoburbs in the San Gabriel Valley (see Zhou, Tseng, and Kim 2008). Also note that the election of

Barack Obama as the forty-fourth president of the United States and his appointment of three Asian Americans to his cabinet and several as federal judges has generated tremendous political enthusiasm in the Asian American community and could increase Asian American political participation and incorporation.

Some recent studies pay attention to civic engagements beyond political participation among Asian Americans (Lien, Conway, and Wong 2004; Ramakrishnan 2008). For example, using the 2006 CPS data, Ramakrishnan (2008) showed that Asians volunteered in organizational activities at a lower rate (18 percent) than whites (31 percent) and blacks (19 percent), but higher than Latinos (14 percent). Asians also volunteered the fewest hours per year. Japanese showed the highest rate of voluntarism in organizational activities (25 percent), while Hmongs had the lowest rate (13 percent), and Koreans (22 percent), South Asians (22 percent), Filipinos (21 percent), Chinese (17 percent), and Vietnamese (14 percent) fell somewhere in between. However, these statistics lump Asian immigrants and their offspring together. Not much information on the voluntarism of Asian immigrants exists. The available data from the 2006 CPS revealed that Asian immigrants (the first generation) volunteered in organizational activities at a lower rate (17 percent) than the second generation (20 percent) and the third or later generation (29 percent).

An appraisal: which theory of adaptation works better?

A number of theories can guide our understanding of the adaptation experience of post-1965 Asian immigrants and their children. Classic assimilation theory, formulated by Park ([1937] 1950) and later by Gordon (1964), envisages a gradual loss of the new immigrant group's culture and institutions and its complete assimilation into the dominant Anglo culture and institutions. Melting-pot theory, molded by Gordon, foresees the fusion of both the dominant and immigrant groups and their cultures into a new group and culture. Cultural pluralism theory, also articulated by Gordon, recognizes the partial assimilation of the new group into the dominant culture, but underscores the maintenance of ethnic culture and the coexistence of both the dominant and ethnic cultures. Segmented assimilation theory, put forward by Portes and Zhou (1993), rejects a straight-line assimilation process and a pattern of uniform upward mobility and prescribes a nonlinear process and diverse adaptation outcomes. Revisionist assimilation theory, proposed by Alba and Nee (2003), revises the definition of assimilation and major arguments of classic assimilation theory, but reaffirms the importance of assimilation in the life of immigrants and their children.

Which theory better captures the adaptation experience of post-1965 Asian immigrants and their children? For cultural adaptation, the available evidence on language and religious assimilation and retention presented in this chapter confirms the validity of cultural pluralism theory. Post-1965 Asian immigrants experience a high degree of language assimilation but, not surprisingly, an overwhelming majority of them also maintain their native languages. For children of Asian immigrants, the degree of language assimilation is even higher, as the majority of them speak English only or undergo total language assimilation; yet, nearly 30 percent still speak their native languages at home. Religious assimilation is also very high, but not total. Data from GSS 1972–2008 indicate that more than half of the post-1965 Asian immigrants had become Christians, but around 30 percent kept their ethnic religions and 18 percent were non-believers. The religious assimilation of native-born Asians was slightly higher than that of their foreign-born counterparts, but still around one-fifth affiliated with a non-Christian religion and about a quarter remained non-religious. Also consistent with what segmented assimilation theory and revisionist assimilation theory suggest, there are large variations in language and religious assimilation and retention across ethnic groups. Gender differences in cultural assimilation are relatively minor.

In terms of socioeconomic adaptation, by and large segmented assimilation theory appears to do a better job, as we observe diverse mobility patterns of socioeconomic performance measured by educational attainment, occupational distribution, personal income, self-employment, and poverty. Collectively, post-1965 Asian immigrants on average surpassed native-born non-Hispanic whites in rates of college completion, advanced degree possession, and professional job attainment; they were similar or close to the latter group in managerial occupational attainment rate, personal income, and entrepreneurship, but had a higher poverty rate. Compared with US-born non-Hispanic whites, children of Asian immigrants also attained a higher rate in college completion, advanced degree possession, professional and managerial job attainment, but had a lower personal income, a lower entrepreneurship rate, and a higher poverty rate. From the first generation to the second generation, upward, downward, and static mobility patterns are all present, as are significant gender differences in mobility patterns. However, the evidence also points to some limitations of segmented assimilation theory. The mobility pattern of second-generation Filipinos is an excellent example. Second-generation Filipinos have undergone a very high degree of acculturation, with a very high rate of total language assimilation, a very low rate of native-language retention, and a high rate of Christianization. However, they have fared worse or much worse than their immigrant parents in personal income and the rates of college completion, professional job attainment, self-employment, and poverty. This pattern of fast acculturation together with a downward socioeconomic mobility is not captured by the three possible outcomes of second-generation mobility described by Portes and Zhou (1993).

Data on intermarriage are also consistent with the argument of cultural pluralism theory. Asian immigrants out-marry at significant rates, and at a very high rate for those from countries with US military involvement. US-born Asians out-marry at a much higher rate and certainly reach the "large scale" level referred to by Gordon, although still less than half of all US-born Asians are involved. Asian women are more exogamous than Asian men. They frequently marry whites, but inter-ethnic marriages among Asian groups have been on the rise in recent decades. The evidence suggests partial assimilation and the blurring as well as the retention of boundaries.

Cultural pluralism theory remains the most powerful of all

the theories with respect to identificational adaptation, as partial assimilation into the host identity and partial retention of ethnic identities characterize the experiences of new Asian immigrants and their offspring. Generation by generation, Asian immigrants and their progeny are more likely to develop an American identity based on the host country such as "American," "Asian American," and ethnic American. However, familial, cultural, and emotional ties to the Asian homelands make severing their roots difficult, especially for the immigrant generation and, to some extent, the second generation. More importantly, the experiences of prejudice, discrimination, and hostility have constantly reminded them that their ethnic identity is real rather than symbolic, because they are treated differently. Hence, retaining "Asian" or an ethnic label before the American identity becomes the natural thing to do. The government's racial lumping and the self-interest of Asian Americans have also contributed to the emergence and circumstantial embracement of the "Asian American" identity.

The fact that none of the adaptation theories addresses political adaptation does not indicate their total irrelevancy. By extension, we can see the pertinence of cultural pluralism theory here. In terms of citizenship acquisition, post-1965 Asian immigrants have demonstrated the highest naturalization rate among all immigrant groups, signaling a strong first stride toward full social membership and political assimilation. However, based on the rates of voter registration and voting turn-out, new Asian immigrants and their progeny seem to have made a smaller stride in political participation. In other words, collectively they have become partly assimilated into the American political system, but they still have a long way to go before full political integration.

Overall, classic assimilation theory and melting-pot theory seem to have little potency in modeling the adaptation experience of post-1965 Asian immigrants and their children, but cultural pluralism theory appears to be the most powerful. Segmented assimilation theory and revisionist assimilation theory are also useful in certain domains.

7

Conclusion

The preceding chapters have presented a great deal of information on Asian immigration to the United States. This final chapter is not devoted to providing a detailed summary of the findings because summaries can be found in the concluding sections of the previous chapters. Rather, it is intended to revisit the three important themes of the book: explanations of Asian immigration, its impacts on American society, and the adaptation of immigrants. It does so by examining the extent to which the findings are congruous with the predictions of the theories presented or the claims made in the literature. Finally, it discusses some possible future trends in Asian immigration to the United States and the need for future research.

Explanations of Asian immigration

As reviewed in chapter 2, the existing explanations of Asian immigration to the United States are highly inadequate. Incorporating the valuable elements of push–pull theory, economic models, sociological models, and integrated theories, this book puts forward a new theory – macro–micro interactive and cumulative causation theory. According to this theory, three clusters of conditions must be present to bring about immigration: disparities between sending countries and the receiving country in economic, political, social, and/or environmental conditions; multilevel connections linking the sending countries with the receiving country and linking potential migrants with their social networks (e.g., families, friends, communities, and ethnic institutions) in the countries of origin and destination; and both immigration and emigration policies of the sending and receiving countries. These three sets of factors influence immigration cumulatively and interactively.

The evidence presented in chapters 3 and 4 appears to lend strong support to the proposed theory. In the pre-1965 era, the disparities between the major Asian sending countries (China, Japan, Korea, the Philippines, and India) and the United States were undeniable realities. In particular, differences in economic and political conditions exerted the greatest impact. The contrast between the economic crises or hardships and in some cases political turmoil in the Asian countries and economic opportunities and political stability in America motivated Asians to move. Foreign involvement or colonization activated the effect of such disparities by uprooting farmers or peasants from their lands, aggravating the economic, political, and social conditions in the Asian sending countries, and creating opportunities for contacts and migration. The great demand for cheap migrant labor in the American West and Hawaii propelled deliberate recruitment, which brought the Asians over. Once the migration flows started, the social networks of Asian immigrants across borders helped sustain the movements. Open-door US immigration policies generally led to large or significant Asian immigration at the onset, despite some restrictions on the entry of Chinese women in the earlier period. But whenever there was exclusion or restriction, Asian immigration decreased or came to a halt. The emigration restrictions in some countries, such as China and Japan during the Gentlemen's Agreement, also had some impact on Asian immigration.

Since 1965, the substantial differences between Asian countries (except for Japan) and the United States in employment, income, quality of life, political stability, individual freedom, democracy, and children's educational opportunities have continued to push Asians out of their homelands and pull them to America. Functioning as push and pull factors, high levels of US economic, military, political, and/or cultural involvements in some Asian countries have been critical in producing large numbers of economic migrants, political refugees, and international marriages and adoptees. Immigrants' social networks across the borders in the forms of kinship, friendship, and ethnic organizations and communities have generated new immigrants and sustained Asian immigration. Changes in US immigration policy since 1965 have played a crucial role in the phenomenal increases in new Asian immigration. The lack of exit controls in most Asian countries has also facilitated Asian immigration.

Macro–micro interactive and cumulative causation theory is proposed to account for Asian immigration to the United States. However, its significance may be beyond this field. The basic ideas of intercountry disparities, intercountry linkages, cross-border immigrant social networks, and immigration and emigration policies, as well as the cumulation and interaction of these factors, are important in the explanation of any international movement of people.

Impacts of Asian immigration on American society

The impact of immigration on the United States has been a focus of highly contentious public discourse. Critics of immigration charge that post-1965 immigration has lowered the quality of the US labor force, adversely affected the employment and wages of native workers, imposed a financial burden on American taxpayers, weakened US national strengths and interests, and increased population and environmental pressures. Proponents of immigration counter that it has supplemented the US labor force for many businesses, had little impact on the employment and wages of native workers at the national level, contributed more in tax revenues than its costs, strengthened US national interests, and had little detrimental effect on the US population or environment. Where does post-1965 Asian immigration fit into this debate? Overall, is it a positive or a negative thing for America?

The data presented in this book suggest that, economically, post-1965 Asian immigration has enhanced the quality of the US labor force because new Asian immigrants are on average much more educated and skilled than the natives. Because of their educational and occupational backgrounds, they are less likely to compete with the less educated, less-skilled segment of the US labor force such as low-class African Americans – a main concern of immigrant–native job competition. Moreover, there is direct and indirect evidence that new Asian immigration has helped job creation in America via investment and the operation of businesses. In terms of welfare participation, the evidence shows that, apart from the refugee population, post-1965 Asian immigrants are less likely to be a public charge than the natives.

As shown in chapter 5, post-1965 Asian immigration has contributed to US national strengths and interests in daily life, medicine, science and technology, and sports. Although it has added about 9.6 million Asians to the US population, its impact on the country's population growth is relatively small. Nevertheless, together with immigration from Latin America, it has transformed the racial or ethnic composition and relations of the population as a whole. There is no evidence that new Asian immigration has degraded the environment in America.

By and large, most of the evidence points to the positive effects of post-1965 Asian immigration on US society. The evidence does not directly and totally repudiate the arguments of critics or support the arguments of proponents since the scope is different. However, it does shed light on the impact of immigration. Within the scope of our examination – immigration from Asia – there is no support for the anti-immigration arguments. Perhaps a differential approach can better capture the reality.

Asian immigrant adaptation in perspective

The traditional approach to the adaptation of immigrants and their progeny is classical assimilation theory, which portrays the gradual relinquishment of ethnic culture and institutions, the eventual total assimilation of new immigrant groups into the dominant culture and institutions, and a straight-line upward socioeconomic mobility generation by generation. However, the evidence on the adaptation experience of new Asian immigrants and their children presented in this book seems to be incongruous with the predictions of this theory because ethnic cultures and institutions have not been completely lost, assimilation has never been total, and socioeconomic mobility has not always been straight-line.

Nor is melting-pot theory, which envisions the biological and cultural fusing of the host and immigrant groups and the creation of something totally new, an apt description of Asian immigrant adaptation. While biological melting via intermarriage is taking place, the part that has already melted is still relatively small. In 2000, the proportion of the Asian population that was of mixed race was only 13.9 percent, which was higher than the comparable figure of 2.4 percent for the total US population. Few would claim that, with 2.4 percent mixed-race population, the United States as a whole is a biological melting pot. Even for Asians, the degree of biological blending was still relatively low. Undoubtedly, certain Asian cultural elements, such as food and perhaps traditional medicine, have been incorporated into American culture, but no one can claim the creation of a totally new culture. Overall, the fusion of Asians and all other groups and the creation of a totally new group and culture are still quite remote.

The cultural pluralism perspective, sometimes known as the ethnic resilience perspective, appears to hold potency for Asian immigrants and their children in a number of areas, including cultural, structural, marital, identificational, and political adaptation. The strong evidence of partial language assimilation and partial retention of ethnic languages and religions is well documented in chapter 6. Residential assimilation has been transpiring, but is not total. In terms of marital assimilation, both endogamous and exogamous trends are present, although the latter has been gaining momentum over time and generations. Identification with the host has been increasing over generations, but ethnic identification and attachment have remained very significant. New Asian immigrants and their children have undergone only partial incorporation into the American political system.

Segmented assimilation theory and revisionist assimilation

theory are also useful in capturing the diverse and "bumpy-line" patterns of socioeconomic mobility of Asian immigrants and their offspring. They are also instrumental in describing the variations across groups and generations in cultural, marital, and identificational adaptation.

The future of Asian immigration

In this book, we have learned the past and present of Asian immigration to the United States. A natural follow-up question is: What will happen to Asian immigration in the future? Any prediction about the future is precarious because of possible changes in economic, political, and social developments in Asia, the United States, and the world; in immigration and emigration policies; in people's behavior; and in other unpredictable events. Nevertheless, for scholarly research and policy planning it is instrumental to outline some important possible trends.

Several trends in future Asian immigration to the United States are highly likely based on macro–micro interactive and cumulative causation theory, present-day reality, and the assumptions that the current demographic trends and US immigration policy will continue. First, considerable Asian immigration is likely to continue. Since 1965, Asia has been the second largest source of immigrants after Latin America. The number of Asian immigrants has increased steadily, from 201,412 in the period 1966–9 to 1.3 million in the 1970s, 2.4 million in the 1980s, 2.6 million in the 1990s, and 3.1 million in the first decade of the twenty-first century. It is highly likely that we will see continual increases at least in the next several decades. This prediction is grounded in the belief that there will be continuous large disparities between most Asian countries and the United States, ongoing close ties between many Asian nations and the United States, expanded migrant social networks across the borders, continuing US pro-immigration policy, and lack of emigration restrictions in Asia. In the corresponding periods, the number of Latin American immigrants rose from 618,177 in 1966–9 to 1.8 million in the 1970s,

2.6 million in the 1980s, and nearly 5 million in the 1990s, but dropped to about 4.3 million in the decade 2000–9. The unusually high levels since the 1990s were the outcome of the amnesty program for undocumented immigrants authorized by the IRCA of 1986. Notice that the number of Asian immigrants grew much faster than the number of Latin American immigrants before the 1990s. Hence, it is possible that, at some point in the future, the level of legal immigration from Asia may be on a par with that of Latin America or may overtake it as the largest sending region.

Second, while China, India, the Philippines, Vietnam, and Korea are likely to remain the major sending countries, several other Asian countries may emerge as large suppliers of immigrants. China has been undergoing tremendous economic and social transformation and magnetizing the return of Chinese students studying abroad and migrants from other countries, but there is no sign that "the America fever" is fading. Although there could be slowdown in emigration decades from now, as the no. 1 demographic giant with a population size of more than 1.3 billion, China will easily fill the immigration spots made available to it under the current US immigration system. Likewise, India, with close to 1.2 billion people, will have no problem filling up its available immigration quota. India could very well become the largest supplier of Asian immigrants in the near future because of greater demographic and economic pressures, on top of other factors predicted by macro–micro interactive and cumulative causation theory. The Philippines had been the largest Asian sending country until the 1990s and is likely to remain a principal immigrant supplier in the foreseeable future on account of its especially close connections with the United States, the level of intercountry disparities, the existing social networks, and its huge population (92 million as of 2009). A latecomer among Asian sending countries but making rapid inroads because of the phenomenal influx of refugees and its population of almost 86 million as of 2009, Vietnam is poised to remain one of the top five countries of Asian immigration. While remaining high currently, Korean immigration is likely to decline or level off in the years to come, largely because of the narrowing gaps between South

Korea and the United States in economic, political, and social conditions, although other conditions predicted by macro–micro interactive and cumulative causation theory remain favorable to immigration. Another possibility is fluctuating levels of Korean immigration contingent upon the economic conditions of the country. One uncertainty is the prospect of reunification between North Korea and South Korea, which could completely alter the prediction. Japanese immigration is likely to remain at a relatively low level with fluctuations contingent upon Japan's economy. However, Pakistan and Bangladesh, with their large populations (168 million for Pakistan and 162 million for Bangladesh as of 2009), could eventually move into a top spot. Other potential new sending countries to watch are Thailand, Indonesia, Nepal, and perhaps Myanmar (formerly Burma).

Third, immigrant transnationalism is very likely to rise and expand in the Asian immigrant communities in the near future. As discussed in chapter 4, perhaps the most important characteristic here is the rise of a transmigrant class who lives a life across national boundaries (Yang 2006a). The number of Asian transmigrants will continue to grow, and the scope of immigrant transnationalism is likely to broaden to most large Asian immigrant communities. Accelerating economic and cultural globalization, continuing proliferation of dual citizenship, increasing transnational labor movement, advances in air transportation and communication technology, and the rational choice of immigrants to maximize their life chances are the major driving forces of this trend.

Fourth, the United States is likely to remain the largest recipient country of Asian immigration in the world. Historically, many Asians migrated to other countries. For instance, the majority of Chinese migrants settled in Southeast Asia. Many Indians moved to Southeast Asia, countries in the Indian subcontinent, and South Africa. Since 1945, a number of Asians (mostly contract laborers) have migrated to the oil production countries in the Middle East, Japan, and the Asian NICs (Castles and Miller 2009; Massey et al. 1998), but North America, Oceania, and Europe have increasingly become their primary destinations. The United States has been the top Asian immigrant receiving country at least since the 1980s, way ahead of countries such as Germany, Canada, Australia, the United Kingdom, New Zealand, and the Netherlands (UNDESA 2006). It is expected that it will continue to attract the largest number of Asian immigrants in the near future.

Fifth, the proportion of Asian immigrants will shrink while the proportion of US-born Asians will increase. According to the recent population projections made by the Pew Research Center (Passel and Cohn 2008), new Asian immigrants will play a decreasing role in Asian population growth in the United States, and the fertility of Asian immigrants already here and their descendants will play an increasing role. By 2050, immigrants will make up only 47 percent of the total Asian population while the native born will rise to 53 percent.

Finally, the impact of Asian immigration on US society is likely to increase in the future. As demonstrated in chapter 5, its impact on US total population growth has been increasing, contributing more than 9 percent in the period 1990–2000. Asians are projected to increase to 34.4 million or nearly 9 percent of the total US population by 2050 (see chapter 5) and further to 75.2 million or 13.2 percent of the population by 2100 according to an earlier projection by the US Census Bureau (see Yang 2006b). With the expansion of the Asian population comes a greater purchasing power, a higher demand for consumer products, and a bigger market. Also anticipated will be a growing diversity in Asian foods, medicines, and cultures, and a larger pool of talent in science and technology, arts and entertainment, sports, and many professions. It can be expected that more Asian immigrants and especially their US-born children will join the political arena.[1] Increasingly, the Asian electorate is much more likely to act as a swing vote in elections in localities and states of Asian concentration and perhaps in the future even at the presidential level (Yang 2002). Inspired by the victory of Barack Obama in the 2008 presidential election, more and more US-born Asians will aim for the US presidency. We may very well see the election of the first US president of Asian descent in the twenty-first century.

Closing remarks

Our time is the "age of migration" (Castles and Miller 2009). Asian immigration to the United States is part of this global migration. This book mainly tells the stories of post-1965 Asian immigrants. Since the immigration reform in 1965, millions of Asians such as those reported in chapter 1 have crossed the Pacific Ocean to adopt the United States as their new homeland. While the story of each new immigrant is unique, their experiences are very similar. They all have come for a better life in America. Through the media, communications with their social networks at home and in America, working for multinational corporations or on US military bases, and education in US schools, prospective Asian migrants learned the differences between their homelands and America in income, quality of life, individual freedom, political system, college education opportunities, and so forth. They were inspired to pursue something better for themselves and their families. Sponsorship of their relatives in America, connections with their former US bosses/supervisors, colleagues, or teachers, marriage with US servicemen, adoption by American families, and graduate training in American universities helped them realize their dreams of immigration. Unlike their pre-1965 predecessors, the new Asian immigrants have been greeted by a much more favorable environment. Post-1965 US non-discriminatory, pro-family reunification, and pro-skills immigration policy has kept the door open for Asians. US policy has also enabled millions of refugees from Indochina and other countries to enter the United States and adjust their status. With a couple of exceptions, few Asians were held back from leaving their countries. Once in America, these new immigrants have helped create jobs through their investments and businesses, diversified the American diet through Asian restaurants and supermarkets, improved American health through traditional Asian medicines, enhanced the US position in science and technology, and strengthened US sports and national interests. These new Asian immigrants and their children have become largely assimilated into American culture, but have retained some of their traditional cultures; they have moved up socioeconomically to be on a par with or close to the levels of non-Hispanic whites; they have registered a relatively higher level of entry into white middle-class neighborhoods; their intermarriage rates, especially among women and the US born, are quite high; they have constructed and reconstructed their identities, reflecting both ethnic and American identities; and they have become partially integrated into the US political system, but still have a long way to go before attaining full integration.

One of the major goals of this book is to develop a new theory of Asian immigration to the United States and to assess its utility. Another chief goal is to appraise the impacts of post-1965 Asian immigration on US society, a lacuna in the literature. Still another is to evaluate the extent to which theories of immigrant adaptation resonate with the actual experience of new Asian immigrants. This book represents the first attempt to develop a synthetic theory of Asian immigration that takes into consideration multilevel processes, multiple causes, initiating and sustaining forces, and historical and contemporary flows. It is also the first book that systematically examines post-1965 Asian immigration to the United States. Through well-researched quantitative historical data and the reassessment of historical analyses, it demonstrates the interconnectedness of historical Asian immigration flows driven by the demand for cheap labor on the West Coast of the United States and Hawaii. It provides a vast amount of the latest generalizable quantitative data on post-1965 Asian immigration. Overall, it is a unique contribution to the literature on Asian immigration to the United States.

However, a volume of this modest length cannot address every issue pertinent to Asian immigration, and even those covered here may not have been discussed in depth. For example, more information has been provided for the major Asian immigrant groups – the Chinese, Japanese, Filipinos, Indians, Koreans, and Vietnamese – but much less on smaller groups (the reader interested in those smaller groups is referred to other works).[2] For many smaller groups, the key constraint is not the length of the book but the exiguity of research. Another limitation is that ideal data for certain topics are not available. For instance, since direct measures of the fiscal and labor market impacts of *Asian* immigration on US society are almost non-existent, only indirect assessment of these impacts has been made.

Several items should be on the agenda of future research on this subject. First, the experiences of underrepresented Asian immigrant groups unquestionably call for further inquiries before some generalizations can be made. Second, generalizable survey research on Asian immigrant transnationalism is very much needed. Third, in-depth research on the undocumented immigration of Asians other than Chinese remains a lacuna. Fourth, research on Asian immigrant structural assimilation requires more attention in the future. Finally, collecting and analyzing data concerning the impacts of Asian immigration on America should be a top priority.

Notes

Preface

1 Based on the author's calculation using the 1965–2009 data from the Department of Homeland Security (DHS), but excluding immigrants from the Middle East countries located on the continent of Asia. In 2010, the total number of post-1965 Asian immigrants should be around 10 million. To dovetail with the term "Asian American" used by the US government, the term "Asian" in this book does not include Middle Easterners from Asia.

2 The other major source of post-1965 immigration is Latin America.

Chapter 1 Introduction

1 Only summaries of these stories are presented here. Readers interested in further details of Asian immigrant stories are referred to Bhatia (2007), Chan (2006), Lee (1991, 2008), Ling (2007), Min and Kim (1999), and Tenhula (1991), among others.

2 Real name.

3 Details of her experience can be found in the epilogue of Zhou (2010).

4 *Epoch Times* (Dallas edition) in Chinese, March 19, 2010, p. B3.

5 Adapted from Ling (2007: ch. 10).

6 Adapted from Bhatia (2007).

7 Adapted from Ling (2007: ch. 6).

8 Adapted from Chan (2006: ch. 12).

9 Adapted from Tenhula (1991: ch. 3).

10 Adapted from Jeong (1999).

11 Real name.

12 Based on the January–March 2010 catalog of Hsu's Ginseng Enterprises.

13 Real name.

14 Based on Tabuchi (2008), *China Daily* (2008), and other news reports.

15 Zhou (2010).

16 Ling (2007: ch. 6).

17 Jeong (1999).

18 Adapted from Shamita Das Dasgupta, "Within the South Asian Community," in Lee (2008).

19 Adapted from a letter written by Jeong Dae to the Fort Worth *Star-Telegram* in 2009.

20 Asian Indians or East Indians were classified as "Hindu" between 1920 and 1940 and became "other" in the 1950–70 US censuses (Nobles 2000). "Other" was subsequently classified as "white" (Espiritu 1992: 124).

21 Excluding Hawaiians from the category "Pacific Islander" would make the remaining "Non-Hawaiian Pacific Islander" category too small. Additionally, such a small number of people would make it difficult to obtain adequate sample data at the state and local levels without employing costly oversampling methods (OMB 1997b).

22 Many Asian Pacific Islander organizations have been established, including the National Coalition for Asian Pacific Islander American Community Development, the Asian Pacific American Legal Center, the Asian Pacific American Bar Association, the Asian and Pacific Islander American Scholarship Fund, the Asian and Pacific Islander American Health Forum, the Asian Pacific American Institute for Congressional Studies, the Asian Pacific American Labor Alliance, the Asian Pacific American Chamber of Commerce, and the Asian American Studies Center and Leadership Education for Asian Pacifics at UCLA. These organizations hold national and regional conferences, undertake research and publish on relevant issues, advocate for and provide services to the Asian Pacific American communities, and/or offer scholarships, internship, and leadership development opportunities.

Chapter 2 A Theory of Asian Immigration

1 See chapter 5 for more details.

2 However, since intervening obstacles are hard to predict on any wide scale, researchers tend to lump them together with the costs of moving and focus on the desire to move (Weeks 2008).

3 An article in the *New York Times* reported that about 1.5 million Taiwanese lived in mainland China (Kahn 2004). While this number was likely to include temporary migrants, according to statistics from the Taiwan Ministry of Interior (see Ng 2009) permanent emigrants were estimated at close to 300,000 as of 2004. Economic and political instability in Taiwan, and business opportunities and incentives as well as low housing prices in China, are among the main reasons for this movement. Statistics from the South Korean embassy in Beijing revealed that, by 2007, more than 700,000 South Koreans resided in China (see Ying 2007). Business opportunities, easier lifestyles, and cheap food and housing largely explain this migration.

4 This theory is sometimes labeled "segmented labor market theory" in the literature (see, for example, Massey et al. 1998).
5 Although transnationalism has gained increasing popularity in international migration research, it has not been labeled as a theory of international migration either in the literature or for my own theory. This approach is more appropriate when addressing the question of how immigrants adapt *after* migration rather than the question of why international migration takes place.
6 Unlike demographic pressure, which influences migration only indirectly, political conditions and environmental hazards can affect migration both directly and indirectly.
7 A lack of immigration/emigration control or restriction could be considered a non-intervention migration policy.
8 This theory does not argue that all disparities must be present simultaneously in order for immigration to occur. Rather, it maintains that one or more of these disparities must exist to cause immigration.
9 Similarly, this theory requires no simultaneous presence of economic, political, military, and cultural linkages, but one or more of these linkages.

Chapter 3 Pre-1965 Asian Immigration

1 For details of the Red Turban Revolt in the Pearl River Delta in 1854–5; see Wong (1976).
2 In the renegotiation of the Burlingame Treaty of 1868, the Qing government agreed in 1894 to accept the provisions of the Geary Act. In return, the United States permitted the return of Chinese laborers who had left temporarily and who had a family or property in the country valued at $1,000. However, in 1904 the Qing government declined to renew the treaty. As a result, Congress reenacted the Chinese exclusion laws indefinitely (Hing 1993: 26).
3 The group started with 149, but one man died en route. Eventually, 141 men, six women, and one child arrived safely (Conroy 1953).
4 The notes were not published until 1939, despite the fact that their terms were widely known.
5 The Emergency Quota Act of 1921 set the annual quota of immigration from any country at 3 percent of the foreign-born population from that country residing in the United Sates in 1910, but the Immigration Act of 1924 reduced the quota to 2 percent in 1890, as determined by the US Census of 1890.
6 Sometimes referred to in the literature as the Oriental Exclusion Act, this provision was part of the Immigration Act of 1924 rather than a separate Act.
7 The Supreme Court ruling on the *Takao Ozawa* v. *United States* case (1922)

240

determined that Ozawa, being Japanese and having been born in Japan, was not a free white person and therefore was ineligible for naturalization.

8 The Asia-Pacific Triangle consisted of Japan, China, Korea, the Philippines (then under US control), Indonesia, Malaysia, Singapore (then a British colony), Siam, Vietnam, Laos, Cambodia, Burma, India, and Ceylon. The Immigration Act of 1924 barred or restricted immigrants from these "undesirable" national origins.

9 The War Brides Act of 1945 and the GI Fiancées Act of June 29, 1946, did not have much effect on these arrivals because, before the McCarran–Walter Act of 1952, Japanese were still ineligible for immigration under the Immigration Act of 1924.

10 Yoo and Chung (2008: 3) reported that 46 percent of these Amerasian children had mixed blood of Korean and European Americans and 13 percent of Korean and African Americans.

11 The term "came via British Columbia" does not necessarily mean that they settled in Canada before moving to the United States.

Chapter 4 Post-1965 Asian Immigration

1 A total of thirty-four countries were identified as adversely affected, as evidenced by a decline in their total immigration after the 1965 Act went into effect.

2 I did not include fiscal year 1965, ended on September 30, because, passed on October 3, 1965, the Immigration and Nationality Act of 1965 had no effect on the immigration statistics in that year. "Post-1965" means after fiscal year 1965 or fiscal year 1966 and after.

3 The CSPA, sponsored by US Representative Nancy Pelosi and signed into law on October 9, 1992, allowed adjustment to the status of permanent resident (as employment-based immigrants) by nationals of the People's Republic of China who were in the United States after June 4, 1989, and before April 11, 1990. It made permanent a temporary ban on deportation of Chinese nationals created by President George H. W. Bush with Executive Order 12711. The stated purpose of the CSPA was to prevent political persecution of Chinese students in the aftermath of the Tiananmen protests of 1989.

4 The INS published no data on sex ratios for fiscal years 1980 and 1981 for any country, leading to the broken lines on the graph. The data are also unavailable for Japan and Pakistan for certain years.

5 An MSA is an urban community with a core city and 50,000 or more residents.

6 Li (2009) rightly made a distinction between new suburban ethnoburbs and traditional inner-city ethnic enclaves. Nonetheless, in my view, the terms "suburban ethnic town" (e.g., suburban Chinatown, suburban Koreatown)

and "ethnoburb" may be used interchangeably, and the former can perhaps be more easily understood by ordinary people.

7 The patterns for 2008 and 2009 were similar.

8 Similar terms in the literature are "professional migration" – often used as an abbreviation of the lengthy phrase "migration of professional, managerial, technical, and related workers" – "migration of the highly trained," and "migration of talent and skills."

9 The number in 1992 included Taiwan, and the number in 2007 included Hong Kong and Macao.

10 The DHS data do not separate H-1B workers from other temporary workers, but an overwhelming majority of Asian temporary workers hold H-1B visas.

11 The data after 2002 do not specify the specific categories of apprehension.

12 The percentage totals do not add up to 100 because of rounding errors.

Chapter 5 Impacts of Asian Immigration on US Society

1 The formula is: (difference between two census periods in foreign-born population ÷ difference between two census periods in total population) × 100.

2 This number includes Hispanics because Hispanic was not a separate category in the 1960 census.

3 Using the 2000 census data as the base of projections, the total adds up to more than 100 percent because individuals may report being of mixed race.

4 The lower limit is set at twenty-five because general and college education has normally been completed by this age. My analysis using the 5 percent PUMS data from the 2000 census produced the same patterns.

5 Data on investor immigrants are not made available by the DHS after 2001.

6 As shown in chapter 4, more than 90 percent of post-1965 Asian immigrants settled in urban areas. Hence, the assumption of the urban–rural distribution is conservative.

7 Asian-owned firms are those in which Asians own 51 percent or more of the stock or equity of the business.

8 Welfare use represents only the cost side of the fiscal impact, not its revenue or benefit.

9 Samuel Ting was born prematurely in Michigan while his Chinese parents were visiting the United States and went back to China with his parents when he was two months old. He did not return to the United States until he was twenty. He was a US citizen by accident and a de facto immigrant.

10 The results of the 2006 Program for International Student Assessment (PISA) showed that fifteen-year-old American students scored on average 489 out of 1,000 points on the science portion of the test, 11 points below the average of the thirty countries in the Organization for Economic Cooperation and Development. In math, US students had a lower average score than students

in twenty-three countries, the same average score as two countries, and a higher average score than four countries. See Gold (2007) for details.

Chapter 6 Adaptation of Asian Immigrants and their Children

1 Assimilation into social institutions and organizations was not considered by Gordon at the time.

2 The evidence cited by Kwon (2008: 60–1), based on pre-departure surveys of Korean immigrants, also corroborates this finding.

3 The data including both single race and two or more races are essentially the same for Asians.

4 However, the race variable in the CPS does not contain separate categories to distinguish the three generations for each Asian ethnic group. Hence, individual analyses by generation for different Asian groups cannot be performed.

5 The 5 percent PUMS data from the 2000 census reveal that Vietnamese (17.3 percent) trailed slightly behind native-born non-Hispanic whites (19.1 percent) in 2000, but the increase in the Vietnamese college completion rate between 2000 and 2006–8 (29.4 percent) was remarkable.

6 Active labor force refers to those aged sixteen to sixty-four who are not in the military or unemployed. Restricting the age range to those aged twenty-five to sixty-four (see Min 2006b) will artificially inflate the self-employment rate and, including those in the military and the unemployed, will underestimate the rate.

7 This speculation gains credence if we compare the 5 percent PUMS from the 2000 census and the 2006–8 ACS. In 1999, US-born Koreans, Indians, and Vietnamese were way behind native-born non-Hispanic whites in personal income (not shown). However, six to eight years later, the gap had narrowed markedly.

8 The data were weighted so that the results can be generalized to the population as a whole.

9 The dissimilarity index can be interpreted as the percentage of either group that would have to move to another neighborhood in order to achieve a population distribution that reflects the distribution of that particular metropolitan area.

10 Iceland and Scopilliti did not separate out the Pacific Islanders, but their number was very small.

11 Using the 2001–6 ACSs, Min and Kim (2009) recently found that restricting the analysis to Asians born in the US after 1965 Japanese rendered the most exogamous group and largely lowered the rate of Koreans.

12 The percentages for "not sure" and "refused" were omitted.

13 Espiritu (1992: 14) defined Asian American panethnicity as "the development of bridging organizations and solidarities among several ethnic and immigrant groups of Asian ancestry." This definition seems to underscore

organizations and solidarity at the collective level, but my definition applies to both collective and individual levels and includes identity and all Asian subgroups.

14 Instrumentalism is also called "circumstantialism," because it views ethnicity as an instrumental adaptation to shifting economic and political circumstances.

15 In fact, Michelle Kwan is 100 percent American, since she was born and raised in Torrance, California. Apart from her physical appearance, she was no different from other seventeen-year-old American teenagers.

Chapter 7 Conclusion

1 The record-breaking appointments to the Obama administration of many government officials, including three cabinet members (Secretary of Commerce Gary Locke, Secretary of Energy Steven Chu, and Secretary of Veteran Affairs Eric Shinseki), and the election to Congress in 2008 of Judy Chu as the first female member of the House of Representatives of Chinese descent and Anh Joseph Cao as the first member of the House of Representatives of Vietnamese descent, following the six members of Congress of Asian descent, offer encouraging signs of growing Asian American political representation.

2 Fortunately, there are a number of books covering smaller or underrepresented groups. For instance, Joanna Scott (1989) compiled a collection of oral histories of Indochinese refugees; Sucheng Chan's (1994) edited volume tells the stories of the Hmong in America; Jeremy Hein's (1995) book examines the experiences of refugees from Vietnam, Laos, and Cambodia; and Huping Ling's (2008) edited book includes essays on Hmong, Mong, Thai, Indonesian, Burmese, Tibetan, and Kashmiri immigrants.

References

Akiba, Daisuke (2006) "Japanese Americans," pp. 148–77 in *Asian Americans: Contemporary Trends and Issues*, ed. Pyong Gap Min. 2nd edn, Thousand Oaks, CA: Pine Forge Press.

Alba, Richard, and Victor Nee (2003) *Remaking the American Mainstream.* Cambridge, MA: Harvard University Press.

Angel Island Association (2009) "Angel Island State Park: Immigration Center," www.angelisland.org (accessed September 2009).

AsianWeek (1996) "Asian Americans on the Issues: The Results of a National Survey of Asian American Voters," 23 August.

Barnes, Patricia, Eve Powell-Griner, Kim McFann, and Richard L. Nahin (2004) *Complementary and Alternative Medicine Use among Adults: United States, 2002.* Washington, DC: US National Center for Complementary and Alternative Medicine.

Barraclough, Geoffrey (1978) *The Rise of the United States to World Power, 1867–1917.* London: Times Books.

Basch, Linda, Nina Glick Schiller, and Cristina Szanton Blanc (1994) *Nations Unbound: Transnational Projects, Postcolonial Predicaments, and Deterritorialized Nation-States.* Basel: Gordon & Breach.

Bautista, Veltisezar (1998) *The Filipino Americans from 1763 to the Present: Their History, Culture, and Traditions.* Farmington Hills, MI: Bookhaus.

Bhatia, Sunil (2007) *American Karma: Race, Culture, and Identity in the Indian Diaspora.* New York and London: New York University Press.

Bhattacharyya, Maitrayee (2005) "Community Support for Supplemental Education," pp. 249–72 in *Supplemental Education: The Hidden Curriculum of Higher Academic Achievement*, ed. E. W. Gordon, B. L. Bridglall, and A. S. Meroe. Lanham, MD: Rowman & Littlefield.

Bonilla-Silva, Edward (2004) "From Bi-racial to Tri-racial: Towards a New System of Racial Stratification in the USA," *Ethnic and Racial Studies* 27(6): 931–50.

References

Borjas, George (1990) *Friends or Strangers: The Impact of Immigrants on the US Economy*. New York: Basic Books.

—— (1992) "National Origin and the Skills of Immigrants in the Postwar Period," pp. 17–48 in *Immigration and the Work Force*, ed. George Borjas and Richard Freeman. Chicago: University of Chicago Press.

—— (1995) "Immigration and Welfare, 1970–1990," *Research in Labor Economics* 14: 251–80.

Boyd, Monica (1989) "Family and Personal Networks in International Migration: Recent Developments and New Agendas," *International Migration Review* 23: 638–80.

Brodkin, Karen (1999) *How Jews Became White Folks and What That Says about Race in America*. Brunswick, NJ: Rutgers University Press.

Butcher, Kristen, and Anna Piehl (1998) "Cross-City Evidence on the Relationship between Immigration and Crime," *Journal of Policy Analysis and Management* 17: 457–93.

Cain, Bruce, and Roderick Kiewiet (1986) "California's Coming Minority Majority," *Public Opinion* 9: 50–2.

Cain, Bruce, Roderick Kiewiet, and Carole Uhlander (1991) "The Acquisition of Partisanship by Latinos and Asian Americans," *American Journal of Political Science* 35: 390–442.

Carter, Susan, Scott Gartner, Michael Haines, Alan Olmstead, Richard Sutch, and Gavin Wright (2006) *Historical Statistics of the United States: Earliest Times to the Present*, Vol. 1. New York: Cambridge University Press.

Castles, Stephen, and Mark Miller (2009) *The Age of Migration: International Population Movements in the Modern World*. 4th edn, New York: Guilford Press.

Chan, Sucheng (1991) *Asian Americans: An Interpretive History*. New York: Twayne.

—— ed. (1994) *Hmong Means Free: Life in Laos and America*. Philadelphia: Temple University Press.

—— ed. (2006) *The Vietnamese American 1.5 Generation: Stories of War, Revolution, Flight, and New Beginnings*. Philadelphia: Temple University Press.

Chan, Willington (2002) "Chinese American Business Networks and Trans-Pacific Economic Relations Since the 1970s," pp. 145–61 in *The Expanding Roles of Chinese Americans in US–China Relations*, ed. Peter Koehn and Xiaohuang Ying. Armonk, NY: M. E. Sharpe.

Chang, Edward, and Russell Leong (1994) *Struggle toward Multiethnic Community: Asian American, African American, and Latino Perspectives*. Seattle: University of Washington Press.

Chen, Carolyn (2008) *Getting Saved in America: Taiwanese Immigration and Religious Experience*. Princeton, NJ: Princeton University Press.

Chen, Jack (1980) *The Chinese of America*. San Francisco: Harper & Row.

Cheng, Lucie, and Edna Bonacich, eds (1984) *Labor Immigration under*

Capitalism: Asian Workers in the United States before World War II. Berkeley: University of California Press.

Cheng, Lucie, and Philip Yang (1996) "Asians: The 'Model Minority' Deconstructed," pp. 305–44 in *Ethnic Los Angeles*, ed. Roger Waldinger and Mehdi Bozorgmehr. New York: Russell Sage Foundation.

—— (1998) "Global Interaction, Global Inequality, and Migration of the Highly Trained to the United States," *International Migration Review* 32(3): 626–53.

Chin, Ko-Lin (1999) *Smuggled Chinese: Clandestine Immigration to the United States.* Philadelphia: Temple University Press.

China Daily (2008) "'Iron Hammer' Still Pounding," January 22.

Choy, Bong-youn (1979) *Koreans in America.* Chicago: Nelson-Hall.

Choy, Catherine Ceniza (2003) *Empire of Care: Nursing and Migration in Filipino American History.* Durham, NC, and London: Duke University Press.

Conroy, Hilary (1953) *The Japanese Frontier in Hawaii, 1868–1898.* Berkeley: University of California Press.

Coolidge, Mary ([1909] 1969) *Chinese Immigration.* New York: Arno Press.

Cornwell, Derekh (2006) *Naturalization Rate Estimates: Stock vs. Flow.* Washington, DC: Department of Homeland Security, Office of Immigration Statistics.

Daniels, Roger (1988) *Asian America: Chinese and Japanese in the United States since 1850.* Seattle: University of Washington Press.

DaVanzo, Julie (1981) "Microeconomic Approaches to Studying Migration Decisions," pp. 90–129 in *Migration Decision Making: Multidisciplinary Approaches to Microlevel Studies in Developed and Developing Countries*, ed. G. F. De Jong and R. W. Gardner. New York: Pergamon Press.

DHS (Department of Homeland Security) (2002) *2002 Yearbook of Immigration Statistics.* Washington, DC: Government Printing Office.

——(2003) *2003 Yearbook of Immigration Statistics.* Washington, DC: Government Printing Office.

—— (2007) *2007 Yearbook of Immigration Statistics.* Washington, DC: Government Printing Office.

Espenshade, Thomas, and Katherine Hempstead (1996) "Contemporary American Attitudes toward US Immigration," *International Migration Review* 30: 535–70.

Espina, Marina (1988) *Filipinos in Louisiana.* New Orleans: A. F. Laborde.

Espiritu, Yen Le (1992) *Asian American Panethnicity: Bridging Institutions and Identities.* Philadelphia: Temple University Press.

—— (1994) "The Intersection of Race, Ethnicity, and Class: The Multiple Identities of Second-Generation Filipinos," *Identities* 1: 234–73.

—— (2008) *Asian American Women and Men: Labor, Laws, and Love.* 2nd edn, Lanham, MD: Rowman & Littlefield.

—— (2009) "Emotions, Sex, and Money: The Lives of Filipino Children of Immigrants," pp. 47–71 in *Across Generations: Immigrant Families in America*, ed. Nancy Foner. New York: New York University Press.

References

Espiritu, Yen Le, and Thom Tran (2002) "'Việt Nam, Nựớc Thội' (Vietnam, my Country): Vietnamese Americans and Transnationalism," pp. 367–98 in *The Changing Face of Home: The Transnational Lives of the Second Generation*, ed. Peggy Levitt and Mary Waters. New York: Russell Sage Foundation.

Essman, Elliot (2007) "Chinese Cuisine in the United States," www.lifeintheUSA.com/food/chinese.htm (accessed June 2009).

Faiola, Anthony (2006) "Putting the Bite on Pseudo Sushi and Other Insults," *Washington Post*, November 24.

Fang, Di (1996) "Japan's Growing Economic Activities and the Attainment Patterns of Foreign-Born Japanese Workers in the United States, 1979 to 1989," *International Migration Review* 30(2): 511–34.

Fong, Timothy (1994) *The First Suburban Chinatown: The Remaking of Monterey Park, California*. Philadelphia: Temple University Press.

Gans, Herbert (1999) "The Possibility of a New Racial Hierarchy in the Twenty-First-Century United States," pp. 371–90 in *The Cultural Territories of Race: Black and White Boundaries*, ed. M. Lamont. Chicago: University of Chicago Press.

Geertz, Clifford (1973) *The Interpretation of Culture*. New York: Basic Books.

Glazer, Nathan, and Daniel Moynihan (1975) "Introduction," pp. 1–27 in *Ethnicity: Theory and Experience*, ed. Nathan Glazer and Daniel Moynihan. Cambridge, MA: Harvard University Press.

Glenn, Evelyn (1986) *Issei, Nisei, Warbride: Three Generations of Japanese American Women in Domestic Service*. Philadelphia: Temple University Press.

Glick, Clarence (1980) *Sojourners and Settlers: Chinese Migrants in Hawaii*. Honolulu: Hawaii Chinese History Center and University of Hawaii Press.

Gold, Maria (2007) "US Teens Trail Peers around World on Math-Science Test," *Washington Post*, December 5, p. A07.

Gold, Steve (2004) "From Jim Crow to Racial Hegemony: Evolving Explanations of Racial Hierarchy," *Ethnic and Racial Studies* 27(6): 951–68.

Gordon, Milton (1964) *Assimilation in American Life*. New York: Oxford University Press.

Greeley, Andrew (1974) *Ethnicity in the United States: A Preliminary Reconnaissance*. New York: John Wiley.

Greenberg, Stanley (1980) *Race and State in Capitalist Development*. New Haven, CT: Yale University Press.

Griswold, Wesley (1962) *A Work of Giants: Building the First Trans-Continental Railroad*. New York: McGraw-Hill.

Hagan, John, and Alberto Palloni (1998) "Immigration and Crime in the United States," pp 367–87 in *The Immigration Debate*, ed. James Smith and Barry Edmonston. Washington, DC: National Academy Press.

Hall, Kermit (1999) *The Oxford Guide to United Supreme Court Decisions*. Oxford and New York: Oxford University Press.

Hamermesh, Daniel, and Frank Bean (1998) *Help or Hindrance: The Economic*

Implications of Immigration for African Americans. New York: Russell Sage Foundation.

Hecker, Andrew (1992) *Two Nations: Black and White, Separate, Hostile, Unequal*. New York: Charles Scribner's Sons.

Hein, Jeremy (1995) *From Vietnam, Laos, and Cambodia: A Refugee Experience in the United States*. New York: Twayne.

Hing, Bill Ong (1993) *Making and Remaking Asian America through Immigration Policy, 1850–1990*. Stanford, CA: Stanford University Press.

Hing, Bill Ong, and Ronald Lee (1996) *The State of Asian Pacific America: Reframing the Immigration Debate: A Public Policy Report*. Los Angeles: LEAP Asian American Public Policy Institute and UCLA Asian American Studies Center.

Hoefer, Michael, Nancy Rytina, and Bryan Baker (2008) *Estimates of the Unauthorized Immigrant Population Residing in the United States: January 2008*. Washington, DC: Department of Homeland Security.

Hsu, Will (2005) "Hsu's Ginseng Enterprises, Inc.: Foreign Currency Risks and Hedging in a Small Business," http://people.hbs.edu/mdesai/IFM05/Hsu.pdf (accessed December 2009).

Huddle, Donald (1993) *The Costs of Immigration*. Washington, DC: Carrying Capacity Network.

Hu-DeHart, Evelyn (1999) "Introduction," pp. 1–28 in *Across the Pacific: Asian Americans and Globalization*, ed. Evelyn Hu-DeHart. Philadelphia: Temple University Press.

Hurh, Won Moo, and Kwang Chung Kim (1990) "Religious Participation of Korean Immigrants in the United States," *Journal for the Scientific Study of Religion* 29: 19–34.

Hwang, Sean Shong, and Rogelio Saenz (1990) "The Problem Posed by Immigrants Married Abroad on Intermarriage Research: The Case of Asian Americans," *International Migration Review* 24: 63–76.

Hwang, Sean-Shong, Rogelio Saenz, and Benigno E. Aguirre (1994) "Structural and Individual Determinants of Outmarriage among Chinese-, Filipino-, and Japanese-Americans in California," *Sociological Inquiry* 64: 396–414.

—— (1997) "Structural Assimilationist Explanations of Asian American Intermarriage," *Journal of Marriage and the Family* 59(3): 758–72.

Iceland, John (2009) *Where We Live Now: Immigration and Race in the United States*. Berkeley, CA: University of California Press.

Iceland, John, and Melissa Scopilliti (2008) "Immigrant Residential Segregation in US Metropolitan Areas," *Demography* 45(1): 79–94.

Ichioka, Yuji (1988) *The Issei: The World of the First Generation Japanese Immigrants, 1885–1924*. New York: Free Press.

Ignative, Noel (1995) *How the Irish Became White*. New York: Routledge.

Ingram, Scott, and Christina Girod (2004) *The Indian Americans*. San Diego: Lucent Books.

References

INS (Immigration and Naturalization Service) (1966) *1966 Annual Report: Immigration and Naturalization Service.* Washington, DC: Government Printing Office.

—— (1971) *1971 Annual Report: Immigration and Naturalization Service.* Washington, DC: Government Printing Office.

—— (1982) *1982 Statistical Yearbook of the Immigration and Naturalization Service.* Washington, DC: Government Printing Office.

—— (1991) *1991 Statistical Yearbook of the Immigration and Naturalization Service.* Washington, DC: Government Printing Office.

—— (1992) *1992 Statistical Yearbook of the Immigration and Naturalization Service.* Washington, DC: Government Printing Office.

—— (2001) *2001 Statistical Yearbook of the Immigration and Naturalization Service.* Washington, DC: Government Printing Office.

INS Office of Policy and Planning (2003) *Estimates of the Unauthorized Immigrant Population Residing in the United States: 1990 to 2000.* Washington, DC: Immigration and Naturalization Service.

Isaacs, Harold R. (1975) *Idols of the Tribe: Group Identity and Political Change.* New York: Harper & Row.

Jacobson, Matthew (1999) *Whiteness of a Different Color: European Immigrants and the Alchemy of Race.* Cambridge, MA: Harvard University Press.

Jain, Sushil (1975) *East Indians in Canada.* Ottawa: Canadian Historical Association.

Jensen, Joan (1988) *Passage from India: Asian Indian Immigrants in North America.* New Haven, CT, and London: Yale University Press.

Jeong, Alex (1999) "A Handicapped Korean in America," pp. 69–74 in *Struggle for Ethnic Identity: Narratives by Asian American Professionals,* ed. Pyong Gap Min and Rose Kim. Walnut Creek, CA: AltaMira Press.

Jeung, Russell (2005) *Faithful Generations: Race and New Asian American Churches.* New Brunswick, NJ: Rutgers University Press.

Johnson, James, and Melvin Oliver (1989) "Interethnic Minority Conflict in Urban America: The Effects of Economic and Social Dislocations," *Urban Geography* 10: 449–63.

Kahn, Joseph (2004) "Taiwan Voters Weighing How Far to Push China," *New York Times,* March 18.

Kauanui, J. Kēhaulani (2008) *Hawaiian Blood: Colonialism and the Politics of Sovereignty and Indigeneity.* Durham, NC, and London: Duke University Press.

Kibria, Nazli (2002) *Becoming Asian American: Second-Generation Chinese and Korean American identities.* Baltimore and London: Johns Hopkins University Press.

—— (2006) "South Asian Americans," pp. 206–27 in *Asian Americans: Contemporary Trends and Issues,* ed. Pyong Gap Min. 2nd edn, Thousand Oaks, CA: Pine Forge Press.

References

—— (2009) "Marry into a Good Family: Transnational Reproduction and Intergenerational Relations in Bangladeshi American Families," pp. 98–113 in *Across Generations: Immigrant Families in America*, ed. Nancy Foner. New York: New York University Press.

Kim, Bok-Lim (1977) "Asian Wives of US Servicemen: Women in Shadows," *Amerasia Journal* 4(1): 91–115.

Kim, Claire (2000) *Bitter Fruits: The Politics of Black-Korean Conflict in New York City*. New Haven, CT: Yale University Press.

Kim, Illsoo (1987) "Korea and East Asia: Premigration Factors and US Immigration Policy," pp. 327–45 in *Pacific Bridges: The New Immigration from Asia and the Pacific Islands*, ed. James Fawcett and Benjamin Carino. New York: Center for Migration Studies.

Kitano, Harry, Wai-Tsang Yeung, Lynn Chai, and Herbert Hatanaka (1984) "Asian American Interracial Marriage," *Journal of Marriage and the Family* 46(1): 179-90.

Koehn, Peter, and Xiao-huang Yin, eds (2002) *The Expanding Roles of Chinese Americans in US–China Relations*. Armonk, NY: M. E. Sharpe.

Korea Times (2009) "Body Launched to Promote Korean Food Abroad," May 4.

Kritz, Mary, and Hania Zlotnik (1992) "Global Interactions: Migration Systems, Processes, and Policies," pp. 1–16 in *International Migration Systems: A Global Approach*, ed. Mary Kritz, Lin Lean Lim, and Hania Zlotnik. Oxford: Clarendon Press.

Kwon, Okyun (2008) "The Religiosity and Socioeconomic Adjustment of Buddhist and Protestant Korean Americans," pp. 60–80 in *Religion and Spirituality in Korean America*, ed. David Yoo and Ruth Chung. Urbana and Chicago: University of Illinois Press.

Kwong, Peter (1997) *Forbidden Workers: Illegal Chinese Immigrants and American Labor*. New York: New Press.

Laguerre, Michael (2009) "Network Governance of Asian American Diasporic Politics," pp. 119–33 in *The Transnational Politics of Asian Americans*, ed. Christian Collet and Pei-te Lien. Philadelphia: Temple University Press.

Lai, Him Mark (2004) *Becoming Chinese American: A History of Communities and Institutions*. Walnut Creek: AltaMira Press.

Lai, Him Mark, Genny Lim, and Judy Yung (1999) *Island: Poetry and History of Chinese Immigrants on Angel Island, 1910–1940*. Seattle: University of Washington Press.

Lasker, Bruno (1969) *Filipino Immigration to Continental United States and to Hawaii*. New York: Arno Press.

Lau, Estelle (2006) *Paper Families: Identity, Immigration Administration, and Chinese Exclusion*. Durham, NC, and London: Duke University Press.

Lee, Erika (2004) "American Gatekeeping: Race and Immigration Law in the Twentieth Century," pp. 119–44 in *Not Just Black and White: Historical and Contemporary Perspectives on Immigration, Race, and Ethnicity in the United*

References

States, ed. Nancy Foner and George Fredrickson. New York: Russell Sage Foundation.

Lee, Everett (1966) "A Theory of Migration," *Demography* 3: 47–57.

Lee, Jennifer (2000) "Immigrant and African American Competition: Jewish, Korean, and African American Entrepreneurs," pp. 322–44 in *Immigration Research in a New Century: Multidisciplinary Perspectives*, ed. Nancy Foner, Ruben Rumbaut, and Steve Gold. New York: Russell Sage Foundation.

Lee, Jennifer, and Frank Bean (2004) "Intermarriage and Multiracial Identification: The Asian American Experience and Implications for Changing Color Lines," pp. 51–66 in *American Youth: Culture, Identity, and Ethnicity*, ed. Jennifer Lee and Min Zhou. New York: Routledge.

Lee, Joann, ed. (1991) *Asian Americans: Oral Histories of First to Fourth Generation Americans from China, the Philippines, Japan, India, the Pacific Islands, Vietnam and Cambodia*. New York: New Press.

—— ed. (2008) *Asian Americans in the Twenty-First Century: Oral Histories of First to Fourth Generation Americans from China, Japan, India, Korea, the Philippines, Vietnam, and Laos*. New York: New Press.

Lee, Matthew, Ramiro Martinez, Jr., and Richard Rosenfeld (2001) "Does Immigration Increase Homicide? Negative Evidence from Three Border Cities," *Sociological Quarterly* 42: 559–80.

Lee, Sharon, and Monica Boyd (2008) "Marrying Out: Comparing the Marital and Social Integration of Asians in the US and Canada," *Social Science Research* 38: 311–29.

Lee, Sharon, and Marilyn Fernandez (1998) "Trends in Asian American Racial/ Ethnic Intermarriage: A Comparison of 1980 and 1990 Census Data," *Sociological Perspectives* 42: 323–42.

Lee, Sharon, and Keiko Yamanaka (1990) "Patterns of Asian American Intermarriage and Marital Assimilation," *Journal of Comparative Family Studies* 21: 287–305.

Levitt, Peggy (2007) *God Needs No Passport: Immigrants and the Changing American Religious Landscape*. New York: New Press.

Lewis, Arthur (1954) "Economic Development with Unlimited Supplies of Labor," *Manchester School of Economic and Social Studies* 22: 139–91.

Li, Wei (1998) "Anatomy of a New Ethnic Settlement: The Chinese Ethnoburb in Los Angeles," *Urban Studies* 35(3): 479–501.

—— (2009) *Ethnoburb: The New Ethnic Community in Urban America*. Honolulu: University of Hawaii Press.

Liang, Zai (1994) "Social Contact, Social Capital, and the Naturalization Process: Evidence from Six Immigrant Groups," *Social Science Research* 23: 407–37.

Liang, Zai, and Naomi Ito (1999) "Intermarriage of Asian Americans in the New York City Region: Contemporary Patterns and Future Prospects," *International Migration Review* 33: 876–900.

References

Lien, Pei-te (2004) "Asian Americans and Voting Participation: Comparing Racial and Ethnic Differences in Recent US Elections," *International Migration Review* 38(2): 493–517.

—— (2008) "Political and Civic Engagement of Immigrants," pp. 47–74 in *The State of Asian America: Trajectory of Civic and Political Engagement: A Public Policy Report*, Vol. 5, ed. Paul Ong. Los Angeles: LEAP Asian Pacific American Public Policy Institute.

Lien, Pei-te, and Tony Carnes (2004) "The Religious Demography of Asian American Boundary Crossing," pp. 38–51 in *Asian American Religions: The Making and Remaking of Borders and Boundaries*, ed. Tony Carnes and Fenggang Yang. New York: New York University Press.

Lien, Pei-te, Margaret Conway, and Janelle Wong (2003) "The Contours and Sources of Ethnic Identity Choices among Asian Americans," *Social Science Quarterly* 84(2): 461–81.

—— (2004) *The Politics of Asian Americans: Diversity and Community*. New York: Routledge.

Light, Ivan, and Edna Bonacich (1988) *Immigrant Entrepreneurs: Koreans in Los Angeles, 1965–1982*. Berkeley: University of California Press.

Lim, Nelson (2001) "On the Back of Blacks? Immigrants and the Fortunes of African Americans," pp. 186–227 in *Strangers at the Gates: New Immigrants in Urban America*, ed. Roger Waldinger. Berkeley: University of California Press.

Lim, Younghee, and Stella Resko (2003) "Immigrants' Use of Welfare after Welfare Reform: Cross-Group Comparison," *Journal of Poverty* 6(4): 63–82.

Ling, Huping (1998) *Surviving on the Gold Mountain: A History of Chinese American Women and their Lives*. Albany: State University of New York Press.

—— (2007) *Voices of the Heart: Asian American Women on Immigration, Work, and Family*. Kirksville, MO: Truman State University Press.

—— ed. (2008) *Emerging Voices: Experiences of Underrepresented Asian Americans*. New Brunswick, NJ, and London: Rutgers University Press.

Liu, Haiming, and Lianlian Lin (2009) "Food, Culinary Identity, and Transnational Culture: Chinese Restaurant Business in Southern California," *Journal of Asian American Studies* 12(2): 135–62.

Louie, Vivian (2004) *Compelled to Excel: Immigration, Education, and Opportunity among Chinese Americans*. Stanford, CA: Stanford University Press.

Lovegren, Sylvia (1995) *Fashionable Food: Seven Decades of Food Fads*. New York: Macmillan.

MacDonald, John S., and Leatrice MacDonald (1974) "Chain Migration, Ethnic Neighborhood Formation, and Social Networks," pp. 226–36 in *An Urban World*, ed. Charles Tilly. Boston: Little, Brown.

Mangiafico, Luciano (1988) *Contemporary American Immigrants: Patterns of Filipino, Korean, and Chinese Settlement in the United States*. Westport, CT: Praeger.

References

Martinez, Ramiro, Jr. (2002) *Latino Homicide: Immigration, Violence and Community*. New York: Routledge.

—— (2006) "Coming to America: The Impact of the New Immigration on Crime," pp. 1–19 in *Immigration and Crime: Race, Ethnicity, and Violence*. New York: New York University Press.

Massey, Douglas (1990) "Social Structure, Household Strategies, and the Cumulative Causation of Migration," *Population Index* 56: 3–26.

Massey, Douglas, Rafael Alarcón, Jorge Durand, and Humberto González (1987) *Return to Aztlan: The Social Process of International Migration from Western Mexico*. Berkeley: University of California Press.

Massey, Douglas, Joaquín Arango, Graeme Hugo, Ali Kouaouci, Adela Pellegrino, and Edward Taylor (1993) "Theories of International Migration: A Review and Appraisal," *Population and Development Review* 19: 431–66.

—— (1998) *Worlds in Motion: Understanding International Migration at the End of the Millennium*. Oxford: Clarendon Press.

Massey, Douglas, Luin Goldring, and Jorge Durand (1994) "Continuities in Transnational Migration: An Analysis of Nineteen Mexican Communities," *American Journal of Sociology* 99(6): 1492–533.

Mazumdar, Sucheta (1984) "Punjabi Agricultural Workers in California, 1905–1945," pp. 549–78 in *Labor Immigration under Capitalism*, ed. Lucie Cheng and Edna Bonacich. Berkeley: University of California Press.

McClain, Charles (1994) *In Search of Equality: The Chinese Struggle against Discrimination in Nineteenth-Century America*. Berkeley: University of California Press.

Mei, June (1984) "Socioeconomic Origins of Emigration: Guangdong to California, 1850 to 1882," pp. 219–47 in *Labor Immigration under Capitalism: Asian Workers in the United States Before World War II*, ed. Lucie Cheng and Edna Bonacich. Berkeley: University of California Press.

Melendy, Howard Brett (1977) *Asians in America: Filipinos, Koreans, and East Indians*. Boston: Twayne.

Min, Pyong Gap (1988) *Ethnic Business Enterprise: Korean Small Businesses in Atlanta*. New York: Center for Migration Studies.

—— (1993) "Korean Immigrants' Marital Patterns and Marital Adjustments," pp. 287–99 in *Family Ethnicity: Strength in Diversity*, ed. H. P. McAdoo. Newbury Park, CA: Sage.

—— ed. (1995) *Asian Americans: Contemporary Trends and Issues*. Thousand Oaks, CA: Sage.

—— (1996) *Caught in the Middle: Korean Communities in New York and Los Angeles*. Berkeley: University of California Press.

—— ed. (2002) *Second Generation: Ethnic Identity among Asian Americans*. Walnut Creek, CA: AltaMira Press.

—— ed. (2006a) *Asian Americans: Contemporary Trends and Issues*. 2nd edn, Thousand Oaks, CA: Pine Forge Press.

—— (2006b) "Korean Americans," pp. 230–59 in *Asian Americans: Contemporary Trends and Issues*, ed. Pyong Gap Min. 2nd edn, Thousand Oaks, CA: Pine Forge Press.

—— (2006c) "Settlement Patterns and Diversity," pp. 32–53 in *Asian Americans: Contemporary Trends and Issues*, ed. Pyong Gap Min. 2nd edn, Thousand Oaks, CA: Pine Forge Press.

Min, Pyong Gap, and Joann Hong (2002) "Ethnic Attachment among Second-Generation Korean Americans," pp. 113–28 in *Second Generation: Ethnic Identity among Asian Americans*, ed. Pyong Gap Min. Walnut Creek, CA: AltaMira Press.

Min, Pyong Gap, and Chigon Kim (2009) "Patterns of Intermarriages and Cross-Generational Intermarriages among Native-Born Asian Americans," *International Migration Review* 43(3): 447–70.

Min, Pyong Gap, and Dae Young Kim (2005) "Intergenerational Transmission of Religion and Culture: Korean Protestants in New York," *Sociology of Religion* 66: 263–82.

Min, Pyong Gap, and Jung Ha Kim, eds (2002) *Religions in Asian America: Building Faithful Communities*. Lanham, MD: AltaMira Press.

Min, Pyong Gap, and Rose Kim, eds (1999) *Struggle for Ethnic Identity: Narratives by Asian American Professionals*. Walnut Creek, CA: AltaMira Press.

Mishra, Sangay (2009) "The Limits of Transnational Mobilization: Indian American Lobbying Groups and the India–US Civil Nuclear Deal," pp. 107–18 in *The Transnational Politics of Asian Americans*, ed. Christian Collet and Pei-te Lien. Philadelphia: Temple University Press.

Myrdal, Gunnar (1957) *Rich Lands and Poor*. New York: Harper & Row.

Nagel, Joane (1994) "Constructing Ethnicity: Creating and Recreating Ethnic Identity and Culture," *Social Problems* 41(1): 152–68.

—— (1996) *American Indian Ethnic Renewal: Red Power and the Resurgence of Identity and Culture*. New York: Oxford University Press.

Nakanishi, Donald (1991) "The Next Swing Vote: Asian Pacific Americans and California Politics," pp. 25–54 in *Racial and Ethnic Politics in California*, ed. Bryan Jackson and Michael Preston. Berkeley, CA: Institute of Governmental Studies.

Ng, Sam (2009) "Taiwanese Gold Rush to China," www.atimes.com/atimes/China/FF30Ad04.html (accessed August 2009).

Nobles, Melissa (2000) *Shades of Citizenship: Race and the Census in Modern Politics*. Stanford, CA: Stanford University Press.

Nordyke, Eleanor (1977) *The Peopling of Hawaii*. Honolulu: University Press of Hawaii.

North, David, and Marian F. Houston (1976) *The Characteristics and Role of Illegal Aliens in the US Labor Market: An Exploratory Study*. Washington, DC: Linton.

Okamoto, Dina G. (2007) "Marrying Out: A Boundary Approach to

References

Understanding the Marital Integration of Asian Americans," *Social Science Research* 36: 1391–414.

Oliver, Melvin, and James Johnson (1984) "Interethnic Minority Conflict in an Urban Ghetto: The Case of Blacks and Latinos in Los Angeles," *Research in Social Movements, Conflicts, and Change* 6: 57–94.

OMB (Office of Management and Budget) (1997a) "Revisions to the Standards for the Classification of Federal Data on Race and Ethnicity," Federal Register Notice, October 30; www.whitehouse.gov/omb/fedreg_1997standards (accessed August 2010).

—— (1997b) "Recommendations from the Interagency Committee for the Review of the Racial and Ethnic Standards to the Office of Management and Budget concerning Changes to the Standards for the Classification of Federal Data on Race and Ethnicity." Federal Register, September 7; www.census.gov/population/www/socdemo/race/Directive_15.html (accessed September 2009).

Omi, Michael, and Howard Winant (1986) *Racial Formation in the United States.* New York and London: Routledge.

Ong, Paul, and Tania Azores (1994) "Health Professionals on the Front Line," pp. 139–63 in *The State of Asian Pacific America: Economic Diversity, Issues, and Policies,* ed. Paul Ong. Los Angeles: LEAP Asian Pacific American Policy Institute and UCLA Asian American Studies Center.

Ong, Paul, and David Lee (2001) "Changing of the Guard? The Emerging Immigrant Majority in Asian American Politics," pp. 153–72 in *Asian Americans and Politics,* ed. Gordon Chang. Stanford, CA: Stanford University Press.

Ong, Paul, Edna Bonacich, and Lucie Cheng (1994) *The New Asian Immigration in Los Angeles and Global Restructuring.* Philadelphia: Temple University Press.

Park, Edward, and John Park (2005) *Probationary Americans: Contemporary Immigration Policies and the Shaping of Asian American Communities.* New York: Routledge.

Park, Lisa Sun-Hee (2005) *Consuming Citizenship: Children of Asian Immigrant Entrepreneurs.* Stanford, CA: Stanford University Press.

Park, Robert ([1937] 1950) "The Race Relations Cycle in Hawaii," pp. 188–95 in *Race and Culture,* Vol. 1, ed. E. C. Hughes et al. Glencoe, IL: Free Press.

Passel, Jeffrey (1994) *Immigrants and Taxes: A Reappraisal of Huddle's "The Cost of Immigrants."* Washington, DC: Urban Institute.

Passel, Jeffrey, and D'Vera Cohn (2008) *US Population Projections: 2005–2050.* Washington, DC: Pew Research Center.

Patterson, Wayne (1988) *The Korean Frontier in America: Immigration to Hawai'i 1896–1910.* Honolulu: University of Hawaii Press.

Peffer, George A. (1986) "Forbidden Families: Emigration Experiences of Chinese Women under the Page Law, 1875–1882," *Journal of American Ethnic History* 6: 28–46.

References

Petras, Elizabeth (1981) "The Global Labor Market in the Modern World Economy," pp. 44–63 in *Global Trends in Migration: Theory and Research on International Population Movements*, ed. Mary M. Kritz, Charles B. Keeley, and Silvano M. Tomasi. New York: Center for Migration Studies.

Piore, Michael J. (1979) *Birds of Passage*. New York: Cambridge University Press.

Pomerantz, Linda (1984) "The Background of Korean Emigration," pp. 277–315 in *Labor Immigration under Capitalism: Asian Workers in the United States before World War II*, ed. Lucie Cheng and Edna Bonacich. Berkeley: University of California Press.

Portes, Alejandro (2003) "Conclusion: Theoretical Convergencies and Empirical Evidence in the Study of Immigrant Transnationalism," *International Migration Review* 37(3): 874–92.

Portes, Alejandro, and Robert Bach (1985) *Latin Journey: Cuban and Mexican Immigrants in the United States*. Berkeley: University of California Press.

Portes, Alejandro, and Rubén Rumbaut (1990) *Immigrant America: A Portrait*. Berkeley: University of California Press.

—— (1996) *Immigrant America: A Portrait*. 2nd edn, Berkeley: University of California Press.

—— (2001) *Legacies: The Story of the Immigrant Second Generation*. Berkeley and New York: University of California Press and Russell Sage Foundation.

—— (2006) *Immigrant America: A Portrait*. 3rd edn, Berkeley: University of California Press.

Portes, Alejandro, and John Walton (1981) *Labor, Class, and the International System*. New York: Academic Press.

Portes, Alejandro, and Min Zhou (1993) "The New Second Generation: Segmented Assimilation and its Variants among Post-1965 Immigrant Youth," *Annals of the American Academy of Political and Social Science* 530: 74–98.

Posadas, Barbara (1999) *The Filipino Americans*. Westport, CT: Greenwood Press.

Qian, Zhenchao, Sampson Lee Blair, and Stacey Ruf (2001) "Asian American Interracial and Interethnic Marriages: Differences by Education and Nativity," *International Migration Review* 35: 557–87.

Ramakrishnan, Karthick (2008) "Political Participation and Civic Voluntarism," pp. 31–46 in *The State of Asian America: Trajectory of Civic and Political Engagement: A Public Policy Report*, Vol. 5, ed. Paul Ong. Los Angeles: LEAP Asian Pacific American Public Policy Institute.

Ravenstein, Ernest (1889) "The Laws of Migration," *Journal of the Royal Statistical Society* 52: 241–301.

Roediger, David (1991) *Wages of Whiteness*. London: Verso.

Rogers, Robert (1996) *Destiny's Landfall: A History of Guam*. Honolulu: University of Hawaii Press.

Rumbaut, Rubén, Roberto Gonzales, Golnaz Komaie, Charlie Morgan, and Rosaura Tafoya-Estrada (2006) "Immigration and Incarceration: Patterns and Predictors of Imprisonment among First- and Second-Generation Young Adults," pp. 64–89 in *Immigration and Crime: Race, Ethnicity, and Violence*, ed. Ramiro Martinez, Jr., and Abel Valenzuela, Jr. New York: New York University Press.

Sarna, Jonathan (1978) "From Immigrants to Ethnics: A New Theory of Ethnicization," *Ethnicity* 5: 370–8.

Sassen, Saskia (1988) *The Mobility of Labor and Capital: A Study in International Investment and Labor Flow*. Cambridge: Cambridge University Press.

Saxenian, AnnaLee (1999) *Silicon Valley's New Immigrant Entrepreneurs*. San Francisco: Public Policy Institute of California.

Schaefer, Richard (2008) *Racial and Ethnic Groups*. 11th edn, Upper Saddle River, NJ: Pearson Prentice Hall.

Scott, Joanna (1989) *Indochina's Refugees: Oral Histories from Laos, Cambodia, and Vietnam*. Jefferson, NC: McFarland.

Segal, Uma (2002) *A Framework for Immigration: Asians in the United States*. New York: Columbia University Press.

Shinagawa, Larry, and Gin Yong Pang (1996) "Asian American Panethnicity and Intermarriage," *Amerasia Journal* 22: 127–52.

Silva, Noenoe (2004) *Aloha Betrayed: Native Hawaiian Resistance to American Colonialism*. Durham, NC, and London: Duke University Press.

Simon, Julian (1981) "What Immigrants Take from and Give to the Public Coffers," in *US Immigration Policy and the National Interest: Staff Report of the Select Commission on Immigration and Refugee Policy*. Washington, DC: Government Printing Office.

Simon, Julian, and Ather Akbari (1995) "Educational Trends of Immigrants into the US," paper presented in the 1995 annual meeting of the Population Association of America, San Francisco.

Sjaastad, Larry (1962) "The Cost and Returns to Human Migration," *Journal of Political Economy*, Supplement 70: 80–93.

Skerry, Peter (2000) *Counting on the Census: Race, Group Identity and the Evasion of Politics*. Washington, DC: Brookings Institution Press.

Smith, James, and Barry Edmonston, eds (1997) *The New Americans: Economic, Demographic, and Fiscal Effects of Immigration*. Washington, DC: National Academic Press.

Speer, William (1853) *China and California*. San Francisco: Marvin & Hitchcock.

Spickard, Paul (2009) *Japanese Americans: The Formation and Transformations of an Ethnic Group*. Rev. edn, Piscataway, NJ: Rutgers University Press.

Stark, Oded, and David Bloom (1985) "The New Economics of Labor Migration," *American Economic Review* 75: 173–8.

Stark, Oded, and Edward Taylor (1989) "Relative Deprivation and International Migration," *Demography* 26: 1–14.

—— (1991) "Migration Incentives, Migration Types: The Role of Relative Deprivation," *Economic Journal* 101: 1163–78.

References

Sung, Betty Lee (1990) *Chinese American Intermarriage*. New York: Center for Migration Studies.

Tabuchi, Hiroko (2008) "Return of the 'Iron Hammer,'" *Wall Street Journal*, August 9.

Takaki, Ronald (1989) *Strangers from a Different Shore: A History of Asian Americans*. New York: Penguin Books.

Tenhula, John (1991) *Voices from Southeast Asia: The Refugee Experience in the United States*. New York and Landon: Holmes & Meier.

Thomas, William, and Florian Znaniecki (1918–20) *The Polish Peasant in Europe and America*, ed. Eli Zaretsky. Kila, MT: Kessinger.

Tienda, Marta, and Leif Jensen (1986) "Immigration and Public Assistance Participation: Dispelling the Myth of Dependency," *Social Science Research* 15: 372–400.

Tilly, Charles, and C. Harold Brown (1967) "On Uprooting, Kinship, and the Auspices of Migration," *International Journal of Comparative Sociology* 8: 139–64.

Todaro, Michael (1969) "A Model of Labor Migration and Urban Underdevelopment in Less Developed Countries," *American Economic Review* 59: 138–48.

Tsai, Shih-Shan Henry (1986) *The Chinese Experience in America*. Bloomington: Indiana University Press.

Tuan, Mia (1999) *Forever Foreigners or Honorable Whites?* New Brunswick, NJ: Rutgers University Press.

Uchida, Yoshiko (1987) *Picture Bride*. Seattle: University of Washington Press.

UNDESA (UN Department of Economic and Social Affairs) (2006) *International Migration Flows to and from Selected Countries: 2005 Revision*. New York: UN Department of Economic and Social Affairs, Population Division.

United Nations (2008) *Per Capita GNI at Current Prices – US Dollars*, http://data.un.org (accessed March 2009).

—— (2009) *Human Development Indices: A Statistical Update 2008*, http://data.un.org (accessed March 2009).

US Bureau of the Census (2000) *Projections of the Resident Population by Age, Sex, Race, and Hispanic Origin: 1999 to 2100 (NP-D1-A)*. Washington, DC: US Bureau of the Census.

—— (2005) "Texas Becomes Nation's Newest 'Majority-Minority' State," www.census.gov/newsroom/releases/archives/population/cb05-118.html (accessed August 2010).

—— (2007) "More than 300 Counties Now 'Majority-Minority,'" www.census.gov/newsroom/releases/archives/population/cb07-113.html (accessed August 2010).

—— (2010) "Facts for Features: Asian/Pacific American Heritage Month: May 2010," www.census.gov/newsroom/releases/archives/facts_for_features_special_editions/cb10-ff07.html (accessed June 2010).

US Immigration Commission (1911) *Report of the Immigration Commission:*

References

Statistical Review of Immigration 1820–1910, Immigrant Distribution 1850–1900. Washington, DC: Government Printing Office.

US Secretary of Defense (1996) *Proliferation: Threat and Response.* Washington, DC: US Government Printing Office.

van den Berghe, Pierre (1981) *The Ethnic Phenomenon.* New York: Elsevier.

Vertovec, Steven (1999) "Conceiving and Researching Transnationalism," *Ethnic and Racial Studies* 22(2): 447–62.

Waldinger, Roger (1997) "Black/Immigrant Competition Re-assessed: New Evidence from Los Angeles," *Sociological Perspectives* 40: 365–86.

Waters, Mary (1990) *Ethnic Options: Choosing Identities in America.* Berkeley: University of California Press.

Weeks, John (2008) *Population: An Introduction to Concepts and Issues.* 10th edn, Belmont, CA: Thompson Wadsworth.

Williams, T. K. (1991) "Marriage between Japanese Women and US Servicemen since World War II," *Amerasia Journal* 17(1): 135–54.

Wong, Bernard (1998) *Ethnicity and Entrepreneurship: The New Chinese Immigrants in the San Francisco Bay Area.* Boston: Allyn & Bacon.

—— (2006) *The Chinese Immigrants in Silicon Valley: Globalization, Social Networks, and Ethnic Identity.* Lanham, MD: Rowman & Littlefield.

Wong, J. Y. (1976) *Yeh Ming-ch'en: Viceroy of Liang Kuang, 1852–8.* New York and London: Cambridge University Press.

Wong, Morrison (1989) "A Look at Intermarriage among the Chinese in the United States in 1980," *Sociological Perspectives* 32(1): 87–107.

Yancey, William, Eugene Erikson, and Richard Juliani (1976) "Emergent Ethnicity: A Review and Reformulation," *American Sociological Review* 41(3): 391–403.

Yang, Fenggang (1999) *Chinese Christians in America: Conversion, Assimilation, and Adhesive Identities.* University Park: Pennsylvania State University Press.

Yang, Philip (1994) "Explaining Immigrant Naturalization," *International Migration Review* 28(3): 449–77.

—— (1995) *Post-1965 Immigration to the United States: Structural Determinants.* Westport, CT: Praeger.

—— (1999) "Quality of Post-1965 Asian Immigrants," *Population and Environment* 20: 527–44.

—— (2000a) *Ethnic Studies: Issues and Approaches.* Albany: State University of New York Press.

—— (2000b) "The 'Sojourner Hypothesis' Revisited," *Diaspora* 9(2): 235–58.

—— (2001) "Professionals and the Brain Drain," pp. 641–8 in *Encyclopedia of American Immigration,* ed. James Ciment. New York: M. E. Sharpe.

—— (2002) "Citizenship Acquisition of Post-1965 Asian Immigrants," *Population and Environment* 23(4): 377–404.

—— (2004) "Generational Differences in Educational Attainment among Asian Americans," *Journal of Asian American Studies* 7(1): 51–71.

References

—— (2006a) "Transnationalism as a New Mode of Immigrant Adaptation: Preliminary Evidence from Chinese Transnational Migrants," *Journal of Chinese Overseas* 2(2): 173–92.

—— (2006b) "Future Prospects of Asian Americans," pp. 292–316 in *Contemporary Trends and Issues*, ed. Pyong Gap Min. 2nd edn, Thousand Oaks, CA: Pine Forge Press.

Ying, Ding (2007) "The Korean Mergence: More South Koreans are Heading to China for Better Lives and Business and Academic Opportunities," *Beijing Review* no. 34, August 23.

Yinger, J. Milton (1961) "The Assimilation Thesis," *Daedalus* 90(2): 247–62.

Yokoyama, Y. (1989) "Social Adjustment Issues among Japanese Wives of Businessmen and Visiting Scholars in the Seattle Area," unpubd PhD dissertation, University of Washington.

Yoo, David, and Ruth Chung (2008) "Introduction," pp. 1–17 in *Religion and Spirituality in Korean America*, ed. David Yoo and Ruth Chung. Urbana and Chicago: University of Illinois Press.

Yuh, Ji-Yeon (2002) *Beyond the Shadow of Camptown: Korean Military Brides in America*. New York: New York University Press.

Zhang, Sheldon (2008) *Chinese Human Smuggling Organizations*. Stanford, CA: Stanford University Press.

Zhao, Xiaojian (2002) *Remaking Chinese America: Immigration, Family, and Community, 1940–1965*. New Brunswick, NJ: Rutgers University Press.

—— (2010) *The New Chinese America: Class, Economy, and Social Hierarchy*. New Brunswick, NJ: Rutgers University Press.

Zhou, Min (1992) *Chinatown: The Socioeconomic Potential of an Urban Enclave*. Philadelphia: Temple University Press.

—— (1997) "Growing up American: The Challenge Confronting Immigrant Children and Children of Immigrants," *Annual Review of Sociology* 23: 63–95.

—— (1998) "'Parachute Kids' in Southern California: The Educational Experience of Chinese Children in Transnational Families," *Educational Policy* 12: 682–704.

—— (2004) "Are Asian Americans Becoming 'White'?" *Contexts* 3(1): 29–37.

—— (2009a) "Chinese Schools and the Ethnic System of Supplemental Education," pp. 148–66 in Min Zhou, *Contemporary Chinese America: Immigration, Ethnicity, and Community Transformation*. Philadelphia: Temple University Press.

—— (2009b) "Conflict, Coping, and Conciliation: Intergenerational Relations in Chinese Immigrant Families," pp. 21–46 in *Across Generations: Immigrant Families in America*, ed. Nancy Foner. New York: New York University Press.

—— (2010) *The Accidental Sociologist in Asian American Studies*. Los Angeles: UCLA Asian American Studies Center Press.

Zhou, Min, and Carl Bankston III (1998) *Growing up American: How*

References

Vietnamese Children Adapt to Life in the United States. New York: Russell Sage Foundation.

—— (2006) "Delinquency and Acculturation in the Twenty-First Century: A Decade's Change in a Vietnamese American Community," pp. 117–39 in *Immigration and Crime: Ethnicity, Race, and Violence,* ed. Ramiro Martinez, Jr., and Abel Valenzuela, Jr. New York: New York University Press.

Zhou, Min, and Myungduk Cho (2010) "Noneconomic Effects of Ethnic Entrepreneurship: Evidence from Chinatown and Koreatown in Los Angeles, USA," *Thunderbird International Business Review* 52(2): 83–96.

Zhou, Min, and Susan Kim (2006) "Community Forces, Social Capital, and Educational Achievement: The Case of Supplemental Education in the Chinese and Korean Immigrant Communities," *Harvard Educational Review* 76: 1–29.

Zhou, Min, Yen-fen Tseng, and Rebecca Y. Kim (2008) "Rethinking Residential Assimilation through the Case of Chinese Ethnoburbs in the San Gabriel Valley, California," *Amerasia Journal* 34(3): 55–83.

Zhou, Min, Jennifer Lee, Jody Vallejo, Rosaura Tafoya-Estrada, and Yang Sao Xiong (2008) "Success Attained, Deterred, and Denied: Divergent Pathways to Social Mobility among the New Second Generation in Los Angeles," *Annals of the American Academy of Political and Social Science* 620 (November): 37–61.

Zolberg, Aristide (1989) "The Next Waves: Migration Theory for a Changing World," *International Migration Review* 23: 403–30.

Index

Index

Index

Index

Index

Index

Index

Index

Index

Index

Index